eating
NEW ORLEANS

eating
NEW ORLEANS

**From French Quarter Creole Dining
to the Perfect Poboy** *Pableaux Johnson*

More than
100
Essential
Louisiana
Eating (&
Drinking)
Experiences

The Countryman Press
Woodstock, Vermont

First Edition

Library of Congress Cataloging-in-Publication Data has been applied for.

ISBN 0-88150-629-X

Cover design by Mucca Design
Text design and composition by Carol Jessop, Black Trout Design
Interior photography by the author
Maps and illustrations by Jeff Goodwin and Pableaux Johnson,
© 2005 The Countryman Press
Cover photo courtesy of Corbis

Published by The Countryman Press, P.O. Box 748, Woodstock, VT 05091

Distributed by W. W. Norton & Company, Inc., 500 Fifth Avenue,
New York, NY 10110

Printed in the United States of America

10 9 8 7 6 5 4 3 2 1

to Ariana
with love and extra gravy

ACKNOWLEDGMENTS

Though there's only one name on the cover of this book, the whole project flat out wouldn't have happened without the assistance and dedication of a broad network of friends, colleagues, and family. Throughout the writing process, they helped keep me focused, sane, and informed through countless phone conversations, lunch meetings, and caffeine-fueled editing sessions.

Lolis Eric Elie and Fred Thompson fielded more than their fare share of late-night phone calls and review drafts. If this project had credits rolling at the end, they'd both be listed as "Producer." Mr. Elie gave me a native's perspective and valuable context throughout. Fred acted as esteemed counsel from both New York City and North Carolina.

A group of local writers also contributed their time, energy and viewpoints to this project. Brett Anderson never hesitated to launch into long restaurant discussions at the drop of a hat. Sara Roahen was always graciously open for an amorphous conceptual riff or an early-morning meeting. I'm grateful for their willingness to act as sounding boards and valued sources.

Then there's the family folks. My sisters, Charlotte Paulsen and Elaine Johnson, are the touchstones; adoptees Annie, Will, and Molly Bates for the bayou-side support; all the far-flung Heberts for the book's foundation. Thanks to my father, Joe Blanco, for the continued tradition of six-hour kitchen table conversations. Thanks to my aunt Mary Minor Hebert, who got the whole damned thing started.

The crew at The Countryman Press were a lot more patient than they had to be. Profound thanks to my editor, Richard Fumosa, for helping me through the rookie mistakes. The many, many rookie mistakes.

There are others worth mentioning—Robb Walsh for his always-welcome unsolicited advice, Smiley Pool and Kirk Tuck for photographic nudges, Cynthia Joyce for her extra set of eyes, Joan Greenfield and Dominque Singer for their thoroughly urban hospitality and all my editors for their lessons over the years.

And of course, most of all to my wife, Ariana French. She's a lot better than I deserve, and her patience and support through this project more than confirm that fact.

And to the city of New Orleans—a place that's so easy to love. I only put a fraction of its beauty in this book. Next time, just a little more . . .

contents

CHAPTER 1

CITY OF APPETITES: EATING NEW ORLEANS

CHAPTER 2

THE BIG PICTURE: NEIGHBORHOODS, LOGISTICS, AND FINDING YOUR WAY

Tourist Tips

CHAPTER 3
THE RESTAURANTS

Classics

Morning Food

The Sweet Stuff: Praline Shops and Snowball Stands

Market Groceries: Neighborhood and Open-Air Markets

CHAPTER 4
BARS AND CLUBS

CHAPTER 5
BAYOU BACKROADS

APPENDIX
THE LOUISIANA PANTRY—LOCAL INGREDIENTS AND RESOURCES

INTRODUCTION

The fascination usually starts with a single well-told food story.

Right after you book a flight to New Orleans, someone—friend, co-worker, brother-in-law—calls with a restaurant recommendation that seems to go on for hours. It's not so much a straight recommendation—"Sit by the window. The veal's really good."—but an epic tale of overstuffed shrimp poboys or turtle soup spiked with a glug of sherry. It could be the story of a lost weekend salvaged with spicy Bloody Marys or a sensual description of sublime butter-sauced pompano topped with a mountain of sautéed crabmeat. And more often than not, it includes a critical phrase: "Everybody else was a local. We were the only tourists in the place."

Stories like these can transform an average business trip into a culinary mission. For travelers on their way to the Crescent City, it's like hearing tell of hidden treasure—the perfect meal in a city known for its exotic ambience and stellar restaurant scene. If the experience lives up to its billing, the place becomes the first step in exploring the rich food traditions of New Orleans.

Great "table stories" have an ecstatic quality that stops just short of evangelical "saved by Jesus" narratives. Sensual descriptions of flavor and texture border on the erotic. If the storyteller happens to be the cook, they'll include an informal recipe and a short tutorial on technique ("Then you cook the onions in that grease. Real slow, until they get good and brown"). Enthusiastic grunts and momentary trance states aren't uncommon, as the sensory echoes of a perfect crawfish bisque or turtle soup rack the mind, body and tastebuds.

At the end, audience and performer alike are primed for a good meal and longing to recreate that perfect experience. They can be headed for a restaurant dining room or their home kitchen, but every person leaves the performance with a hearty appetite and a focus on the next good meal.

Growing up in the south Louisiana town of New Iberia, I heard the rural counterparts to the city stories—which butcher made rice-stuffed boudin with just the right amount of pepper, where to buy shrimp fresh off the boats in Delcambre, why your grandmother made okra gumbo instead of using a roux. It was the same storytelling reflex in a rural setting: you were either talking about a fantastic meal or eating a fantastic meal. Sometimes both.

Years later, I moved back to Louisiana and found the food stories of New Orleans as compelling (and delicious) as ever. As a journalist and restaurant reviewer, I've had the good fortune to eat my way across the city, exploring its edible traditions and restaurants one bowl, plate and meal at a time. I've consumed countless variations of classics (gumbo, shrimp remoulade, bread pudding and down through the menu), dined at the über-formal "temples of Creole gastronomy" and tasted how ambitious young chefs constantly reinterpret the traditions and dishes of the city.

And in between meals, I've found so many things to love about this town. *Eating New Orleans* is a collection of these food stories: the ones that leave us hungry and longing, the ones that help us understand the Crescent City and its edible legacy.

how to USE THIS BOOK

Eating New Orleans is a hungry explorer's guide to the city's legendary restaurant scene, distinctive food culture and renowned barrooms. The book takes readers to the eateries where authentic Louisiana cuisine lives and breathes, from the French Quarter's white-linen Creole standbys to the funky family-owned joints that locals call home.

Equal parts travel book and food guide, *Eating New Orleans* delves into the city's lesser-known neighborhoods and provides plenty of tips for the well-fed traveler. Maps and browse-friendly lists provide valuable context while short features explain the city's distinctive specialty dishes, native ingredients and signature celebrations.

Chapter 1 (City of Appetites: Eating New Orleans) gives an overview of the city's restaurant scene, with brief discussions of south Louisiana's two distinctive native cuisines—Creole and Cajun—and how the modern tourist economy affects the way we eat.

Chapter 2 (The Big Picture: Neighborhoods, Logistics, and Finding Your Way) focuses on the logistics and practical aspects of exploring New Orleans. It contains a collection of neighborhood descriptions and maps that help demystify the city's often puzzling layout and explain why a normal compass just doesn't work in this town.

Chapter 3 (The Restaurants), the review section, represents the bulk of the book. The reviews are grouped by type instead of by name or neighborhood—the better to give a feel for the city's distinctive restaurant genres (oyster bars, poboy shops, etc.). Each section also contains magazine-style sidebars that explain classic New Orleans dishes, unfamiliar ingredients or other topics of interest.

The hundred or so restaurants represent different incarnations of New Orleans native food traditions—in other words, the food you'd have a hard time getting anywhere else. It's a selective list that includes classics, newcomers, neighborhood bars and fine dining establishments, but since its focus is on distinctive local foods, it doesn't contain listings for Mexican taquerias, sushi bars or restaurants specializing in Thai-California fusion.

Eating New Orleans is also admittedly city-centric. Though there are many notable restaurants outside of Orleans Parish in the outlying suburbs, there are very few listed in these pages. Given the in-town nature of most travelers, this seemed like the logical focus.

Also, I realize that there are fewer restaurants in these pages than in the hearts of its readers. I am one man with one gullet. That's just the way it goes.

A few notes on the review listings:

Addresses and Logistics
Restaurant addresses are given with cross streets for easy taxicab translation. Websites are listed only if the restaurant maintains its own domain (i.e. www.eatingneworleans.com).

Zone

In Chapter 2, I divide the city into nine broad zones for easy navigation. They tend to be larger than individual neighborhoods, but the names will make sense to most locals.

Meals

Since exact opening and closing times can change unexpectedly, the listings tell you which *meals* that the restaurants serve (lunch Monday through Friday, etc.). If an establishment is open 24 hours, it's listed as such.

Fancy Factor

The Fancy Factor is a simple rating system that ranks a restaurant's dress code and level of formality. It has three broad categories—high-, middle-, and lowbrow—that capture the overall vibe of a place from the "anything goes" dives to the upscale establishments where the maître d' acts as de facto fashion enforcer. Just for accuracy's sake, two intermediate levels (high- and low-middlebrow) round out the ratings.

Tourist-town dress codes tend to be a mixed bag, especially in subtropical climes that encourage a "shorts and flip-flops" aesthetic. Formal "dressing for dinner" is becoming less common in modern times, much to the chagrin of locals and members of older generations, who consider sports coats to be a little too casual for a nice evening out. Most restaurants that "suggest" a dress code focus specifically on men. (Go figure.) Semicoded buzz phrases ("business casual," "everyday sophisticated") are pretty common in the middlebrow and high-middlebrow range and translate to "no jeans, no tennis shoes, shirts with a collar, please."

> **Highbrow**—Strictly formal by contemporary standards. The most common buzz phrase, "coat and tie required for gentlemen," also assumes that the fellas will act accordingly. Sit up straight, because your grandmother might be watching.

> **Middlebrow**—One step above everyday kick-around clothing (collared shirts, no blue jeans, no tennis shoes, no shorts). Buzz phrases: "business casual," "coats and ties optional," "upscale casual."

> **Lowbrow**—Anything goes and the house couldn't care less. Guys can wear a tie-dyed tank top, saffron sarong and gladiator helmet if that's what's clean. Odds are your server won't even blink twice, as long as you tip well.

> **Nobrow**—A catchall category for retail establishments and other places where your wardrobe isn't an issue.

As a general rule, I tend to err on the formal side once you get to the high-middlebrow range, mostly for reasons of comfort. Though it's not uncommon for restaurants to seat parties who don't quite make the wardrobe cut, this situation can make for awkward cross-room glances. I'd rather have you a bit overdressed than feeling out of place in worn-out jeans and flip-flops. Or asking for a table at Antoine's in a Day-Glo NO FAT CHICKS T-shirt and matching Speedo. Unless that's your thing. In that case, knock yourself out.

Price Range
The prices listed are for entrées on the respective dinners during the fact-checking period of this book: early November 2004.

Caveats and Bonus Points
For the sake of convenience, *Eating New Orleans* assumes that each of the modern tourist-friendly restaurants follows this broad set of practical guidelines:

- accepts major credit cards
- closes on Monday
- has on-street parking
- closes at roughly 10 PM
- isn't particularly savvy to special-needs diners (vegetarians especially)

Caveats and bonus points alert you to establishments that don't provide these basics (caveat: cash only) or go above and beyond restaurant norms (bonus points: valet parking, open late-night).

Chapter 4 (Bars and Clubs) delves into the city's active cocktail and nightclub scene. The twenty-five thumbnail reviews represent about 0.00000001 percent of the fine watering holes in this bar-crazy town. In other words, just a few to get you started. The reviews are arranged by neighborhood—the better to encourage bar crawls that don't require a designated driver. A series of cocktail features describe some of New Orleans' signature drinks and contributions to international cocktail culture. It follows a similar format to the restaurant review section, but more bar-centric. All the categories are pretty self-explanatory (address, vibe, peak times, music, games). Note: for the games section, only communal bar games are included (pool, foosball, pinball, etc.). Video poker and video golf are not included in this category. Especially video golf. God, how I hate video golf . . .

Chapter 5 (Bayou Backroads) is a special trip out to the coastal countryside for the truly dedicated fans of things Cajun. Based out of the de facto regional capital of Lafayette, the chapter has thumbnail descriptions of notable restaurants in the small towns that dot south Louisiana's bayou country, coastal prairie and coastline.

The **Appendix** (Louisiana Pantry, Glossary) contains descriptions and resources for Louisiana ingredients as well as the traditional glossary and index.

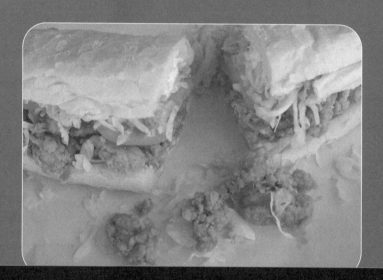

chapter 1
CITY OF APPETITES
Eating New Orleans

It's always exciting when the foodfolks come to town.

Whether they're in for a weeklong convention or a long weekend of pure indulgence, dedicated eaters come to New Orleans with a noble mission—to learn about the city's fascinating, distinctive food culture one plate at a time.

First-timers arrive in New Orleans armed with guidebook recommendations, cooking -show inspiration and the unbridled enthusiasm of hungry puppies. They're just starting their collection of perfect Louisiana meals and start their quest with a long weekend in the French Quarter, scarfing down a series of firsts: first gumbo, first jambalaya, first beignets, first poboy. There might be a few adventure foods thrown in for good measure (fried alligator, boiled crawfish) and a few high-octane frozen daiquiris to wash it all down.

Veterans hit the city with the same manic energy, but a different agenda. They know that any trip to New Orleans is measured in meals instead of days, and that the three-meal "breakfast/lunch/dinner" format might cost them valuable eating opportunities. The veterans need to relive great past meals as they explore neighborhoods outside the tourist-heavy Quarter. Not satisfied with the usual concierge suggestions, veterans are always on the prowl for new leads—asking cabbies, waiters and streetcar drivers where *they'd* go for lunch on Wednesday or for the perfect soft-shell crab. In between new experiences, they head back to their own secret spots, hoping to recreate perfect experiences in this idiosyncratic culinary capital.

Creole and Cajun: Compare and Contrast

We'll cover each in depth elsewhere (see pages 3–4), but here's a quick overview showing the broad differences between Louisiana's two most renowned native traditions. (Though many of the lines have blurred in modern times, these should give you a sense of the basic boundaries.)

	CREOLE	CAJUN
ORIGIN	New Orleans (city food) active restaurant culture	rural south Louisiana (country food) traditionally a home-kitchen cuisine
FLAVORS	flavors sophisticated, subtle	bolder, but balanced
PREPARATIONS	often complex with French-influenced sauces	slow-cooked one-pot recipes
SOME TYPICAL DISHES	Creole gumbo (see page 43) speckled trout meunière shrimp Clemenceau red beans and rice, fried seafood, turtle soup au sherry shrimp remoulade jambalaya (with tomato)	Chicken and andouille sausage gumbo (dark roux), boiled crawfish red beans and rice, white beans crawfish étouffée, fried seafood jambalaya (without tomato) boudin (rice sausage, see page 235)
TOMATOES IN GUMBO AND JAMBALAYA	yes	no
COMMON COOKING FAT	butter	lard
SAUSAGE	sausage chaurice, smoked	andouille, boudin

Give 'Em What They Want: Tourist Town Cuisine

Somewhere around the mid-1980s as the Cajun Hot movement was reaching its peak, New Orleans enjoyed new popularity as a "destination dining city" and Cajun food became the biggest draw in town.

Then in late 1985, the "oil bust" hit Louisiana as low petroleum prices crippled the state's oil-based economy, making the New Orleans economy even more dependent on the tourist trade. Twenty years later, tourism and related activities in the hospitality industry are New Orleans' biggest moneymakers (see below for more information).

By the time New Orleans made the shift from port city to tourist town, the line between Cajun and Creole was already thoroughly blurred. Cajun restaurants popped up in the French Quarter, run by businessmen hoping to capitalize on this potentially profitable case of mistaken identity.

And unfortunately for the long-standing Creole tradition, New Orleans is chanting the tourist town mantra:

Give 'Em What They Want.

It's a tourist town truism. If you've got a certain amount of money in your pocket—say fifty bucks—and you're looking for Cajun food, then someone will indeed sell you some version of Cajun food. (Of course, the same goes for sushi in Saskatchewan or burritos in Bangkok, but you get the idea.) Tourists expect to find Cajun food—and lo and behold—they find it.

The down side of tourist food is that it's often no better than the stuff you'd get back home in a generic shopping mall food court. And in the case of chain restaurant infiltration, it's often the EXACT SAME food you'd get back in your local mall.

Locals love it when traveling foodfolks come to the city, because it gives us an opportunity to show off some of what New Orleans does best. It gives us a chance to talk about our favorite restaurants, learn more about the city's evolving restaurant scene and remember the delicious traditions that we might take for granted sometimes.

All this to say, if you're headed to New Orleans and you're here to eat, then you're already among friends. Your curiosity and passion for good food is your backstage pass to one of the best food cities in the world.

A SENSE OF PLACE

Every year, New Orleans plays host to over 8 million visitors eager to sample the best food the city has to offer: refined Creole standards, rustic Cajun specialties and the creative contemporary dishes served up in the city's trendiest bistros.

Makes you hungry just thinking about it.

New Orleans' restaurants are as big a draw for the city as its legendary nightclub and music scenes. Travelers and tourists alike fill the city's dining rooms to get a taste of the city, and in many cases, the cuisines that you just can't find anywhere else.

Creole and Cajun: City and Country

South Louisiana's two distinctive regional cuisines—Creole and Cajun—are the driving forces behind the city's reputation as a restaurant town. Each of these culinary traditions has its own history, cultural influences and classic dishes. As recently as the 1970s, the two were considered as fundamentally distinct as their respective native cultures.

In simplest terms, Creole is the food of a vibrant port city—a sophisticated cuisine that blends diverse influences from three centuries of international trade and cultural cross-pollination. Marked by butter-rich sauces and reliance on fresh-caught seafood from the nearby Gulf of Mexico, Creole cuisine often bears a striking resemblance to continental French cooking (as typified in old-line Creole recipes) while still showing significant influence from West Africa (okra-thickened gumbos, red beans and rice). Early in the city's history, classical cooking techniques of early French aristocrats melded with those of African slave cooks, and the rich natural larder of the fledgling colony provided plentiful raw materials for the distinctive style. Other ethnic groups—among them Italians, Spaniards, Germans, Caribbean islanders and Croatians—influenced the city's evolving cuisine. As the "food of the city," Creole cooking is marked by rich sauces, smooth textures and subtle spices. (For a more complete discussion, see page 2.)

Cajun food, in contrast, is a more rustic cuisine that developed in the swampy countryside of south Louisiana. The originators of this unique cuisine were the Acadians,

Cajun Comes to the City

Compared to New Orleans' native Creole foods, Cajun cookery is a *Jeanny*-come-lately cuisine that moved from the Louisiana countryside in the mid-1970s.

Though home cooks prepared some dishes in the Cajun repertoire, the Crescent City restaurant scene didn't really embrace Louisiana's native "country food" until Paul Prudhomme (see opposite page) introduced a few dishes from his native Opelousas at Commander's Palace. His debut of simple but boldly spiced "country food" at a fancy Garden District eatery attracted enthusiastic diners and a wave of local and national press. By combining the two native traditions, Prudhomme brought Cajun traditions to the city, and though he went to pains to call his personal creations "Louisiana food," the label "Cajun food" became the default for all cuisine regardless of its region of origin.

In the mid-1980s, Louisiana's economy shifted from petroleum to tourism, and the "Cajun Hot" trend became an important part of New Orleans' public image. Somewhere in the marketing plan, Creole cuisine lost its caché and was eclipsed by its country cousin.

Almost thirty years later, you can see this mistaken identity as tourist restaurants offer "authentic Cajun specialties" in the center of New Orleans' historically Creole *Vieux Carré*.

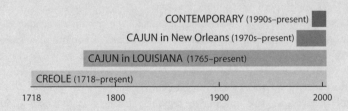

new orleans culinary timeline

Paul Prudhomme

Even though Cajun food was a staple in rural Louisiana kitchens for hundreds of years, it took a high-spirited boy from the prairie town of Opelousas to bring it to the world.

Paul Prudhomme brought the trademark dishes of Cajun cooking to New Orleans and through constant appearances on the TV talk-show circuit, became the representative of a previously undiscovered American cuisine. He introduced the diners to the wonders of Cajun cuisine: savory gumbos, buttery crawfish étouffée and jambalaya chunky with deep-smoked andouille sausage and plump Gulf shrimp. He demonstrated one of his signature dishes—a spicy, quick-seared preparation called "blackened redfish"—and touched off a nationwide mania for bolder flavors and new spice combinations. Dressed in chef's whites and a matching floppy cap instead of a toque, "Chef Paul" charmed audiences with natural charisma, quick wit and dishes that were at once approachable and exotic.

By the early 1980s, Prudhomme was an easily recognizable icon—one of America's first celebrity chefs (or at least the first professional chef to walk out of the kitchen and in front of the cameras) and the one most closely identified with a single culture and cuisine. In the minds of many, Chef Paul was the embodiment of then-trendy Cajun cuisine. The enthusiastic crowds followed him first to Commander's Palace (see page 91) and then to his French Quarter restaurant K-Paul's Louisiana Kitchen (see page 113). Twenty-five years later, Prudhomme has shifted focus from K-Paul's kitchen to other enterprises, most notably his work with his Magic Seasonings spice company. His early work helped bring the word "Cajun" into the international mainstream and still influences the New Orleans restaurant scene today.

French refugees from maritime Canada who arrived in Louisiana during the late 1700s. The Acadians (whose group name eventually Anglicized to "Cajuns") adapted their elemental one-pot dishes to the swamps, prairies and waterways of coastal Louisiana. They settled in small, mostly French-speaking communities and lived in relative isolation until the mid-twentieth century. The simpler "one-pot" cuisine of the Cajuns featured bolder spices than their Creole counterparts, and also made use of readily available ingredients whether they be the freshwater seafood (including the trademark crawfish) in bayou country, Gulf seafood along the coast or barnyard favorites (pork, smoked sausage, chicken) in the flat coastal prairie. (For a more complete discussion, see page 229.)

Paul Prudhomme's "Louisiana Food"

Until the 1970s, Creole and Cajun cuisines developed more or less independently. There was some cultural exchange between city and country, but mostly in home-cooking traditions. But that would all change in 1970s, when an itinerant chef from the Cajun prairie town of Opelousas accepted a job at a white-tablecloth Creole restaurant.

Paul Prudhomme, the charismatic culinary figure who would become the country's first celebrity chef, drew on his native Cajun traditions and his mastery of French technique (Creole and classical) to create a personal style he called "Louisiana food." Many of Prudhomme's trademark dishes—blackened redfish, cream sauces flavored with spicy Cajun tasso—were his own eclectic creations, but were considered by many to be authentically Cajun.

South of the South: French Louisiana

Even though Louisiana is traditionally considered part of the American South, the French Colonial culture and unique history of New Orleans and Cajun Country qualify the southern half of the state as its own distinctive region that goes beyond Mason-Dixon geography.

Consider French Louisiana a small Franco-Caribbean nation that shares a common border with the United States.

In cultural terms, Louisiana is divided into three distinct cultural zones: New Orleans, the biggest port and independent city-state; Acadiana, southern land of the Cajuns; and northern Louisiana, the only section that can be accurately called the "Deep South."

Geographically, of course, Louisiana *is* part of the "Deep South"—a term often applied to the group of states from coastal South Carolina to the eastern border of Texas. (It's tough to argue with compass directions, after all.) Culturally, though, Louisiana differs significantly from the other states in the region (Alabama, Georgia, Mississippi and South Carolina), which all share a host of common cultural features. States of the Deep South were settled by English immigrants, Scotch-Irish settlers and slaves brought over from the coast of West Africa. They have been historically rural, agricultural and often poverty-stricken. And in terms of religion, they are dominated by conservative strains of evangelical Protestantism.

All these characteristics are found in northern Louisiana, but they don't reflect the Franco-Catholic cultures of New Orleans and Cajun Country. French Louisiana's colonial experience separates it from the states of the Anglo-American "Bible Belt" in terms of history, culture and demographics. And it's the separation that gives French Louisiana its unique cultural flavors.

Strangely enough, from anywhere in French Louisiana, you need too drive due north to get to the American South.

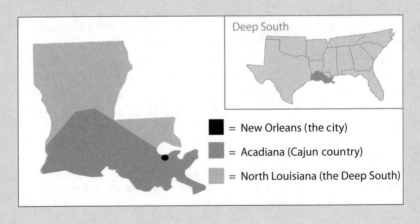

Deep South

■ = New Orleans (the city)

▇ = Acadiana (Cajun country)

▇ = North Louisiana (the Deep South)

At Commander's and then later at his own restaurant, K-Paul's Louisiana Kitchen, Prudhomme gained a national reputation for his cooking and made Cajun food one of the hottest food trends of the 1980s. A darling of the national TV talk shows, he demonstrated his signature dishes, told Louisiana stories and introduced Cajun culture to an international audience.

And when tourists arrived in New Orleans, they knew exactly what they wanted: Cajun food.

EATING WELL IN THE CRESCENT CITY

We'll close out this section with a few strategies for making the most out of your eating tour of the city; a few helpful guidelines to start you on your way.

Get Beyond the Quarter

The French Quarter is a great place, but as the neighborhood with the highest concentration of tourists, it's got a matching concentration of tourist traps. Even if it's your first time to the city, you should make sure and eat in neighborhoods with a higher house-to-hotel ratio.

Beware "Authentic"

Any menu should contain the word "authentic" or its synonyms once. Maybe twice. If an item is listed as "Authentic Cajun Jambalaya with Real Alligator Sausage from a secret Cajun family recipe," all the references to "real" make it seem fake. It's like a boyfriend saying, "I love you. Really."

Eating with the Seasons

Even though most of the world divides its year according to the weather patterns, Louisiana natives put an edible twist on the winter/spring/summer/fall continuum.

As the old joke goes, Louisiana has its OWN seasons: oyster, crawfish, crab and shrimp.

Being a subtropical, swampy kind of place, Louisiana has a mild climate with a year-round growing season. The term "hard freeze" doesn't get a lot of play in south Louisiana.

Of course, a long growing season doesn't mean that certain trademark foods aren't better at certain times of the year. Live crawfish, for example, are their at peak during the springtime, while early summer is when tangy Creole tomatoes are so good they can make a grown man weep.

All this to say that the tourist food factor is in effect: beware the restaurant that wants to sell you boiled crawfish in September.

Here's a quick chart—broad groupings based on peak season—to help you eat with Louisiana's distinctive food-based seasons.

SEASON	SEAFOOD	PRODUCE
WINTER	oysters some live crawfish	satsumas and Louisiana citrus Greens (turnip, collard, etc.)
SPRING	live crawfish soft-shell crabs	Ponchatoula strawberries Creole tomatoes (through early summer) dewberries (wild blackberries)
SUMMER	crab pompano early shrimp	sweet corn, peaches watermelon, Louisiana blueberries okra
FALL	shrimp flounder	irliton (vegetable pear) Opelousas sweet potato

Saving Louisiana's Traditional Foods: The Slow Food Movement's Ark of Taste

Part culinary movement, part workaday philosophy, Slow Food International is a global organization dedicated to battling the spread of fast food and a "convenience over taste" mindset that they see as endemic in modern industrialized societies.

For the Slow Food crowd, the dinner table is both a place of pleasure and a chance to revive traditional products and regional dishes. Their culinary call to arms states that "Our defense should begin at the table with Slow Food. Let us rediscover the flavors and savors of regional cooking and banish the degrading effects of Fast Food."

Ten years after its founding in 1986, the group founded the "Ark of Taste," an endangered species list of products (seafoods, grains, fruits, cheeses) the group considered on the brink of modern-day extinction. Like Noah, the project's biblical inspiration, the group pledged to "save the cherished Slow Foods, one product at a time" by raising awareness and creating new markets for the disappearing products.

The American chapter of the group (Slow Food USA) has recognized many Louisiana foods in the Ark, including:

Creole Cream Cheese—A tangy fresh cheese similar to French Neufchâtel (see page 246).
Daube Glacé—A New Orleans Creole preparation of cooked beef chunks suspended in a rich jellied medium.
Hogshead Cheese—Another gelatinous specialty from Louisiana's rich charcuterie tradition. Tender meat from a long-boiled pig's head (hence the name) is ground and cooled into a jellified loaf.
Louisiana Cane Syrup—A sweeter cousin of molasses, cane syrup is a thick, dark syrup made from slow-cooking sugarcane juice in huge cast-iron pots.
Louisiana Heritage Strawberries—The sweet-tart local varieties that thrive across the state, especially in Ponchatoula, the state's strawberry capital.
Roman Chewing Candy—Hand-pulled taffy still sold from a single mule-drawn cart in New Orleans (see page 201).
Tasso—A spicy smoked seasoning meat common in traditional Cajun cooking (see page 235).
Wild Louisiana Catfish—Free-swimming freshwater catfish. A response to the growing industrial aquaculture trade.

For more information on Slow Food's continuing work, visit www.slowfoodusa.org.

Ask Around

Every citizen of New Orleans has got a favorite meal that they love to talk about. Instead of asking a concierge about where they'd recommend, ask cab drivers, house painters or people waiting at the bus stop.

The Home Town Rule

If you recognize a restaurant from back home, pass it by. In a city that's got hundreds of unique dining experiences, it would be a shame to waste one at T.G.I.McFrankley's Burgertorium, even if you're crazy about their Exploding Onion Strips. Don't Worry: You'll find a suitable substitute.

When New Orleans was the capital
of the Spanish Province of Lui-
siana. 1762 — 1803
This street bore the name
CALLE D SAN LUIS

chapter 2
THE BIG PICTURE
Neighborhoods, Logistics, and Finding Your Way

It's been called the most European of American cities, and the northernmost outpost of the Caribbean. By most standards, New Orleans just doesn't *feel* like an American city.

Unlike the boomtowns of the Sun Belt, New Orleans was designed well before the age of the automobile. Many of its streets don't accommodate heavy car traffic comfortably, making it a pedestrian-friendly town reminiscent of European and older American cities. Unlike many of its boomtown counterparts, it's possible to live and work in New Orleans without owning a car.

Much of the modern-day city is surrounded by water—the Mississippi River creating a fast-flowing boundary on three sides and the shoreline of Lake Pontchartrain forming a northern frontier. Rather than forming a rectangular grid, the city's urban plan breaks into irregular shapes—triangular neighborhoods contain streets that disappear after a few blocks, grand boulevards follow the gentle curve of the river.

With a population of about 500,000 inside the city limits, it's about the size of Charlotte, North Carolina, or Columbus, Ohio. (Add the metropolitan suburbs, and the population registers at approximately 1.5 million.) In modern times, it's been a poor city with its share of urban problems caused by endemic poverty. Fifty years ago, the economy was powered by offshore oil drilling; a century before that by a flourishing international shipping trade.

Today, New Orleans is a cultural center, tourist town and (as all good foodfolks know) an international culinary destination.

BEYOND BOOBS AND BEADS: THE MARDI GRAS MYSTIQUE

Like any other modern-day tourist town, New Orleans thrives by attracting travelers. Other American cities can rely on a familiar landmark as their icon—San Francisco has the Golden Gate Bridge, New York the Statue of Liberty. New Orleans sells its carefree reputation and ability to throw a good party.

New Orleans has a different image—the nonstop party atmosphere that most people associate with Mardi Gras. Without a soaring structure to put on our postcards, we build our marketing plans and ad campaigns encouraging visitors to come get

Crescent City vs. Big Easy

A quick note on nicknames: despite the fact that marketing types use the term constantly, "The Big Easy" isn't considered a local's preferred nickname for New Orleans. Among natives, "Crescent City" is the most commonly used alternative, or simply "home."

The Big Easy came into common usage sometime in the 1980s, as many smaller cities were trying to find a riff on New York's "Big Apple" moniker. Though it's rumored to be linked to an early-twentieth-century dance hall, the phrase (and usage thereof) is the conversational equivalent of off-season Mardi Gras beads: the mark of an outsider.

The Crescent City makes more sense because of New Orleans' placement on the curving riverbank. Before it was possible to drain the swamps behind the French Quarter, the city grew along the riverbanks in an elongated crescent shape. That, and the fact that it sounds a lot better.

Beads out of Season

It's completely proper to wear elaborate, glittering beads in the city, but only during the actual Carnival season (see page 33). On the way to and from Mardi Gras parades, you're likely to see the entire population festooned with huge and elaborate faux jewelry caught from last year's floats and worn with pride. The shiny plastic trophies are part of the city's biggest theatrical celebration and are most importantly flung to the audience free of charge.

During the other ten or eleven months of the year, Mardi Gras beads are seen as the mark of the not-so-savvy conventioneer and folks who just don't understand the city. Given the preponderance of tchotchke shops in the Quarter, it's inevitable that some people will shell out five or ten dollars a string for necklaces decorated with comically big Christmas ornaments, interlocking plastic marijuana leaves or the logo of a favorite sports team. Unlike the tourist tradition of "getting lei'd" in Hawaii, some establishments (casinos, museums) will provide a few shiny strands custom-embossed with a corporate logo or two. But be advised that it's like wearing Mickey Mouse ears while walking around downtown LA.

Words to the wise: resist the urge.

their taste of the Carnival spirit—complete with elaborate floats, shiny beads and dancing in the streets. The city's food and musical traditions play an integral part in this Mardi Gras caricature—usually quick shots of spicy boiled crawfish and a brass band second-lining down a picturesque French Quarter alleyway.

We sell New Orleans as one big party that never lets up—a year-round Mardi Gras that kicks off the second you step off the plane. The sales job has been so successful that Bourbon Street is now synonymous with "outta-town exhibitionism"—*carte blanche* to do things you wouldn't DARE do in your own hometown. Get drunk on the streets. Flash your breasts for a few glittery trinkets. Stay out all night and sleep in past noon.

Try doing *that* back home in Terre Haute.

The arrangement has advantages and its downsides—it brings in much-needed revenue, but it also turns New Orleans' distinctive culture into just another commodity. For a fee, any organization can hire an event-planning company to throw a private "Mardi Gras– themed parade" any time of year.

The mystique convinces people that there's really nothing beyond the French Quarter, and in some ways, it's just like home. And most importantly, that *anything* can be had for a price.

The tourist trade requires year-round access to signature foods whether or not they're pulled from nearby waters or harvested from local fields. Your crawfish might be shipped in from Sacramento, and as a result you'll be charged a premium price for an experience that's a pale reflection of the real thing when it's in season.

The good news is that there's a whole world of authentic experience beyond the neon-lit establishments that peddle our carnival-like caricature. And once you know what to look for, the tourist traps are surprisingly easy to avoid.

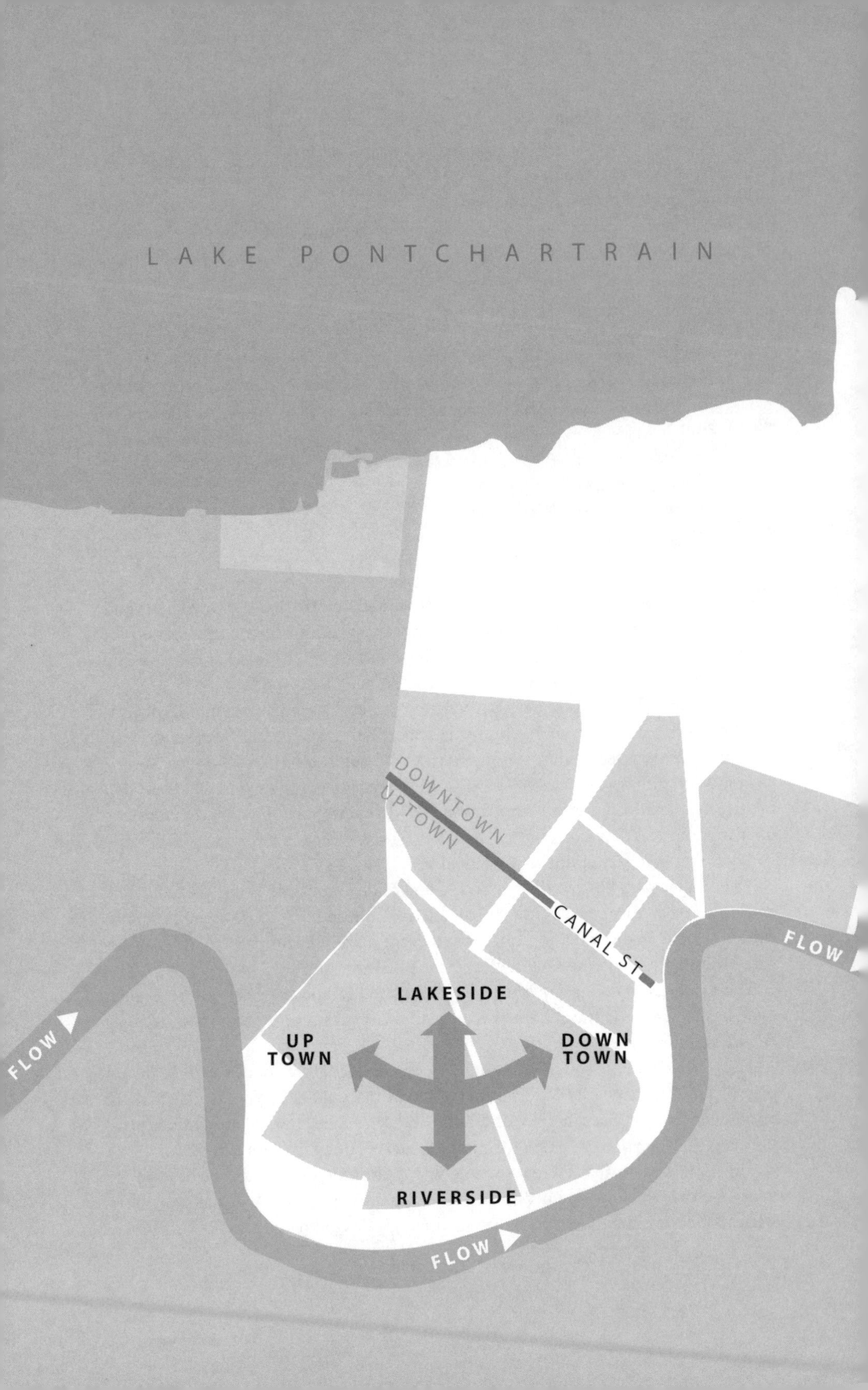

LAKE PONTCHARTRAIN

DOWNTOWN
UPTOWN

CANAL ST

FLOW

FLOW

LAKESIDE

UP
TOWN

DOWN
TOWN

RIVERSIDE

FLOW

New Orleans Compass Points

Navigating New Orleans can make you crazy if you let it. Actually, it only *really* drives you crazy if you think about it in typical compass terms.

The answer to any "How do you get to . . ." query will almost never include reference to the usual compass directions (North/South/East/West) but instead substitute their New Orleans equivalents (Lakeside/Riverside/Downtown/Uptown). If you can wrap your mind around this, you're halfway to becoming a local.

Understanding the Lakeside/Riverside axis is fairly easy—the lake sits to the north of the city and the Mississippi's lowest point is functionally south. (None of the streets run straight along this axis, hence the "functional" designation.)

Grasping Uptown/Downtown, however, requires you know a little about the river itself. New Orleans is tucked into a little oxbow of the river, which flows west to east before heading south on the far side of the city. The terms "Uptown" and "Downtown" are linked to the direction of the river's FLOW, in this case Uptown means upriver and Downtown means downriver (against or with the flow of the river, respectively). See map.

Since New Orleans was once a much smaller city, the dividing line between the sections of town was Canal Street, the grand boulevard that currently separates the French Quarter from the Central Business District. Everything to the curving east of Canal is considered Uptown (upriver) and everything to the wiggly west is Downtown (downriver).

LAY OF THE LAND: THE NEIGHBORHOOD ZONES

If you spend your whole New Orleans trip in the French Quarter, then map reading is a breeze. Any destination is a few turns and twelve blocks away, tops. Any set of directions will include only three directions (left, right or straight) and life couldn't be simpler.

But expand your view beyond the orderly grid of the Quarter and things get a lot more complicated. For one, the Quarter doesn't really look like itself on a city map—instead of being aligned in a perfect page-sized grid, it's tilted off to one side, pointing almost due northwest (or southeast, depending on your perspective). The rest of the streets (familiar names like Magazine, Broad or Tchoupitoulas) form a complex maze bounded by the U-shaped bend of the Mississippi to the gently arcing south shore of Lake

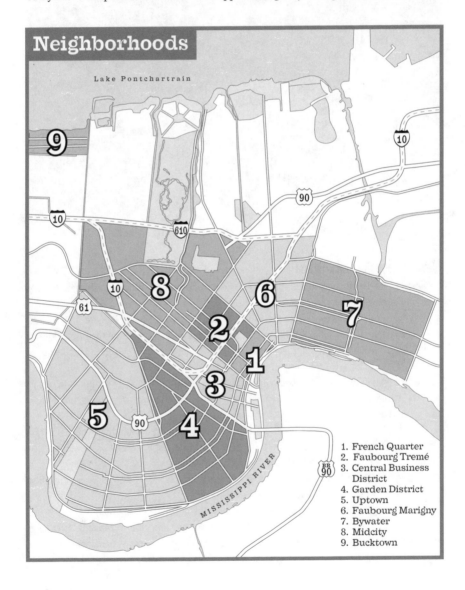

Neighborhoods

Lake Pontchartrain

MISSISSIPPI RIVER

1. French Quarter
2. Faubourg Tremé
3. Central Business District
4. Garden District
5. Uptown
6. Faubourg Marigny
7. Bywater
8. Midcity
9. Bucktown

Pontchartrain. Some neighborhoods are made up of mostly straight streets, while others look more like wagon wheels.

In other words, it's pretty easy to get lost in New Orleans.

Navigation is a LOT easier if you split the city up into manageable chunks.

In the review section, we're dividing the city into nine neighborhood clusters that will make sense to any local in town. Some contain single regions (such as the easily delineated French Quarter) while others are combinations of adjacent neighborhoods (such as the Central Business District/Warehouse District cluster).

Natives often refer to the neighborhoods by more specific names based on ward number, housing project or historic subdivision ("Ooooh, that's over between Pigeontown and Hollygrove . . .) but travelers rarely require that level of detail. If you're headed for a dinner at a restaurant in the Riverbend, referring to it as "Uptown" gives your cabbie plenty of information to work with.

THE NEIGHBORHOODS
French Quarter

In the beginning of its colonial era, the French Quarter wasn't just a neighborhood, it was the city itself. When Jean Baptiste Bienville laid out the plan for Nouvelle Orleans, the port city was positioned at a strategic turn in the river, and laid out in even, right-angled blocks. Unlike some western towns whose thoroughfares developed from cattle tracks and footpaths, New Orleans had a precise six-by-twelve-block grid fronting on the river, a prominent public square and earthwork barricades to protect it from attack. The streets were named after French nobility and their patron saints, a flattery that would make it easier to secure financing for the fledgling settlement. Names like St. Ann, Dauphine, Toulouse, Urslines and, of course, Bourbon (named for the royal house instead of the Kentucky liquor). Battlements protected the settlement on three nonriver sides—upriver on what is now Canal Street, downriver on modern-day Esplanade Avenue, and to the rear, the appropriately named Rampart Street.

The boundaries still exist today, and though the neighborhood has undergone countless changes since its initial planning, the French Quarter still maintains a historic character from its early years. Two fires swept through the Quarter during the Spanish

▬ TOURIST TIPS ▬

Oh TAXI!

If you're coming in from a city with single-color taxi fleets, you're likely to be a little confused in the Crescent City. New Orleans is a city of small operations and independent gypsy cabs. A hodgepodge fleet—anything from a late-model minivan to a tattered old Coupe de Ville with the driver's name spelled out with hardware-store adhesive letters.

The general rule of thumb: call United (504-524-9606) or choose your gypsy cabs judiciously. Most restaurants call United.

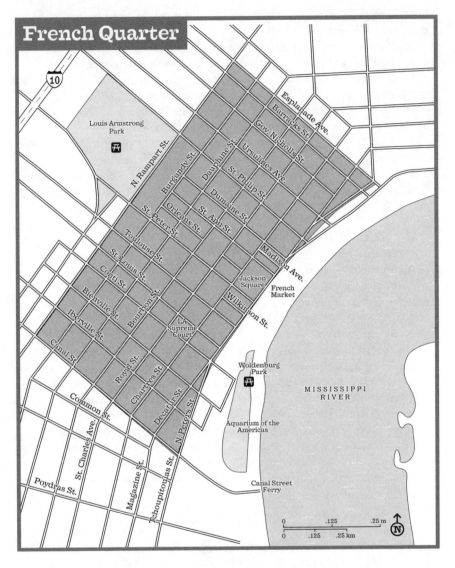

French Quarter

administration (one in 1788 and another six years later), requiring a rebuilding in the Spanish architectural style that included broad galleries with ornate cast iron balconies. As the city developed, the original area, still a bastion of old Creole culture, became known as the Vieux Carré (Old Quarter), and with the arrival of other ruling groups, the French Quarter (to distinguish it from the American and Spanish sections of the growing city).

The modern-day Quarter is a study in almost surreal contrast. Historic market buildings and warehouses have been converted to endless stretches of T-shirt shops packed with five-dollar strings of Mardi Gras beads. Former eighteenth-century residences have mostly gone condo for part-time residents, while a few are cut up into multi-apartment spaces housing longtime Quarter denizens. Sidewalk stoops seem to welcome the walk-

People of the Port: Ethnic Influence

It's tempting to reduce New Orleans' complex history to its flag-flying rulers (French 1718–65, Spain 1775–1800, France 1800–03, United States 1803-present) but as a major trading center, the city was equally shaped by the groups that passed through its port. Here are a few of the major ethnic groups that left their mark on New Orleans and the cuisine of the city.

French/French Creoles—The founders of the city and their descendents. Laid the cultural foundation starting with the city's founding in 1718.

Africans (1700s)—Slaves from Senegal, Gambia, Nigeria and other modern-day west African nations.

Spanish—Administrators and caretakers of the colony. Responsible for much of the historic French Quarter architecture (broad galleries, intricate ironwork). 1765–1800

German—These early settlers came to Louisiana in the 1720s and many settled upriver in present day St. Charles and St. John the Baptist Parishes, also referred to as the Cote Allemandes (the German coast). Farmers, bakers and sausage makers.

Croatians—Immigrants from the Dalmatian coast of the Adriatic sea (former Yugoslavia). Originally settled in the city and coastal Plaquemines Parish in the 1820s. Built Louisiana's oyster industry, contributed their own flavors (garlic, olive oil, etc.) to the local cuisine.

Caribbean—Haitians from the revolution and freed slaves made their way to New Orleans in the eighteenth century.

Irish (two waves—1803–30 and another from 1830–62)—Significant impact on the city, but not so much on its food.

Vietnamese—the newest major immigrant group. After 1975, the Catholic diocese actively aided refugees fleeing Vietnam and resettled them in New Orleans East.

by pedestrian traffic; wrought-iron gateways topped with sharpened spear-tips or colorful shards of broken bottle glass provide dark, artistic protection from would-be intruders. And at all hours of the night, the rhythmic clop of mule hooves echoes off brightly colored shotgun houses and Creole cottages—adding to the romance and mystery of the old city.

The Vieux Carré restaurant scene is a mixed bag, from the rightly famous Creole old-line institutions to corporate chains that would be at home just about anywhere in the U.S. Visitors should be aware that much of the Quarter's prime real estate in the high-traffic tourist areas has been converted to eateries of various types and quality levels. And with the prime space often comes premium prices. When choosing a restaurant in the Quarter, keep this rule of thumb in mind: if a joint *has* a barker out front to lure in the crowds, the food usually *requires* a barker to bring in diners.

CBD/Warehouse District
Neighborhoods: Central Business District, Warehouse District

A short jaunt across Canal Street puts you in a completely different world from the human-scale, historic Vieux Carré. All of a sudden you're surrounded by office towers, modern

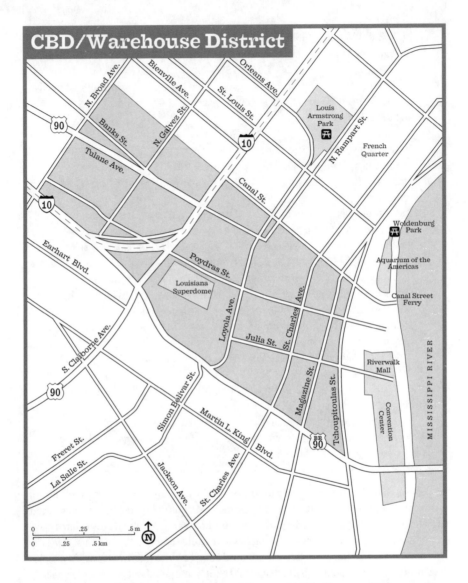

CBD/Warehouse District

N. Broad Ave. · Bienville Ave. · Orleans Ave. · St. Louis St. · 90 · Banks St. · N. Galvez St. · 10 · N. Rampart St. · Louis Armstrong Park · French Quarter · Tulane Ave. · Canal St. · 10 · Earhart Blvd. · Poydras St. · Woldenburg Park · Louisiana Superdome · Aquarium of the Americas · Canal Street Ferry · Loyola Ave. · St. Charles Ave. · Julia St. · Riverwalk Mall · S. Claiborne Ave. · 90 · Simon Bolivar St. · Magazine St. · Tchoupitoulas St. · Convention Center · MISSISSIPPI RIVER · Freret St. · Martin L. King Blvd. · BB 90 · La Salle St. · Jackson Ave. · St. Charles Ave.

0   .25   .5 m
0   .25   .5 km   N

multistory hotels and a vibe that's eerily reminiscent of 1970s Houston. There are a few historic structures sprinkled among the new stuff, but the two neighborhoods in this zone—the Central Business District (CBD) and the Warehouse District—house the city's corporate and modern tourist infrastructure, including the cavernous Ernest Morial Convention Center, cruise ship docking facilities, the Riverwalk mall, and Louisiana's only land-based casino complex. Second only to the Quarter in terms of tourist attractions, this is where the conventioneers roam with conference badges clanking against complimentary corporate-themed Mardi Gras necklaces.

In any other city, the Central Business District would just be called "downtown." Located on the upriver side of Canal Street, it's the home of a mixed bag of architectural styles—

towering 80s-era high-rises, Art Deco drugstores and nineteenth-century Beaux Arts office blocks. Responsible for most of the New Orleans skyline, the CBD changes personality almost block to block—the area near the Louisiana Superdome resembles oil-boom Houston, while sections nearer the Quarter can feel like New York in the 1920s.

Formerly a run-down series of decaying dockside buildings, the Warehouse District started its modern development during the much-maligned 1984 World's Fair, which opened up a stretch of the riverfront to commercial tourist development. In recent years, the renovation has become a hot spot for art galleries, huge tourist hotels, high-dollar loft apartments and warehouse conversions. The Warehouse District is also home to the city's new art and history museums.

The two neighborhoods have their share of upscale hotel restaurants, as well as high-profile contemporary eateries. In the 1990s, an ambitious Commander's Palace alumnus took a chance by opening his first restaurant in a not-so-swanky Warehouse District location, but Mr. Lagasse's gamble paid off, as Emeril's provides a prominent anchor for the neighborhood. Other restaurants and clubs now populate the spit-and-polish hipster zone.

Garden District
Neighborhoods: Garden District, Lower Garden District, Irish Channel, Central City

Next to the Quarter, the Garden District is the most familiar neighborhood to the average tourist, thanks to the grand St. Charles Avenue and its historic streetcar. If a Quarter-bound tourist ventures out of the Old City, they'll hop a train to gawk at the stately Greek Revival mansions and grand Victorian houses of the first American robber

▮TOURIST TIPS▮

Public Transit

City dwellers who depend on public transit in their everyday life (I'm looking at YOU, New Yorkers) will probably spend a lot of time at the bus stop checking their watches and staring up the road. Even though the busses and streetcars technically follow a set timetable, the schedule tends to have a Caribbean feel to it. To be charitable, let's say that it's not quite as  consistent as Switzerland. You might wait for thirty minutes without seeing a bus, only to have three pull up to your stop simultaneously. In other words, when you're on your way to fixed-time dinner reservations, keep your eyes out for a taxicab as a backup.

barons. Fans of modern-day author and vampire promoter Anne Rice stalk the side streets around the writer's former house and walking around the easily accessible above-ground graves of Lafayette Cemetery #1.

The adjacent neighborhoods don't quite have the tourist appeal of this historic "American" neighborhood, but are every bit as significant. Magazine Street cuts through the Lower Garden District with a stretch of renovated shops and peaceful residential areas. Closer to the river, the old Irish Channel neighborhood was the original disembarking point for much of the city's nineteenth-century Irish immigrants following the

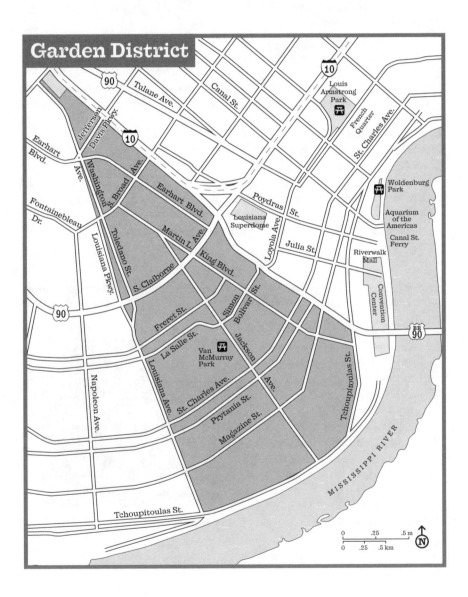

mid-century potato famine. Streets named after the nine Greek muses run through Central City, a historically poverty-stricken neighborhood that's nonetheless home to strikingly beautiful architecture in decay.

Restaurants in these sections run the gamut from neighborhood soul-food joints to old line standbys to barrooms and hidden treasures.

Bourbon Street: Welcome to the Neon Zone

If you're a first-time visitor to New Orleans, there's just no avoiding it.

After hearing so many tales of decadence and city-sanctioned overindulgence, after seeing Mardi Gras video footage and late-night infomercials, after feeling the gravitational pull of near-flammable frozen drinks, questionable "gentleman's clubs" and pedestrian cocktail culture—folks just have to have their own personal Bourbon Street experience. And for that, they've got to hit the Neon Zone.

When visitors hear the phrase "Bourbon Street," they conjure up images of this seven-block stretch of Bourbon between Canal and St. Anne Streets. It's a wonderland of boisterous cover bars, topless clubs, streetside beer vendors and barkers that try to sell the sizzle to anything on two legs. It's the natural habitat of boa-draped bachelorette parties, whooping herds of Greek-lettered students and 14-year-old boys of all ages. Off-hour conventioneers, nice Christian families, porcupine-pierced gutter punks and pneumatic exotic dancers in spray-on shortshorts roam this pedestrian-only zone looking for their personal version of action as bright neon lights bathe it all in a soft, eerie glow.

For first-timers or any attendee of a regional sales conference, the Neon Zone has "moth to flame" appeal—bright, shiny and pretty much unavoidable.

It is also the section of New Orleans most responsible for the city's saucy, somewhat illicit and gloriously tacky reputation. Shot bars. T-shirt shops. Dance clubs. Off-season bead emporiums. Closet-width storefronts that magically contain a thousand churning frozen daiquiri machines. The distinctive smell of stale beer, cigar smoke, grain alcohol, fried foods and various bodily fluids. And sitting on the sidelines, the gigantic steel weenies and half-lidded gazes of the Lucky Dog vendors.

Which is not to say that the Zone doesn't have its share of gems; many of the city's historic old-line Creole restaurants—Galatoire's, Antoine's, Broussard's and Arnaud's to name a few—are either half a block off Bourbon or smack dab in the middle of the boozy affair.

A few blocks closer to Esplanade, Bourbon turns quiet; just another secluded residential street on the downriver end of the historic Vieux Carré. Outside the Zone, even Bourbon Street takes a breather.

If you're here to do the things that you wouldn't *dream* of doing in your own town— New Orleans gives you a brightly lit, no-holds-barred place to go wild for the weekend. But if you want to know the true nature of the city, walk away from the Neon Zone and see New Orleans in a more natural light. No beer goggles required.

Block-to-Block Town

Even if you never leave the French Quarter, you'll soon figure out that New Orleans is a relatively poor city, and that you're never too far away from that aspect of urban reality. To put it in other terms, New Orleans doesn't have well-defined areas of wealth or poverty. It's been described quite poetically as a "block-to-block town" where people of different races and classes live in close proximity. Even the grand mansions on St. Charles aren't far from some of the more destitute sections of Baronne Street.

The city's natural and architectural beauty can make you forget that New Orleans is a three-hundred-year-old city with its share of urban blight and street crime. Don't let a little grit deter you from exploring the city's lesser-known districts, but take care to "keep your city eyes on." For a traveler in an unfamiliar town, a little awareness can go a long way.

Uptown
Neighborhoods: Uptown, Riverbend, Carrollton, University

Just a bit farther upriver, the loose group of neighborhoods are collectively known as "Uptown" more for their direction than uptown. Formerly a series of wedge-shaped plantation grants, the Uptown neighborhoods became early faubourgs (suburbs) before being annexed by the growing city.

As the "long streets" (Tchoupitoulas, Magazine, St. Charles) follow the broad curve of the river, the Uptown neighborhoods seem like a continuation of the Garden District aesthetic, without the prissy, vaguely British name. The streetcar continues down St. Charles, going past streets named for Emperor Napoleon and his great victories (Marengo, Milan, Cadiz, Valence). Uptown is the land of the oaks—mountainous, centuries-old live oaks provide constant shade as they muscle their way through the concrete sidewalks with ease. Narrow streets are lined with shotgun houses—everyday architecture that has stood the test of time, whether or not they're renovated to showcase condition.

The streetcar rumbles past the Tulane and Loyola campuses—two prominent universities sitting side by side and facing the vast, idyllic Audubon Park, which stretches from St. Charles to the river. At Carrollton Avenue, the train hangs a right into the Riverbend neighborhood not far from the Mississippi's towering levee structure.

Though not nearly as compact as the French Quarter, Uptown is home to many of the city's more famous restaurants, especially the house bistros that sprang up in the 1980s. Most are hidden away among the residential neighborhoods and are favorites of locals and tourists savvy enough to explore this tree-shaded section of the city.

Faubourg Tremé

Situated just lakeside of the French Quarter, the Faubourg Tremé (Treh-MAY) is one of the city's most culturally rich neighborhoods, despite the fact that it's currently one of the city's most economically poor. Located just across Rampart from the French Quarter, Tremé is

Uptown

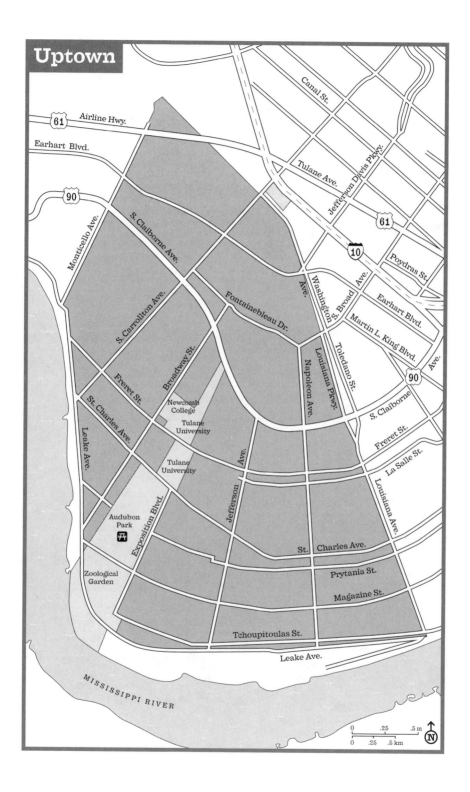

Canal St.

61 Airline Hwy.

Earhart Blvd.

Tulane Ave.

Jefferson Davis Pkwy.

90

61

Monticello Ave.

S. Claiborne Ave.

10

Poydras St.

Washington Ave.

S. Broad Ave.

Earhart Blvd.

Fontainebleau Dr.

S. Carrollton Ave.

Martin L. King Blvd.

Toledano St.

90

Ave.

Louisiana Pkwy.

Napoleon Ave.

S. Claiborne

Broadway St.

Frencht St.

Newcomb
College

Tulane
University

Freret St.

St. Charles Ave.

La Salle St.

Louisiana Ave.

Leake Ave.

Tulane
University

Jefferson Ave.

Audubon
Park

Exposition Blvd.

St. Charles Ave.

Zoological
Garden

Prytania St.

Magazine St.

Tchoupitoulas St.

Leake Ave.

MISSISSIPPI RIVER

0   .25   .5 m
0   .25   .5 km

N

also home of some of the funkier tourist attractions (New Orleans' first cemetery, voodoo queen Marie Laveaux's grave, Louis Armstrong Park at Congo Square), some of the rougher public housing projects in the city—Lafitte, etc.—and a few genre-defining Creole restaurants.

The Tremé is arguably the home of the defining American music, as many historians attribute the birth of jazz to Congo Square, where West African slaves met on Sundays to participate in drum ceremonies according to the French Colonial rules known as the "Code Noir." After Haiti's 1794 revolution, "free persons of color" streamed into the city and settled in the Tremé. In modern times, it is home of the modern second line parade tradition, the Zulu Social Aid and Pleasure Club and many of the hard-working Mardi Gras Indians.

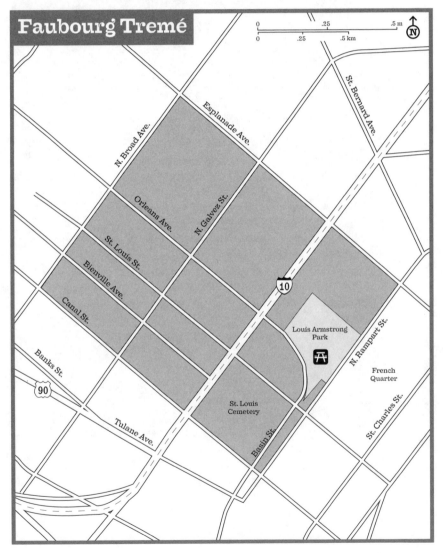

For much of the twentieth century, the Tremé was a flourishing district for the African-American middle class until the construction of the Interstate overpass decimated the businesses along its main commercial artery, North Claiborne Avenue.

Faubourg Marigny
Neighborhoods: Faubourg Marigny, Bywater, St. Roch, 9th Ward
Visually and historically, the Faubourg Marigny is the downriver extension of the French Quarter. A quick jump across Esplanade Avenue—things take a funky turn where the even rectangular blocks change to a more triangular street grid as the geometric urban plan yields to the river and things get a little tougher to navigate.

Formerly home to a thriving Creole population outside the limits of the Quarter, the Marigny has as its border Esplanade Avenue, the "Creole St. Charles"—known for its extravagant and beautiful Creole homes and oak-shaded atmosphere.

The Marigny is the gateway to the downriver sections of the city—where the postcolonial Creoles settled when the Quarter pretty much filled up, and in contemporary times where the city's gay community coalesced and revived the run-down neighborhood. It's a sense of closeness, a sense of "to the curb" building that marks other downtown neighborhoods.

▦ TOURIST TIPS ▦

On Foot
I can tell what you power walkers are thinking. "Wow! New Orleans is so small and flat, we can just hike the whole time. What an opportunity for fitness!"

And while New Orleans is scaled perfectly as an old-school walking city, there are a couple of things you should know about long-distance hiking in the Crescent City.

Navigation—Even for most natives, the city's layout is confusing as hell on the best of days. Once you get outside the very orderly French Quarter and CBD/Warehouse District, the street grid breaks down fairly quickly, and it's easy to get disoriented. I'm not saying that you need to leave a trail of bread crumbs or anything, but a good full-city street map is always helpful if you're taking in the sights by foot.

Sweat Factor—Make no mistake, long-distance walking in New Orleans is a distinctly subtropical experience and usually requires at least one change of clothes and constant rehydration. Many well-intentioned walkers get the hint after a few blocks, when they sweat through their shirts. During the height of summertime, you can pretty much forget it. If you get winded after a spell, take advantage of one of the city's many dark barrooms (cool, soothing, refreshing, aaaaaahhhh . . .).

City Factor—New Orleans is a patchwork town when it comes to development and poverty, so you might plot a linear course between destinations that takes you through some rougher neighborhoods. Stop short of being paranoid, but as in any city, you should operate with your "city rules" in effect. (See "Block-to-Block Town" on page 22.)

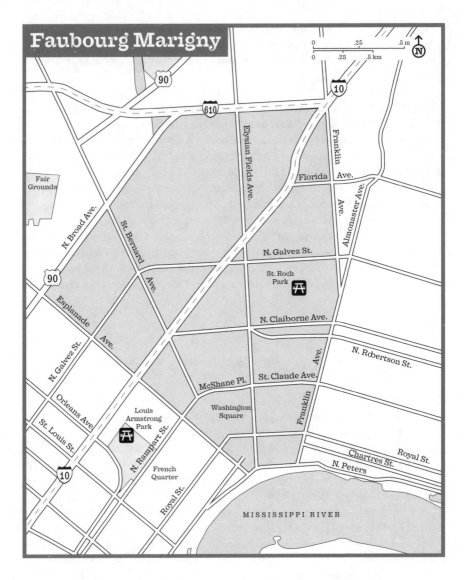

Faubourg Marigny

In recent years, a number of restaurants and notable clubs have sprung up around the neighborhood, especially on bustling Frenchman Street near the river. On Mardi Gras morning, the semi-impromptu St. Anne's Parade gathers on Royal Street in the Marigny, making it the place to see over-the-top costuming without the tourist hoards.

Midcity
Neighborhoods: Esplanade Ridge, Faubourg/Bayou St. John
In modern times, Midcity is best known as the home of the New Orleans Jazz and Heritage Festival, held every April and May at the New Orleans Fairgrounds horse-

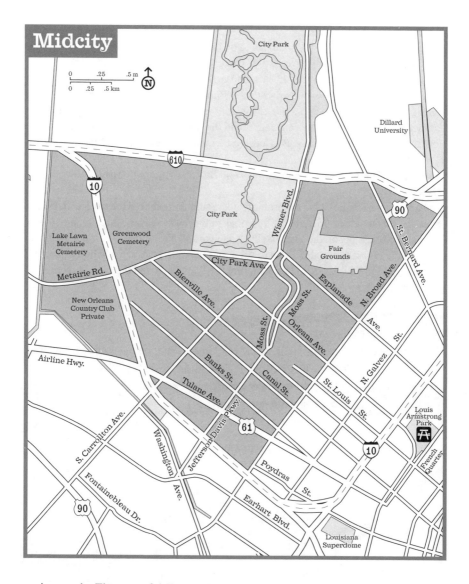

Midcity

0   .25   .5 m
0   .25   .5 km

N

City Park

Dillard
University

610

10

City Park

Lake Lawn
Metairie
Cemetery

Greenwood
Cemetery

Wisner Blvd.

City Park Ave.

Fair
Grounds

90

St. Bernard Ave.

Metairie Rd.

New Orleans
Country Club
Private

Bienville Ave.

Esplanade

N. Broad Ave.

Moss St.

Orleans Ave.

Ave.

St.

Airline Hwy.

Banks St.

Moss St.

Canal St.

St. Louis

N. Galvez

St.

Tulane Ave.

Louis
Armstrong
Park

S. Carrollton Ave.

Washington Ave.

Jefferson Davis Pkwy.

61

10

French
Quarter

Fontainebleau Dr.

90

Poydras
St.

Earhart Blvd.

Louisiana
Superdome

racing track. The peaceful Bayou St. John, the closest natural portage to Lake
Pontchartrain, flows through the Faubourg of the same name and is home to the
Mardi Gras Indians' annual Super Sunday celebrations. New Orleans' other major
green space, Fredrick Law Olmsted's City Park, contains the New Orleans Museum
of Art. A reopened Canal streetcar line makes this area easily accessible from the
Quarter and CBD.

Midcity is home to many of the restaurants made famous by their proximity to
Jazzfest—including many of the legendary bar/grill combinations and semi-hidden
Creole legends.

To the Lake: Bucktown

These neighborhoods hug the south shore of Lake Pontchartrain and tend to resemble the suburbs more than New Orleans' city center. When it comes to restaurants, only one of these has any real local fame—the waterfront community of Bucktown, just across the border of Jefferson Parish. In earlier times, Bucktown was a fishing community—the canals and docks still add to that feel. Many of the informal seafood houses proudly listed their locations as "Bucktown USA"— and the town gave its name to a style of overloaded seafood platter still famous in local restaurants like Deanie's, Sid-Mar, and R&O's.

The Suburbs: Metairie/Kenner, West Bank, Chalmette and New Orleans East

Spreading out from the city in all directions, these suburbs both feed the city and have their own distinct identities. Metairie and Kenner to the west, Algiers, Gretna and Harvey across the Mississippi on the West Bank; Chalmette and New Orleans East farther downriver. These communities are home to some of the city's more active ethnic restaurant scenes, especially the Vietnamese eateries on the West Bank and the Latin American in the western suburbs.

THE CELEBRATIONS
Mardi Gras/Carnival

For many incoming visitors, the annual Mardi Gras celebration represents the glittering soul of the city—a five-day weekend of general debauchery and universal excess

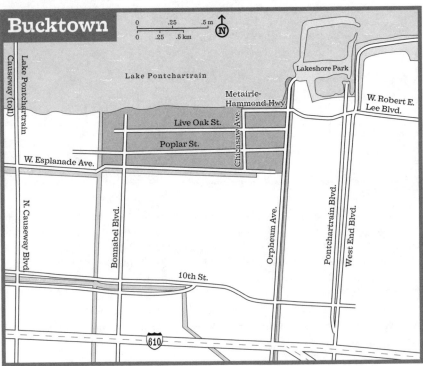

TOURIST TIPS

If You're Driving

By and large, New Orleans is not an auto-centric city. The city streets tend to be on the narrow side and reflect a time when galloping horses were considered high-speed transit.

Slow it down. Even though New Orleans doesn't fit the high-density "concrete jungle" model, the city has plenty of unpredictable street traffic, especially in residential areas. It's good practice for drivers to slow down and stay alert.

Watch your corners. The common practice of "building to the curb" often cuts down visibility for drivers, especially those accustomed to tooling around highway-dependent towns. Keep an eye out for blind corners and timid drivers nosing into traffic.

Left turn, kick turn, Right turn. The city's broad boulevards make for a bizarre turning protocol: if you need to hang a left on a major street, you have to go to the next block, make a U-turn and double back for a *right* turn. It's confusing but cuts congestion at traffic lights. Do it a few times and it'll feel completely natural.

Don't fight the train. On the streetcar boulevards (St. Charles, Carrollton, Canal), the aforementioned kick-turn maneuver often puts your car on top of railroad tracks, so treat the situation with the respect it deserves. Remember your Basic Railroad Physics: **streetcars stop slower than you think.** Before you take a U-turn, check your mirrors and BOTH TRACKS before spinning your wheel. Otherwise, you might spend a chunk of your weekend talking to tow-truck drivers and filling out reams of insurance paperwork.

Parking

Assume that *every* open space is illegal (especially in the French Quarter). Forbidden spaces aren't always marked with signs or painted curbs. New Orleans' complex parking laws involve a set of unwritten (and mostly unposted) rules governing "towable offenses." What seems to be a perfectly clear space may violate one of the following rules:

It's less than 15 feet from a stop sign.

It's less than 3 feet from a driveway.

It's less than 8 feet from a street corner.

And that's just for starters. There are probably a million other statutes on the books that magically qualify your car for immediate removal, extended detention and possible crushing. A solid rule of thumb is to *never park in a space that seems too good to be true.* Safe zones are often (though not always) marked with yellow pavement paint, so check the ground before settling in and locking up.

Find the pound and pay the fee. On the off chance that you DO get towed, you can get in line at the automotive lockup, located under the overpass at **St. Louis and North Claiborne**. If it's any consolation (and it probably isn't) your cab fare to the city impound lot will be reasonable. If you end up in line, be forewarned that the following strategies won't get you off the hook: slick talk, protestations of innocence, righteous indignation or threats of litigation. Pay the fee (cash or credit card) and get on with your life.

culminating in a day of costuming, public drunkenness and trinket-induced nudity. Those visitors (and you know who you are) arrive on Friday and prowl about the French Quarter looking for like-minded revelers, and the bash of a lifetime.

And in this case, they're exactly half right. Mardi Gras—or rather, the variable-length Carnival season—*is* the soul of the city, but not for the obvious "get plowed and skip work" reasons one might assume.

New Orleans is internationally known for its Mardi Gras celebration, but for locals, the fete lasts a good deal longer and goes by a different name: Carnival.

The difference between the two? Usually about twenty days of parades, parties and general revelry.

Technically, the term "Mardi Gras" applies to a single day—the Tuesday before the Catholic feast day of Ash Wednesday, the beginning of the long Lenten season. Forty days of repentance and deprivation before Easter—another vestige of the region's European heritage and active Catholic culture.

So when *is* Mardi Gras? Good question.

Here's a better question. Are you ready for some complex math?

The Carnival season starts every year on a fixed date (January 6, the Feast of the Epiphany or Twelfth Night) and runs until Mardi Gras day, which, since it's linked to Easter, is a "movable feast" —a Catholic celebration that can occur on a different day every year. (Why? Because Easter is linked to the Jewish holiday of Passover, which runs on a lunar calendar.) The differences in the solar and lunar years means that Mardi Gras can fall on any Tuesday between February 3 and March 9 (which explains why

On the Radio

One downside to the whole rental car experience is the soundtrack. Too often the radio's preset buttons are programmed to local commercial stations that pipe in bland pop music or whatever caught the last customer's ear. Should this happen to you, plant your presets on these two stations for audio accompaniment that's appropriate to this distinctive city.

WWOZ (90.7 FM, 24 hours)—Independent community radio broadcasting live from the Faubourg Tremé's Louis Armstrong Park. This amazing listener-supported station pumps out the best of New Orleans native music—from jazz to funky brass-band music to historic rhythm and blues. WWOZ is a primary media sponsor of the Jazz and Heritage Festival and broadcasts much of the event's music live—for those souls not fortunate enough to see the shows in person. Always good for in-depth coverage of the New Orleans music scene.

The Food Show (WSMB, 1350 AM, 4–7 PM Mon–Fri)—Native food writer and restaurant maven Tom Fitzmorris hosts a talk radio show that's particularly suited to New Orleans— three full hours of food talk during peak afternoon drive time. Fitzmorris is an encyclopedic resource of local food knowledge and features interviews with local restaurateurs and chefs, often broadcasting from the local eateries. The call-in segments give locals a chance to sound off on their favorites and to talk food with Tom and his guests.

Nametag Nation: A Conventioneer's Guide to Escaping the Conference Crowd

If you're in New Orleans on business, sometimes you might feel the overwhelming need to escape your co-workers. Nothing personal, but after spending three consecutive days in a hotel conference room or sprawling convention floor, sometimes you would just like to escape the familiar throngs, be they fellow dermatologists, historians or regional sales reps.

So stow your badge, hail a cab and seek out a place where nobody knows your name . . .

Avoid the obvious. Conference-goers usually congregate at "no brainer" gathering spots—convention center restaurants, hotel bars, etc. Make a mental list of these places and cross them off your list.

Eat where they ain't. Being a mostly pedestrian people, conventioneers naturally gravitate toward the high-traffic neighborhoods (French Quarter, Warehouse District near the Convention Center, CBD near the hotels). Grab a cab and head for restaurants in the lesser-known zones: Midcity, Uptown or the Marigny. (see neighborhood listings, page 14)

The magic number is four. If you want to move quickly, limit your escape group to four members. It's the perfect number, since everybody can pack into a cab, last-minute tables are easier to nab and the group doesn't fall prey to the dreaded "I don't know . . . what do YOU want to do" syndrome. (If you get roped into a larger group, break into groups of four rather than waiting for one huge table.)

Invent a family It never hurts to have a convenient "family obligation" excuse ready, just in case. If you need to give your boss the slip, invent a distant family member who insists on taking you out to dinner or a drink. Distant cousins or friends of a sibling work well, since they're not particularly trackable.

your friends in New Orleans are always commenting that Mardi Gras is running "early" or "late" in any given year). It never seems to be right on time, but that's another story.

The parading season—when elaborate floats, clamoring crowds and brass bands take over the city's major thoroughfares—lasts for about three weeks before Mardi Gras day proper, with evening parades most weeknights, and afternoon *and* evening parades on Saturday and Sundays. After two weeks of parades and parties, the celebration culminates with the big parades (Zulu and Rex) and the world's best dress-yourself party—the St. Anne's Parade in the Faubourg Marigny (which invariably spills over into the French Quarter). By early afternoon on the Tuesday, most everybody is looking forward to forty days of Lent just to recover from the excesses of Carnival.

In terms of food traditions, Carnival is a time of general debauchery and abandon—it doesn't matter *what* you eat, as long as there's a lot of it. Given the "farewell to the flesh" theme, there tends to be a lot of meat consumed during Carnival, and because of the often wintery climate, a lot of gumbo and other gut-warming dishes. And understandably, that also goes for cocktails as well.

The most recognizable Carnival food is, ironically, one of the least interesting. Imagine a glazed coffee cake dusted with crunchy sugar dyed in the official Mardi Gras colors (purple, gold and green). This sweet, sometimes goopy seasonal pastry contains a tiny baby figurine hidden somewhere in the cake's sugary filling. At communal "King Cake parties," a random guest gets the lucky slice and "bites the baby" in an edible game of hide-and-seek. Cheers ensue and the "winner" buys the next cake.

New Orleans Jazz and Heritage Festival

When most folks head to New Orleans during the Jazzfest weekends, they go for the music. It's a chance to see umpteen bazillion bands from every possible genre performing in the spacious infield of the Midcity horse track. With twelve stages running full tilt from late morning to early evening, there's never a moment when fantastic music (home-grown or otherwise) doesn't flow across the Fairgrounds, calling shirtless locals and blinding-white midwesterners to celebrate Louisiana's hyper-humid springtime.

But for any food lover, the real action goes on *between* the stages, at an impressive array of food booths set up by restaurants, community organizations and catering companies. Along the rows of identical blue nylon kitchen tents, any culinary explorer can capture New Orleans' cuisine in a microcosm, with specialties from the state's Cajun southwest and a few international influences thrown in for good measure. You can also easily eat yourself into a coma by what normal people consider "lunchtime."

The options can be overwhelming, but luckily, they come in handy appetizer-sized portions. You can wander from booth to booth enjoying everything from straightforward Cajun specialties (deep-fried boudin balls, jambalaya chunky with spicy andouille sausage, too many gumbos to count) to the more refined staples of urban Creole cookery (smothered okra with shrimp, with oyster and artichoke soup and catfish amandine).

As you'd expect, the poboy form adapts seamlessly to the Jazzfest's "movable feast" atmosphere and makes the perfect one-handed meal. Another popular festival food category is the "tiny styrofoam bowl with plastic fork" format. It's the only real way to sample Louisiana's many soup- and stew-based classics, but things get a little dicey in front of the stages, where oblivious listeners sometime mix dancing and dining. (If you've ever seen a "fork to the lip" injury, you'll understand.)

Here are a few of the festival favorites:

Crawfish Monica—The source of many a first-time crawfish addiction. Rotini pasta tossed with a smooth, slightly spicy crawfish cream sauce.

Summer Vacation

If you're the hot-blooded sort who visits New Orleans at the peak of summer, you might be in for a surprise come dinnertime. Many restaurants do as the Parisians do and close down for a couple of weeks during the hot months (usually when convention traffic is at its slowest). If you're planning a trip here in August, call to make sure your favorite restaurants will be serving. Otherwise, you might have to find *new* favorites.

Soft-Shell Crab Poboy—Tempura-crisp soft-shell halved and stuck leg-up inside a length of Leidenheimer's French bread. Looks more like a fully articulated alien pastry than food; start by snapping off the crunchy, buglike legs and munching them one by one.

Cochon de Lait Poboy—Melt-on-the-tongue slices of roast pork layered on a gravy-soaked French roll that maintains the perfect amount of crunch.

Crawfish Bread—Tender crawfish tails with onions, garlic and cheese, wrapped inside a crispy calzone-like crust.

Mango Freeze—A frosty fruit cup that's somewhere between a slush and sorbet, ably hawked by community radio station WWOZ.

Other Festivals

New Orleans also plays host to many other festivals that don't quite have the international reputation of Mardi Gras or Jazzfest, but are big draws nonetheless. Here are a few of them.

Essence Music Festival (July 4th weekend)

Billed as "the largest African-American gathering of musical talent in the world," this broad-ranging musical showcase packs the Superdome over Independence Day weekend.

French Quarter Festival (early April)

A three-day weekend of free music in the French Quarter. Fifteen stages run nonstop.

Satchmo Summerfest (early August)

A hot-weather celebration of Louis Armstrong's musical legacy and the city's jazz heritage.

Southern Decadence (Labor Day weekend)

A regional celebration of gay life, music and culture.

chapter 3
THE RESTAURANTS

Now that you have a feel for the city and a little bit of its cultural history, it's time to dive into the thick of the New Orleans restaurant scene. Your edible tour of the city starts with the old-line Creole establishments and works its way through to the sweetshops and markets that give the city its distinctive sweetness and character. In between, you'll visit some of New Orleans' hidden neighborhood gems, see the city's culinary celebrities and join the quest for the perfect poboy. Through hearty plate lunches and hand-torn loaves of French bread, you'll eat your way through the city's history and its culinary evolution. You'll see that New Orleans has more than its share of transcendent meals, whether you've got three dollars to spend or three hundred.

So without further ado, here are the restaurant stories.

Get crackin'. You've got a *lot* of eating to do.

OLD-LINE creole

The old-line Creole restaurants are the granddaddies of the New Orleans restaurant scene and, luckily for their admirers, are the least susceptible to change. Most are living bastions of old-world formality and gentility— staffed by tuxedo-clad waiters and decorated with polished brass and antique mirrors all around. For generations they've been the regular haunts of New Orleans' elite and they remain cornerstones of the city's international culinary reputation. Like most grandparents, they've successfully resisted modernity for decades, and they're not about to embrace it now.

Many have been serving the same classic seafood-centric Creole menus for well over a century, providing diners with a sense of comfort and culinary continuity. At many of the old-line restaurants, you can often precisely recreate a meal that you remember from fifty years past down to the last delicious detail.

This restaurant category contains some of the fancier restaurants in town and a few neighborhood standbys that are equally resistant to the passage of time. Being appropriately traditional, the old-line restaurants are most likely to maintain old-school "dress for dinner" standards and matching table manners.

Antoine's

713-717 St. Louis St. (at Royal)
504-581-4422

zone: French Quarter
website: www.antoines.com
reservations: recommended

meals: lunch and dinner Mon–Sat,
   closed Sun
specialty: Classic Creole
fancy factor: highbrow
price range: $18–43

caveats: no parking
bonus points: open Monday,
   great for history

Fonde en 1840.

To dine at Restaurant Antoine is to have this simple French phrase burned into your brain. It's printed on every menu page and every plate. It's the omnipresent tag line that reminds you that this cavernous institution on Rue St. Louis is, in fact, the oldest restaurant in New Orleans. It was founded in 1840 by Antoine Alciatore Guste, and has been one of the city's revered old-line institutions ever since.

The long menu echoes the "here first" mentality with a similar phrase: notre creation. The kitchen was first to cook oysters Rockefeller (listed on the bilingual bill of fare as *Huitres en coquille à la Rockefeller*) and a host of other dishes (trout Marguery, oysters Bienville) that haven't received quite the nationwide traction as this popular shellfish concoction—"named for John D., and the color of money" according to the server.

As for the ambience, we'll have to go with "stately." There's a sense of über-formality to the cream-colored main dining room, an eerie glow cast by an unbroken line of incandescent bulbs, a faint gold glow around the whole joint. On a quiet night, one can't help but think *Citizen Kane*'s echo-ridden dining scenes in Xanadu—tuxedo-clad waiters stationed across a huge dining room, padding over occasionally to check on the meal's progress.

The kitchen may be the oldest, but it's far from being the best regarded. There are other old-line kitchens in town that weren't *fonde en 1840* and don't have quite the chronological street cred, but execute the dishes better. For all the pomp of the French/English menu and claims to originality, what's on the plate doesn't quite match the price you pay, even in the Quarter.

The simple classics seem to be the most successful—it's hard to go wrong with the Pompano Pontchartrain—a simple grilled filet of this delicate fish topped with butter-sautéed crabmeat. And Poulet Rochambeau sounds intriguing on the menu, but the two sauces (a sugary brown Rochambeau sauce and thick terragon-laced béarnaise) don't play particularly well together on the plate or palate.

For history buffs, though, Antoine's is almost worth the premium price for its museum-like qualities. Occupying nearly an entire city block, the restaurant is a labyrinth of dining rooms filled with over 160 years of history. There are rooms dedicated to the most historic Mardi Gras krewes (Hermes, Proetus, and of course Rex), the red-walled Mystery Room, and the cavernous annex space. The walls are covered with portraits and signed menus from prestigious guests, including FDR, Whoopi Goldberg, Don Knotts, George Patton and, of course, Pope John Paul II.

Arnaud's

813 Bienville St. (at Bourbon)
866-230-8895

zone: French Quarter
website: www.arnauds.com
reservations: accepted

meals: lunch Mon–Fri, dinner nightly,
 brunch Sun
specialty: Creole classics
fancy factor: highbrow
price range: $21–38

bonus points: range of formality options

At this point in its history, Arnaud's isn't so much a restaurant as a one-block complex. Since opening in 1918, the restaurant has absorbed a number of nearby buildings and created a multiroomed empire that caters to the diverse French Quarter tourist crowd.

Diners seeking the old-school dining experience will gravitate toward the "original" Arnaud's—the fancier of Arnaud's two public dining rooms. Things aren't quite as fancy as they used to be (an evening "jacket and tie" requirement has given way to a more lenient "business casual" guideline), but the tuxedo-clad waiters still work the room with an appropriate air of old-line formality.

Arnaud's caters to novices with a sampler-happy menu that allows diners to taste their way around the Creole classics in small-portion roundups. Dedicates of oysters Bienville (see page 41) can order a full order of the baked shellfish specialty while curious palates can order a sampler that includes one each of five different baked oyster varieties. An entrée sampler features a trio of trademarks: mushroom-sauced

veal tournedos, crab cake, and sautéed crawfish tails in brandy/lobster sauce. A more traditional prix fixe menu lets you build an outstanding meal (a potent shrimp remoulade, rich speckled trout amandine and cup custard) for a reduced price.

If you're in the mood for a little Dixieland with your dinner, Arnaud's more casual Jazz Bistro shares both a menu and kitchen with the quieter main room. (Older folks might remember the Jazz Bistro as the former Richelieu Room.) The live music will add a reasonable surcharge to your bill (about $4 at press time). Same food, more banjoes.

The complex also contains two different bars—the French 75 and the Richelieu—and Remoulade, an oyster bar and informal Cajun/Creole eatery for Bourbon Street's "T-shirt and shorts" crowd.

Broussard's

819 Conti St. (at Bourbon)
504-581-3866

zone: French Quarter
website: www.broussards.com
reservations: recommended

meals: dinner nightly
specialty: updated Creole
fancy factor: highbrow
price range: $26–34

Broussard's doesn't get as much street buzz as its old-line Creole contemporaries, partially because it's the most hidden of the off-Bourbon institutions. Tucked away on Rue Conti, the restored French Quarter mansion has a vibe comparable to its architectural doppelganger Brennan's—similar grand dining rooms, carriageway-to-courtyard conversion and earthy brick seating with views of the lush patio space.

Open as a restaurant since 1920, Broussard's was considered a mainstay of old-line Creole under the direction of chef Nathaniel Burton. As coauthor of a popular 1978 cookbook, Burton committed his culinary philosophy and many of his classic recipes (crabmeat-stuffed flounder, trout amandine, Creole-style stewed rabbit) to print. Written with New Orleans native Rudy Lombard, *Creole Feast: 15 Master New Orleans Chefs Reveal Their Secrets* is a significant historical snapshot of Burton and other legendary Creole cooks, but sadly out of print.

The culinary approach of current chef and owner Gunter Preuss is decidedly more contemporary. His *Delice Ravigote Conti* starter teams a creamy herbed crabmeat salad with a spicy shrimp remoulade and—somewhat untraditionally—a serving of delicate house-cured salmon gravlax. The simple corn and shrimp bisque is fortified with a bit of sweet potato purée—a twist which adds a welcome layer of depth to the already flavorful classic. Gulf fish Pontchartrain teams smothered oyster mushrooms in a buttery sautéed crabmeat and shrimp

Creole 101

It's tempting to look at the butter-sauced seafood dishes of New Orleans and assume that the city's Creole food is simply an American adaptation of classical French technique to New World ingredients. Look at any menu of an old-line Creole restaurant and the evidence seems pretty overwhelming—fish cooked with browned butter sauces or topped with hollandaise, flash-fried potatoes topped with béarnaise, elongated loaves of French bread on every table.

And while the Continental influence is an important component of Creole cuisine, it's only half of the culinary story. The other main influence comes from another part of the Old World—the countries of West Africa.

Look at the other end of the formality spectrum—the everyday dishes of the city—and you'll see a much more pronounced African influence. Gumbos thickened with okra have their precursors in the okra stews found in Senegal and Gambia. Long-cooked red beans and rice are the local adaptation of similar dishes common to West Africa. The slaves that cooked for the ruling classes brought their own foodways to the New World and shaped New Orleans' unique cuisine in the process.

Other ethnic groups who settled in and passed through the busy port also had their effect on the city's cuisine. Italian red sauces are a mainstay of just about every neighborhood eatery. Oysters from primarily Croatian communities in coastal Placquemines Parish—shucked raw at oyster bars or baked into decadent oysters rockefeller—are a mainstay in the city. Caribbean islanders brought spices and peppers to the oceangoing port.

topping. Berlin-born Preuss also has a reputation for top-flight wild game preparations, including a mixed grill of quail, boar sausage and venison served with earthy apples and red cabbage.

Dooky Chase

2301 Orleans Ave. (at N. Miro)
504-821-0600

zone: Tremé
reservations: recommended

meals: lunch and dinner daily
specialty: Creole classics
fancy factor: middlebrow
price range: $11–25

caveats: not a walking location
bonus points: take-out operation in the back

At this point in her career, chef Leah Chase qualifies as one of the city's living legends but you'd never know it to talk with her. In her book *Beyond Gumbo,* food historian and author Jessica B. Harris dubbed Ms. Chase "the doyenne of the African style of Creole cooking in the Crescent City." She's run the kitchen at Dooky Chase's for over sixty years, but still makes the dining room rounds for a little lunchtime conversation.

Dressed in a bright green chef's jacket, Ms. Chase can spellbind you with story. She'll tell you about her childhood in rural Louisiana, why you should use pepper grass in your *gumbo z'herbes* or what makes a Creole gumbo "Seventh Ward" style. An afternoon audience with the charismatic doyenne is an expected benefit at this landmark restaurant in the Faubourg Tremé.

Since its founding as a lunch counter in 1941, Dooky Chase's has been influential in New Orleans' culinary and social history. The restaurant was named for Leah's late father-in-law, Dooky Chase, and converted into a fancier establishment, so much so that it was dubbed the African-American equivalent of Antoine's. Touring black musicians such as Ray Charles would frequent the restaurant after late-night gigs in the city's active nightclub scene. (Charles actually immortalized the place in his cover of Louis Jordan's "Early in the Morning Blues." Mr. Jordan went to Jennie Lou's to get something to eat. Brother Ray went to Dooky Chase.) In the early 1960s, it became known as an integrated meeting place where black and white Civil Rights activists could eat together in the same dining room. Then as now, Ms. Chase was been active supporter of her neighborhood and the larger community.

The building that used to house the sandwich shop still contains Ms. Chase's kitchen and the restaurant's take-out stand. The fancier dining rooms occupy two renovated shotgun houses that also hold the chef's collection of works by African-American artists.

By most accounts the kitchen doesn't hit the high notes it did in its prime, but a little clever strategy can compensate for the menu's lack of consistency. The key is to take a partner and go during the weekday lunch buffet (served Monday–Friday from 11:30 to 3:00). One person should order the buffet while the other orders a couple of selections from the standard menu. On Fridays, the buffet has a few standard dishes, maybe a nice okra gumbo, and fried fish that stand up nicely to steam-table presentation. (If there's fried chicken available, so much

Not-So-Raw Oysters, On and Off the Half Shell

Though they're awfully damned tasty slurped straight from the shell, here are a few traditional oyster dishes you'll find in New Orleans restaurants.

Oysters Rockefeller—Oysters baked on the half shell with puréed greens and breadcrumb mixture flavored with plenty of butter and a hint of Herbsaint (see page 102). Though many recipes use spinach as the green component, the folks at Antoine's say that spinach isn't an authentic ingredient. They play coy with the secret formula, but approximations call for everything from celery leaf to green onion to parsley or watercress and chervil. Served on a bed of hot rock salt.

Oysters Bienville—Another baked half-shell presentation claimed by Antoine's and Arnaud's. Oysters topped with a white and cream sauce studded with mushroom, diced shrimp and peppers. Also served on hot rock salt.

Oysters en Brochette—Shucked oysters wrapped in bacon, threaded on a skewer, then battered and deep fried. Served with a drizzle of butter and squeeze of lemon.

Oyster Stew—A delicate milk- or cream-based soup flavored with onion and oyster liquor (natural liquid inside the shell after shucking). Whole shucked oysters are added just before serving to prevent overcooking.

---

the better. Ms. Chase's is considered among the best in town.) The à la carte diner should request two of the house specialties—a bowl of Mamere's Crab Soup to start and an order of Shrimp Clemenceau. Mamere's soup is a must for anyone who loves crab, with chunks of meat and a light roux base setting off the richest crab stock imaginable. Shrimp Clemenceau is a rapidly disappearing dish, and in Ms. Chase's version, shrimp are quickly sautéed in a garlicky butter sauce and mixed with quick fried cubes of potato, mushrooms and green peas. If you can manage to rotate plates with your dining partner, you'll both get ample tastes of the kitchen's current strong suits.

A note for the pedestrian crowd: though it seems a plausible hike from the French Quarter, Dooky's is located in one of the poorer sections of the city, directly across Orleans Avenue from the Lafitte public housing projects. Public transit or taxicabs are the preferred mode of travel.

Galatoire's
209 Bourbon St.
(at Iberville)
504-525-2021

zone: French Quarter
website: www.galatoires.com
reservations: recommended

meals: lunch and dinner Tues–Sun, closed Mon
specialty: Classic Creole
fancy factor: highbrow
price range: $15–30

Gumbo

So what's it going to be? Do you want a bowl of thin filé gumbo packed with shrimp and quartered crabs, or a complex roux-thickened duck gumbo with chunks of smoky andouille sausage in every spoonful? Or maybe it's Holy Thursday and you're hoping for a bowl of *gumbo z'herbes,* a celebration-specific version thickened with all manner of leafy greens (collard, mustard, carrot tops, beet tops, watercress) cooked down to God's own pot likker.

In south Louisiana, gumbo isn't so much a dish as it is a culinary genre like *stew* or *soup*—a broad category that can include a wide range of core ingredients and cooking techniques. In the broadest sense, gumbo is a savory, thick-bodied middle ground between a stew and a soup—a hearty mélange chunky with the bounty of Louisiana's land, water and sky. Locals demand it when cool winds sweep down from the north, but there are summertime versions that contain the summer-peak crops as well (shrimp and okra, to be precise). Considered Louisiana's gift to the soup course, it's usually served with a scoop or two of fluffy white rice and, in some Cajun households, a scoop of creamy potato salad.

Despite dictionary definitions that contend gumbo must always be thickened with okra—the English word being an adapted version of *ngombo,* the Bantu name for the vegetable—the dish can also be thickened with two other signature Louisiana ingredients: filé powder or roux.

Filé powder is the pulverized leaf of the native sassafras tree. According to some histories, the Creoles learned to use it from the Native American tribes that flourished here before French colonists arrived. The pulverized leaf adds a distinctive herby flavor and a somewhat glutinous quality to gumbo, whatever the ingredients. *Roux* is a browned mixture of fat (usually vegetable oil) and flour that French cooks used to thicken soups, sauces and stews. In gumbo, roux are most often cooked to a deep, dark, chocolate brown consistency, the point at which they provide a strong, nutty flavor to the final product.

Gumbos across Louisiana can contain different ingredients—the rule of thumb being that an area's native gumbo contains whatever the cook can find in their backyard. Down by the coast, that means dark, rich seafood gumbos packed with shrimp, crab and oyster. In the Cajun prairie, the barnyard and smokehouse become the primary inspirations—chicken and andouille sausage or long-smoked tasso versions dominate. Farmhouse ingredients and shellfish often make it into the same pot, but finfish and crawfish rarely make an appearance in a bowl of traditional gumbo. In the city, markets have traditionally acted as the cook's backyard, resulting in distinctive variation on the gumbo theme: Creole gumbo. Leah Chase, chef/owner of Dooky Chase in the Tremé, once described the classic gumbo:

> If you talk to everybody in . . . this area, I'm sure the ingredients would be the same. They'd tell you that it had shrimp, crab, oysters, ham, chicken wing, veal stew meat in it. They would put two kinds of sausage: smoked sausage and for heaven's sake you have to have a chaurice— a fresh hot sausage.

Traditional Creole gumbo gets its distinctive flavor from the wide variety of seafood and meat cooked long and slow, each adding its flavor to the final dish. Its thin consistency comes from both roux ("not too dark, a little darker than peanut butter," Chase says) and filé powder stirred in at the end of the cooking process. Unlike simpler Cajun variations, which are considered everyday food, Creole gumbo is a traditional dish at holiday meals when the whole family gathers to celebrate.

There are countless variations on the gumbo theme, some of which highlight the difference in traditions between city and country cooks. New Orleans cooks might add tomato to the mix, a practice shunned by cooks in Cajun Louisiana.

Since Cajun food rocketed to popularity in the 1980s, there are some native New Orleanians who contend that, where restaurants are concerned, the city's gumbo aesthetic has changed. Instead of the Creole gumbos commonly referred to as "Seventh Ward Style," restaurants now default to a dark roux chicken and andouille gumbo, common to Prudhomme's home around Opelousas but a relative newcomer to the Crescent City. It's a significant sign of changing times and another case of things "just not bein' what they used to be."

caveats: downstairs room "first come, first served," no parking
bonus points: late lunch service

If you're one of those foodfolks who keeps a "things to do before I die" list, a long Friday lunch at Galatoire's should definitely be on that list. It might not happen on your first visit, but on some return trip you should spring for that extra day off work, impossibly early airplane flight, or an extra connection through Atlanta—you won't be disappointed.

A long lunch—and by long I mean four hours or so—is one of the city's best culinary experiences and done right, it's an amazing piece of midday theatre in a century-old New Orleans institution.

Located in the thick of Bourbon Street's Neon Zone, Galatoire's is a step back in time and a delicious reminder of the city's classic Creole roots. The recently renovated dining room is a study in genial formality—where easy charm dominates despite an implied "coat and tie" dress code. (For lunch, it's not a strict requirement, but a gentleman's jacket helps you blend in nonetheless.)

You flat out won't find better people-watching anywhere in town. In the ground-level seating area, banks of waist-high mirrors afford direct and covert views of well-heeled regulars, patter-perfect waitstaff and thunderstruck tourists taking in the spectacle of it all.

Lunchtime at Galatoire's is one of the city's essential eating experiences, both for its decadent, butter-infused seafood dishes and the cultural experience that's as much show business as sustenance. A standard luncheon at Galatoire's routinely take three or four hours, especially on Fridays, when the workweek ends mid-morning and the cocktails flow like water. Once you take your table, you're there for the day. The more extreme lunchers tend to pour themselves into taxicabs while the dinner crowds congregate in the lobby.

Well before noon, an assortment of businessmen, political power brokers, and well-dressed "ladies who lunch" will already be settled into the relaxing ritual of the extended meal. Clutches of

The Reveillon Dinner

If you're traveling around the city during the month of December, you might notice an unfamiliar special offered in restaurants around town.

The modern Reveillon is a revival of a nineteenth-century meal celebrated twice during the holiday season—one simple meal after midnight mass on Christmas Eve, a second lavish feast on New Year's Eve.

Though the tradition is no longer commonly practiced in local homes, some of the city's restaurants have dusted off the custom (in name at least) by offering prix fixe dinner menus on the nights before Christmas (usually December 1–23). Sometimes the menu will be a special old-style Creole spread, but often the Reveillon is just a mix-and-match affair of standard menu items. It might not be particularly traditional, but it fills the seats during a slow month for convention traffic.

professional women, dressed to the nines and shod with impossibly pointy *Sex in the City* slingbacks, toast an early girl's night out with mimosa-filled flutes. Mother-daughter pairs mill about the room, apparently chatting with old family friends. Each conversation contributes to the growing din, and when traditional lunchtime arrives, the room resonates with a dull yet appealing roar. For many of these patrons, this experience is a regular part of their weekly routine—a chance to revel in fine food, to sip a nice Sazerac and to mix business with pleasure.

It's a world that few travelers ever see—attorneys gathering for five-drink lunch meetings, priests dining with parish benefactors, and tuxedo-clad waiters providing seamless service that borders on the theatrical.

Galatoire's encyclopedic menu is a contradictory study in complexity and simplicity, counter to contemporary dish descriptions, where every ingredient has both a listing and geographic pedigree. Each of the five pages lists simple dish names along with a price listing. For any additional information, the old-line system requires that you consult your oracle, ally and all-knowing authority—your server.

Done right, the "waiter as translator" aesthetic can yield an amazing amount of information about the house specialties. The seafood-stuffed eggplant, for example, tends to be a whole lot more seafood than eggplant, while the soufflé potatoes—thin, flash-cooked slices that puff up like crispy pillows—and their fragrant béarnaise sauce are a near-universal appetizer choice.

"My friends, the pompano is very, *very* fresh today," goes the old routine. "But we only have a few filets left . . . How many should I save?"

Classic dishes run the gamut from smooth, spicy Crabmeat Maison (flawless lump meat dressed lightly with a spicy mayonnaise dressing and capers) to *oysters en brochette* (a quick-fried skewer of fat oysters and thick-sliced bacon). Entrée standouts include such standards as trout meunière—a pan-sautéed filet topped with a simple brown-butter sauce (butter, lemon, parsley and a hint of Worcestershire sauce). For a little added crunch, order the amandine variation (identical except for a crunchy almond topping).

Gulf Fish

Many of the traditional Creole seafood dishes in the old-line repertoire require fish that fits a certain flavor profile—usually "delicate, mildly flavored white fish." Luckily, there are plenty of species in the Gulf that fit that description. Here
are a few of the more common varieties likely to show
up on menus and specials lists around town.

Pompano—A small, delicate fish considered by many
to be the tastiest in the Gulf. Usually served broiled, or
en papillote (baked in a parchment wrapper). Most common in summer.

Speckled Trout—Also known as the spotted sea trout. The preferred fish for pan-fried
preparations (meunière, amandine). Not to be confused with common fresh-water
species such as lake, brook or rainbow trout.

Redfish (a.k.a. red drum)—When Paul Prudhomme started blackening this common
fish, skyrocketing demand decimated Louisiana's coastal populations. Commercial
fishing in the gulf halted in 1988, so the fish is fairly rare unless you know a local
sport fisherman. Farm-raised redfish are starting to appear on menus across town,
but some chefs would rather substitute other wild Gulf fish than use the milder-
flavored domesticated fish.

Black Drum—A cousin of the redfish. Commonly substituted for the rare redfish in
popular dishes.

Red Snapper—Another low-oil fish with firm meat and an almost sweet flavor.

Sheepshead—Often considered a "trash fish" by commercial fishermen, this once-
fashionable Gulf fish is making a comeback among younger chefs. Similar to speckled trout.

Mahi Mahi—Despite its Hawaiian name, this colorful Gulf fish is known for its firm
texture and sweet flavor.

Escolar—A more full-flavored, oily fish. Closely related to tuna. Usually grilled.

Wahoo—Another Gulf member of the mackerel family.

Tuna—You might associate this fish with the North Atlantic, but yellowfin tuna also
roam the Gulf and often appear on plates in New Orleans. Firm-fleshed and meaty
in texture.

Also look for are amberjack, grouper triggerfish and tripletail.

Other mealtime traditions include the uncut bread loaves swaddled in pristine white napkins (dig in with your hands), *Crepes Suzettes* for dessert and *Café Brulot* for post-meal recovery (both of which involve dramatic tableside preparation and huge plumes of blue flame).

In the days before the renovation, Galatoire's single ground-floor dining room operated on a strict "no reserva-tions" policy of much local renown. If the Queen of Sheba wanted a table for lunch, she'd wait her turn in line. But thanks to expanded seating on the second floor, advanced planners can reserve upstairs tables most evenings.

But still, you should dress up early and jockey for a lunch table with the rest of the regulars. It'll be an experience you remember the rest of your life.

Restaurant Mandich

3200 St. Claude Ave.
504-947-9553

zone: Bywater
reservations: none

meals: lunch Tues–Sat, dinner Fri–Sat, closed Sun
specialty: Italian and classic everyday Creole
fancy factor: low-middlebrow
price range: $14–26

caveats: irregular hours
bonus points: incredible garlic bread

Another of the "step back in time" establishments that populate the New Orleans restaurant scene, this Bywater standby takes you back to early 1961. Step across the threshold and feel the years drip away. JFK is still in the White House, the Beatles are still playing basements in Hamburg, and somewhere across town, Tennessee Williams is putting the finishing touches on *Night of the Iguana.*

Mandich's location on deep St. Claude pretty much guarantees that you'll never see a conventioneer in the place. Instead, stop in for a Friday lunch and you'll see a thoroughly mixed old New Orleans crowd—older ladies out for a nice midday meal, businessmen from Chalmette digging into oversized steaks ("My doctor said I ain't supposed to be eatin' this, but he ain't here. Make it rare") and cellphone-happy contractors fixing up jobsite problems over steaming bowls of gumbo. Eavesdroppers will soon realize that the accents run thick here: close your eyes and you'll swear you're in Brooklyn.

Breaking Bread

It almost seems like a cruel joke. You're in a fancy restaurant, and after bringing the cocktails, your waiter presents a loaf of pillowy French bread, still hot from the oven. Not *slices* of bread, mind you, but an intact loaf, and not a serrated knife in sight. Is there a special utensil that I'm missing? A bread fork of some kind?

But relax, it's not a joke—even in the toniest of the old-line restaurants, it's completely proper to ditch your utensils, give in to your primal side and tear your desired portion directly from the loaf. Don't worry. The maître d' won't throw you out and nobody will think that your mama didn't raise you right. If you need further encouragement, look around and see the tablecloths of the other diners. They'll be absolutely *littered* with bready shrapnel.

The simple act of breaking bread is visceral and satisfying—fingers cracking through the thin, crunchy crust into an airy interior, still warm from the kitchen—and a shower of crusty particles littering the table linens. And even though Ms. Manners might not approve, just tear into it and let the crumbs fall where they may.

CLASSIC

Café Brulot

The perfect capper to any old-line meal is a tiny cup of Café Brulot—a Creole specialty that qualifies as both cocktail and fiery after-dinner theatre.

Café Brulot is a classic coffee drink consisting of brandy sweetened with a little orange liqueur, then spiced with cinnamon stick, cloves and citrus peel. A silver bowl of the aromatic concoction is touched off with a match and explodes in a controlled ball of liquid-blue flame. Flavors intensify as the alcohol burns off, and your fearless server nimbly ladles flames a foot in the air for added flourish. After a few minutes of pyrotechnic performance, the flames are extinguished with a stream of hot chicory-laced coffee, then served in innocuous demitasse cups. The resulting after-dinner drink is potent, aromatic and soothing to a butter-filled stomach.

The restaurant's been open since 1922, but the ambiance doesn't look like it's changed much since the 60s. The room feels like somewhere between your hard-drinking aunt's dining room and the formerly swanky supper club that time forgot.

The specialties at Mandich fit into the garlicky nether region between Creole Italian and Croatian, with a few standard seafood dishes thrown in for good measure. The term "Bordelaise" crops up a lot on the menu, and can translate to olive oil spiked with green onions and untold cloves of garlic. The waitress talked about original owner John Mandich and his Croatian lineage just as she plunked down a basket of hot garlic bread (the standard lunchtime starch). Freshly toasted and powerful enough to hold Anne Rice's vampire hordes at bay, the crispy slices are absolutely irresistible, so bank on inhaling at least one basket per person.

Besides garlic, the prevailing flavors that emanate from the kitchen—in sauces and soups, anyway—are sugar and cinnamon. The ever-present marinara sauce

and tomatoey turtle soup both have the combination that wakes up your taste buds, but soon gets too cloying for savory dishes. (I suggest sticking with the Bordelaise whenever possible.) Candied yams rely on the same sweet spices, and can easily double as a dessert dish.

The Croatian influence reaches its peak with oysters Bordelaise (fried oysters topped with the garlic sauce) the Creole Italian with the pannéed veal (a milk-fed scallop pounded impossibly thin, then fried-crisp). Dipped in breadcrumbs and quick-fried, the veal weighs a few ounces but covers an entire platter like an oversized meaty cracker, best eaten as "tear and eat" finger food.

Prices tend to be on the steep side ($10–13 for lunchtime poboys with a cup of soup) and beware semi-hidden surcharges for add-ons. The Trout Mandich, a crispy broiled fish, seems reasonable enough at $16, but add crabmeat and the price goes up to the mid-twenties. Split a dish between two diners and your tariff jumps by almost eight bucks.

The Sazerac

Inhale the aromas of a well-made Sazerac and you can smell the history of New Orleans. Spicy-sweet whiskey dominates at first, giving way to the subtle perfume of liquid licorice. A hint of medicinal bitters rises off the pink-tinged surface and a heady kick of alcohol confirms that this is what even locals refer to as a "stout cocktail."

As the city's trademark whiskey drink, the Sazerac is a classic cocktail that New Orleans can definitively call its own. Born in a French Quarter coffeehouse and flavored with home-grown ingredients, the Sazerac is a complex drink with a unique set of rituals and a distinguished local lineage.

In its modern form, the Sazerac is a close cousin of the more universal Old-Fashioned cocktail—bourbon fortified with sugar, aromatic bitters, crushed orange and usually a bright red maraschino cherry. The Sazerac substitutes spicy rye whiskey for the sweeter bourbon and a local anise-based liqueur for the dominant citrus flavors. A dash of concentrated bitters and a subtle lemon twist are aromatic common ground. The result is a long-sipping cocktail with an intriguing, multi-layered bouquet that balances spicy and sweet on the tongue.

The Sazerac is likened to New Orleans both by history and its traditional ingredients. The drink first appeared under its present name in the mid-1850s, when spirits importer and bar owner Sewell Taylor named a sweet brandy and bitters mixture after his establishment, the Sazerac House. Taylor's concoction was originally mixed with *Sazerac-du-Forge et Fils* brandy and bitters invented by local apothecary Antoine Peychaud, who prepared the mix for his customers for years. Sweetened with a little sugar, this combination proved to be immensely popular in the "coffeehouses" (bars) of New Orleans.

A few changes in the recipe developed over time. Not long after Taylor laid claim to the Peychaud's potion, an anonymous bartender began swirling a few drops of a popular herbal liqueur in the glass for added aroma and flavor. The anise-flavored liqueur was absinthe, a controversial spirit that was reputed to cause hallucinations and extreme mania for its drinkers. Absinthe contained a reputedly toxic herb called wormwood, and the pale green liquor was eventually outlawed in most of Europe and the U.S.

Roughly twenty years later, a new owner of the Sazerac House changed the primary liquor from cognac to the most popular spirit of the time, rye whiskey. A U.S. Department of Agriculture ban on absinthe forced a switch to Herbsaint, a locally-produced *liqueur d'anis*, for the necessary flavors without the wormwood.

Bartenders who know their Sazeracs are most often found in the Crescent City, where there is access to this trio of comparatively unusual ingredients: rye, Herbsaint and the deep-red Peychaud's bitters. In a pinch, clove-heavy Angustora bitters can stand in for the deep red Peychaud's variety, as French-made Pernod can replace Herbsaint. But in New Orleans, all bars are stocked with the necessary components and tend to have at least one Sazerac-savvy bartender on duty at any given time. A good rule of thumb is "the older the better," and if they barkeep's nametag says Tony or Louie, you're probably in good hands.

Turtle Soup

If you've ever had a bowl of New Orleans turtle soup, you've tasted one of the city's most distinctive dishes. Rich, spicy and deeply savory, the soup has an earthy richness that comes from (you guessed it) finely diced turtle meat, eye-raising texture from bits of hard-boiled egg and the clean, fragrant aroma of sherry (some cooked into the stock, some poured right before the diner's first spoonful). The at-table flourish of the traditional service question ("More sherry, ma'am?") adds to the theatre of the dish.

Since it calls for an amphibian most people only see in pet stores or on TV nature shows, turtle soup doesn't show up on many menus outside the Crescent City. But the distinctive soup is a hallmark in the more traditional Creole restaurants, whether they're white-linen fancy (Commander's Palace) or neighborhood favorites (Mandina's).

In years before the Endangered Species Act, the turtles of choice were seafaring varieties, but contemporary cooks have since switched to freshwater varieties (farm-raised snapping turtles also locally known as *cowain*). The meat can often be ordered through specialty groceries or well-stocked seafood markets.

Even in farmed form, turtle meat has a distinctly gamey flavor, and is often mixed with more common grocery meats—pork, veal and beef—to take the livery edge off. Home cooks routinely substitute beef round or stew meat for the more expensive *cowain*, making for an acceptable "mock turtle" version.

The current owners, Lloyd English at the bar and his wife Joel in the kitchen, opt for a serving schedule that suits their family life, but can be confusing for some customers (lunches Tuesday through Friday, dinner Friday and Saturday). If you're looking for this particular step back in time, it's best to call ahead.

Mandina's

3800 Canal St. (at N. Cortez)
504-482-9179

zone: Midcity
website: www.mandinas.com
reservations: none

meals: lunch and dinner daily
specialty: Classic everyday Creole
fancy factor: middlebrow
price range: $9–15

caveats: cash only, no reservations
bonus points: open nightly

Even though the menu at this Midcity institution goes on for days, it's tough to get past the speckled trout amandine. It's not particularly fancy, but nearly perfect—a big filet of crispy, pan-fried Gulf fish topped with a mound of toasted almond slices and drizzled with a lemony browned butter sauce. For the first few bites, the dish is an exercise in richness and crunch. Over time, the sauce softens up the nutty crust a bit and eventually soaks into the bed of French fries. Replace the potatoes with the tiny cubed Brabant variety, and this dish could easily play one of the fancier old-line eateries in the French Quarter. But on its clunky stoneware platter, this trout dish, delicate fish topped with a buttery "gravy," is a workaday standby at a neighborhood classic.

Mandina's was my first taste of the city's old-line Creole tradition and remains one of my favorites. Part of the appeal is the room—a decidedly unfussy space that doubles as both bar and main dining area. High ceilings keep the smoke from getting too thick, a few big windows glow with huge neon signs facing Canal Street that brag of its once-novel comfort technology: MANDINA'S— AIR CONDITIONED.

For locals, it's a family joint, the perfect place to celebrate birthdays and not-so-fancy occasions. For an increasing number of travelers, it's a comforting introduction to the sometimes fuzzy middle zone where the old-line Creole cuisine meets neighborhood Italian. On festival weekends, the sidewalk fills with customers waiting patiently for a table and sipping whiskey drinks to pass the time.

Like its white-linen counterparts in the Quarter, Mandina's maintains a few hints of formality—career waiters wear bow ties as they shuffle between tables, plates of toasted French bread arrive with the entrées—but the overall vibe is more rough-and-tumble. This is a place where businessmen come for uncomplicated, comforting dishes and a good stiff cocktail.

The menu mixes solid seafood and Italian options with daily specials that have their own loyal followings. There are red beans on Monday, stuffed veal *bruccialone* with shell pasta on Thursday, and eight different seafood options on Friday. Tuesday brings a dish that's got a cult following among locals—a mountainous portion of tender beef stew. (A waiter nods his approval. "That's a long-shoreman's meal. It'll stay with you 'till supper.") And luckily, the trout is always on the specials list.

The Italian side of the menu isn't quite as strong. A poached link of Italian sausage doesn't add a lot of flavor to the lackluster spaghetti and red gravy. The *bruccialone*, with a spinach and egg stuffing, is more flavorful, but not quite marquee material.

This, of course, brings us back to the Creole side of the equation and to another "don't miss" house specialty—the turtle soup. For visitors, it's a special treat to have an older gentleman deliver this local classic—a shallow bowl of fragrant soup flecked with ground turtle meat, bits of tomato and boiled egg—then offer an extra shot of sherry if you'd like. Out comes the bottle, and a drizzle tops off the dish.

After a couple of bites, you'll understand the trout problem. On future visits, you might *want* to order the gumbo, but you'll have a hard time getting past this soup.

Tujague's

823 Decatur St. (at Madison)
504-525-8676

zone: French Quarter
website: www.tujagues.com
reservations: recommended

meals: lunch and dinner daily
specialty: old-style Creole classics
fancy factor: middlebrow
price range: $33–38

caveats: no à la carte default
bonus points: historic saloon, bar dining

Know this before you go into Tujague's: the boiled beef is not optional. To be fair, neither are three of the other four courses on the set meal (a small salad topped with deep red shrimp remoulade, soup du jour and bread pudding for dessert). You get to choose your entrée from a verbal list of six or so options, and after the soup, you'll get the boiled beef.

Before you make a nasty face, know this: you'll probably love it.

There was a time when this simple dish, a bit odd by modern standards, was a standard in the Creole cook's repertoire. The earliest versions of the *Times-Picayune Creole Cookbook* from the early 1900s have a whole chapter dedicated to *La Bouille*—beef brisket simmered until fall-apart tender, then served with various sauces.

At Tujague's (pronounced TOO-jacks), the sauce of choice is a simple yet potent mix of ketchup and horseradish similar to the standard oyster-bar cocktail sauce. Touch a chunk of the brisket with a fork's edge and the meat collapses into moist shreds on the tiny green-rimmed plate. And though the flavors seem more

British than Creole, you'll probably end up licking your plate and not so secretly longing for seconds.

Tujague's comes by its traditional bent honestly. This Decatur Street restaurant and saloon, founded in 1856, cur-

CLASSIC

Special Spuds

You might recognize them boiled, fried or mashed, but here are a few trademark potato variations commonly found on old-line Creole menus.

Au Gratin—Sliced potatoes baked with cheese, heavy cream and often bread crumbs.

Brabant—Deep-fried potatoes cut in tiny cubes. Traditionally topped with slightly garlicky butter sauce and chopped parsley.

Lyonnaise—Boiled potatoes sautéed with onions and butter until browned. Good mix of starchy and crunchy.

Soufflé—Not so much a side dish as an appetizer. Thin slices of double-fried potato that puff up like crispy balloons and resemble two potato chips welded together at the seam. Served piping hot with a side of béarnaise sauce.

rently ranks as the second-oldest eatery in the city (after Antoine's). Its location a block downriver from Jackson Square puts it in prime tourist territory, yet it's probably the least reconstructed of the French Quarter's old-line establishments. The narrow dining room, which holds maybe twenty tables, is copiously decorated with B-list celebrity photos (Alex Trebeck, Dan Ackroyd, the guy who played Tubbs on *Miami Vice*) and wall-length shadow boxes containing a million or so shot-sized liquor bottles. Go figger.

The restaurant specializes in set-menu meals—five courses are standard—for a reasonable price, with entrées being a bit more modern than you'd expect. Along with a simple broiled drum and steak options, the kitchen offers crawfish pasta or sautéed shrimp and crabmeat ladled over pannéed eggplant. On the whole, the execution isn't particularly strong (soggy shrimp, insipid soup), but the tangy remoulade and savory beef can leave a lasting impression.

Of course, you can avoid the preset menu by stepping next door into Tujague's historic saloon-style barroom. Backed by a huge 19th-century carved mirror, the cypress bar is one of the best afternoon hangouts in the city. And as luck would have it, a damned fine place to get a substantial boiled-beef poboy. With a side dish of that scarlet remoulade, maybe? The set menus stop at the dining room door, and it can't hurt to ask.

NEIGHBORHOOD favorites

At this point in New Orleans' history, no restaurant wears the label "undiscovered" for very long. With plenty of travel writers and video crews prowling the city in search of "the real New Orleans," joints that would have been considered obscure ten years ago decorate their walls with framed articles cut from the glossy lifestyle magazines or the owner shaking hands with hyper-toothy television personalities.

The neighborhood favorites are those places that see the occasional flash of spotlight but don't let it affect them too much. Cable crews might show up for the occasional film shoot, but the owners still cater to a local audience, who by now are accustomed to seeing unfamiliar faces mixed in with the regulars.

Most of the entries in this category will take you outside the well-worn tourist zones and into the city's funkier (and sometimes dicier) neighborhoods. If you're using public transportation, call ahead and ask about the best options.

Camellia Grill

626 S. Carrollton Ave. (at St. Charles)
504-866-9573

zone: Uptown
reservations: none

meals: breakfast, lunch and dinner daily
specialty: short-order diner specialties
fancy factor: lowbrow
price range: $4–8

caveats: expect a wait, cash only, no table
 seating
bonus points: open after hours, breakfast
 anytime

First thing in the morning or well after midnight, the crew at Camellia Grill put on a great show at one of the shallowest stages in town. Take your seat on one of the thirty or so circular stools and you're already deep into the shtick—a waiter/bar back dressed in black bow tie and white shirt welcomes you in with a sense of rapid-fire familiarity:

"HellofellashaveaseatwhatcanIgetcha?"

The Camellia, a late-night standard for many a traveler and insomniac student, keeps its active reputation by serving up dependable diner-style specialties for a hungry and adoring public. Located right where the St. Charles streetcar line makes its dogleg turn up Carrollton Avenue, the building's somewhat weathered plantation façade has become a

landmark for Uptown tourists riding the rails and wary locals hoping to avoid "out the door" lines at peak service times.

From any seat on the curvy Formica lunch counter, you can see all the action—thick milkshakes being whipped to order, burgers sizzling on a double-wide griddle, French fries bubbling in oil. The menu couldn't be any more straightforward—diner-style favorites in the "eggs and sandwiches" genre with a full-service soda fountain thrown in for good measure.

The exposed galley kitchen leaves nothing to the imagination; instead it provides a cutaway view of a working restaurant that beats reality TV hands down. You'll see eggs beaten into a froth in a 50s era milkshake mixer then spilled onto a well-buttered grill with amazing efficiency. Meantime, the grill cooks routinely abuse the cooking hamburgers—piercing them with sharp-cornered spatulas, mashing them flat for a dramatic sizzle—doing everything that could turn the patty into a dry, tasteless puck. But somehow, they arrive on the well-dressed bun as juicy and savory as can be; not fancy but consistently drool worthy.

Of course, the savory aromas of "breakfast anytime" rise above the exposed kitchen's periodic clatter and patter. Regulars expect to smell salty bacon as the milkshake machine whines in quick staccato pulses. Ham on the grill crisps around the edges just as it's swooped onto a platter of scrambled eggs and fries.

A quick glance at the menu shows pride in the dishes that aren't made on the grill or fountain. The "From our Kitchen" section spotlights the house-made chili, lest you think it's poured from a can. (The chili-cheese omelet is an oversized, feather-light wonder that makes a perfect after-bar meal.) The desserts subtly marked as "Our Own" have a similar "Yes, we make them here" familiarity. A hidden standout is the hot house-made apple pie à la mode, in which a wedge of pie is heated on the butter-soaked griddle and picks up just a hint of savory grease from the burgers and bacon that have come before. It's the unexpected interplay of salt and sweet, crunchy and creamy that makes the late-night crowd dream for a break in the line.

Peak times at the grill vary wildly, so you might want to call ahead—weekend breakfast and after-bar shifts draw enthusiastic and patient crowds. If you're craving the pie, you've got no choice but to wait it out—but with a nonnegotiable "cash only" policy, you might just need those few extra minutes to visit a nearby cash machine.

Crescent City Steaks
1001 N. Broad St. (at St. Philip)
504-821-3271

zone: Midcity
website: www.crescentcitysteaks.com
reservations: accepted

meals: lunch and dinner Tues–Sun
specialty: steaks
fancy factor: low-middlebrow
price range: $20–22

caveats: steaks only (but ask nice, they might find something for you)

bonus points: open Sun, über-private booth seating

One look at the bill of fare and it's obvious that Crescent City Steaks is true to its name. While other so-called chop houses have been busy diversifying their menu, this old-school Midcity standard holds the bovine hard line: entrée wise, you can either eat steak or go hungry. No chicken, no salmon, no lobsters in a tank. Don't even bother asking.

Since 1934, this Croatian-owned neighborhood supper club has catered to locals in search of a straightforward meat-and-potatoes experience. And from the looks of the modern-day crowd, things haven't changed much. There are tiny families clustered around four-tops, larger groups in for celebrations and little trysts taking place in the seductive, somewhat claustrophobic curtained booths lining one wall. The vibe is beyond casual and borders on time travel;

flowery curtains, hexagonal tile and all. In any other city, this room would have been converted into a semi-ironic hipster lounge during the mid-90s martini craze, but in this downmarket stretch of Broad Street, the steakhouse is safe from any kind of fashionista incursion.

Get your meat in one of five cuts: rib eye, New York strip, T-bone, filet or multi-person porterhouse. They're all pretty much prepared the same way: cooked to order and served in a pool of melted butter. (Not quite the signature sizzle of other nearby steakhouses, but in the same stylistic vein.) Sides are equally simple—a half dozen varieties of steakhouse potatoes, heated-through canned peas, broccoli and spinach available either naked or smothered in a cheesy but not particularly notable *au gratin* sauce. Start off with a tangy shrimp cocktail and some crunchy, hand-dipped onion rings.

Nothing in the execution will particularly knock your socks off, but if you're looking for a meaty indulgence far from the tourist-beaten track, you've found your place.

Commerce Restaurant

300 Camp St. (at Gravier)
504-561-9239

zone: CBD/Warehouse
reservations: none

meals: breakfast and lunch Mon–Fri
specialty: short-order diner specialties
fancy factor: lowbrow
price range: $3–10

caveats: weekday lunch only

If I had any damn sense at all, I'd keep this one to myself.

I've been eating my way across this city full-time for more than five years and the Commerce is a new find for me. It's one of those CBD lunch counters that's always closed when I'm driving by or always looking abandoned even at peak dining times. Though I pass right in front of it a half-dozen times a week, I can count on one hand the number of times I've seen signs of life through the windows on Camp Street.

But there's something about the red beans at the Commerce that puts me on a mission. They're the kind of simple fare that just about every first-timer searches for. Smooth and creamy, flecked with a little pork and topped with your choice of sausage (hot or smoked). Served in a room that's not blasting zydeco accordion or bathed in neon, this is workaday New Orleans lunch food, and it's the only way to celebrate a Monday if you're wandering anywhere near downtown.

Some things you just gotta share.

The Commerce is a no-frills breakfast and lunch joint that caters exclusively to the CBD crowd (office dwellers and construction crews alike). Only a few non-locals ever find the place despite the fact that it's nearly tourist-perfect: only two blocks from Canal Street and practically surrounded by high-rise hotels. Part of that is probably timing—they're open only for breakfast and lunch, Monday through Friday. Another factor is neighborhood—what self-respecting vacationer wants to venture close to office buildings with French Quarter bars just steps away?

If you find your way to the cafeteria-style ordering area, zero in on the center section—past the poboy zone and deep into plate-lunch territory. That's the steam-table area where you'll find the everyday offerings (red beans, roast beef, spaghetti and meatballs) and the once-a-week specials (including a hearty beef stew on Tuesday and baked chicken on Thursday). You can ask the lovely ladies behind the counter for suggestions, but it's pretty hard to lose. You can up the ante by ordering a side of crispy, shoestring cut sweet potato fries.

Elizabeth's
601 Gallier St. (at Chartres)
504-944-9272

zone: Bywater
website: www.elizabeths-restaurant.com
reservations: none

meals: breakfast and lunch Tues–Sat, closed Sun–Mon
specialty: home-style southern and breakfast favorites
fancy factor: low-middlebrow
price range: $5–7

caveats: no reservations, not particularly walkable
bonus points: roadhouse portions, great desserts, serves calas

Heidi Trull came to New Orleans for Jazzfest, but moved here on the merits of a stuffed chicken wing.

On break from cooking duties in Asheville, North Carolina, Trull and her husband were dining at Emeril Lagasse's NOLA restaurant, and after a single bite, her eyes opened wide and she proclaimed, "I'm not going back."

After stint cooking at NOLA, Trull opened up her place—a simple white frame restaurant in the then-dicey Bywater—and gave it the simple motto "Real Food Done Real Good."

Though Heidi hails from South Carolina, she's carved out an important niche in this historically downmarket neighborhood. When she opened in 1998, she mostly served locals living within easy walking distance and earned a reputation that lived up to the motto.

Elizabeth's is a strictly daytime joint—breakfast and lunch only, with Jazzfest dinners being annual after-dark exceptions. The morning menu presents hearty meals with a distinctly southern pedigree—fluffy fresh-baked biscuits, eggs however you want them, and (of course) true grits. The "Loula May Breakfast Poboy" is a mountain of a meal—scrambled eggs, crispy hot sausage and cheese on a French loaf—dressed with mayo, lettuce and tomato if that's your pleasure.

A couple of Trull's specialties show her respect for local tradition and a penchant for extreme flavors. In a nod to living food history, she's one of the few chefs to offer "old-fashioned calas" on her everyday menu. This light cooked-rice fritter is a disappearing New Orleans specialty, and practically required eating if you take a seat before 10:30 AM (the breakfast/lunch transition). Both crispy and creamy, Trull's calas make a perfect alternative to morning beignets in the Quarter. On the meaty end of the spectrum, her "praline bacon" is a full-bore assault of sugar, salt and smoke. If you're a pork lover with an insatiable sweet tooth, you may never leave the place.

Much of the lunchtime action at Elizabeth's doesn't make it to the regular menu, but lives on the well-worn "daily specials" board. Dessert fiends can usually find a rotating list of home-baked cakes and pies that invariably contains some sugary childhood favorite. Heidi's husband Joe Trull, a former pastry chef at NOLA, turns out damn fine traditional sweets (red velvet cake, lemon chess pie) and ice creams during the summer months.

Gargantuan portions and enticing desserts conspire against light eaters, so you might want to pace yourself if you're going to save room for the sweet stuff (and you should).

A waiter once summed up a meal at Elizabeth's perfectly: "We *specialize* in too much food."

Fiorella's Cafe
45 French Market Pl. (at Gov. Nicholls)
504-528-9566

zone: French Quarter
reservations: none

meals: bonus po lunch and dinner
specialty: fried chicken and New Orleans barfood
fancy factor: lowbrow
price range: $6–16

bonus points: open late, French Quarter delivery

Any after-the-meal story about this funky French Market stalwart starts with a critical question: "Did you sit in the store side or the galley side?"

Located on the downriver end of the Quarter, Fiorella's has two entrances, two addresses, and two different—yet equally funky—aesthetics. Enter from the French Market side and you'll experience a historic if grungy grocery store turned barroom. Enter from the Decatur Street saloon strip and you're sitting in what seems like a surreal former seafood house, complete with New England maritime theme, faux portholes along the starboard wall and a lamp that looks eerily like Ernest Borgnine in nautical drag.

Either way, you're ordering from the same menu—a mixture of unfussy comfort foods that have powered the down-

Trout Meunière and Amandine

You'll find some version of this seafood dish in just about every white-linen restaurant in town, and quite a few of the older neighborhood joints as well. A filet of speckled trout is lightly dredged in flour, pan-sautéed, and topped with a rich brown butter sauce.

Sauce meunière—French for "the miller's wife"—can be a simple preparation (deglazing the pan with lemon, whisking in butter, garnishing with minced parsley) or require an experienced saucier's skill (made with a seafood or beef stock, reduced until thickened, spiced with Worcestershire and lemon, then mixed with butter). Either way, the resulting sauce is versatile enough to be used on a wide variety of seafood dishes.

Another common fish dish, *trout amandine*, is simply trout meunière layered with a crunchy mound of toasted almond slices.

---

town crowd through many an adrenaline-soaked late night and remorseful morning after. Hipster veterans of the latter situation swear by the hefty hamburger steak topped with grilled onions and gravy—just the thing to calm the stomach and provide ballast when you're particularly "sensitive to light." The daily specials follow the local dietary rhythms, including Monday red beans and fried catfish on Friday.

In July of 2004, Fiorella's kitchen got an unexpected nod from *Southern Living* magazine for their fried chicken; the buttoned down home and garden publication pronounced it some of the region's best. And with good reason: the chicken always emerges from the fryer with a wonderfully deep and crunchy crust covering moist, tender birdflesh; a consistent winner even when the kitchen's having an off night.

Franky and Johnny's Restaurant and Lounge
321 Arabella St. (at Tchoupitoulas)
phone:504-899-9146

zone: Uptown
reservations: none

meals: lunch and dinner daily
specialty: boiled seafood, poboys
fancy factor: lowbrow
price range: $6–12

caveats: can get pretty smoky
bonus points: good boiled seafood in season

Naugahyde without irony. Red-and-white plaid vinyl tablecloths. A jukebox that spins old 45s. Ceilings low enough to inspire bomb-shelter fantasies. In nearly every detail, the semi-grungy neighborhood bar a feels like an improvised midwestern speakeasy, hand-built and run by your high-school friend's dad's bowling team.

An unapologetically old-school bar and grill, Franky and Johnny's is nobody's idea of fine dining, but it's a trusty spot for the hungry Uptown lunch crowd and nostalgic Tulane University alumni returning for various sporting events. Walking-distance regulars always seem to be taking refuge in the window-less bar, safe from natural light and basking in the flicker of perpetual ESPN.

Straight-ahead neighborhood fare is the order of the day—and in keeping with the dockside ambiance, portion control isn't an issue. A quick scan of the menu hints at the kitchen's layout—they've got a deep fryer, an extra-wide griddle, and an oversized boiling rig. The fryer churns out tender tempura-crisp shrimp and tender, cornmeal-battered green pepper rings among many, many other options. The griddle turns out respectably juicy pork chops and huge hamburger poboys. The boiling rig runs the crawfish/crab/shrimp cycle according to season. Any Italian dish will be soaked in a sugary "red gravy"; bean dishes mysteriously run on the sweet side as well.

Halpern's Home Furnishings Cafe

1600 Prytania St. (at Terpsichore)
504-566-1707

zone: Garden District
reservations: none

meals: lunch weekdays
specialty: Creole lunch specialties
fancy factor: lowbrow
price range: $5–12

caveats: almost totally hidden
bonus points: almost totally hidden

Most gumbos are pretty easy to analyze, but this one was special.

As restaurant versions go, it was pretty close to perfect and absolutely addictive. For a seafood gumbo, it had all the meaty ingredients of the Seventh Ward Creole style. Thick in texture, it had the deep, nutty roux flavor and the herbal spiciness from the perfect amount of filé. Tiny peeled shrimp and the occasional shard of crab shell floated in the full-bodied broth with a savory aroma of rich seafood stock. Two kinds of sausage—soft, rounded chunks of hot chaurice and firmer-bodied slices of smoked sausage—floated alongside the shrimp, adding just a bit of heat and a multilay-ered porky dimension. The rest of the ingredients added to the flavor without being immediately recognizable—and Miss Gloria will only answer so many questions.

"Don't try to figure out my secret ingredients," she said with a suspicious smile. "I'll go get the rest of your order." Not only is her seafood gumbo some of my favorite in town, it's also the best you're likely to get in ANY furniture store in the country.

New Orleans has a long tradition of destination dining tied to high-dollar shopping, but that practice usually took place on bustling Canal Street. Older locals remember dining at various lunch counters in department stores (Maison Blanche, Goudchaux's, D.H. Holmses', Krauss), and many of the revered Creole cooks such as Austin Leslie list off these stores as important parts of their mental résumés.

In the age of the modern shopping mall and multivendor food court, the local department stores have mostly been con-verted to hotel space, and Miss Gloria car-ries on the tradition in a nearly hidden

Garden District furniture store—Halpern's Home Furnishings. To reach the second-floor dining room, you'll pick your way through a crowded showroom of armoires, sectional sofa suites, and floor-sample upholstered chairs marked down for quick sale. Well-pressed sales staff—expectant but lonely—perk up a bit when the door opens, only to shrink a bit when they realize you're just part of the lunch crowd.

The café is a two-person operation and a model of efficiency. Miss Gloria welcomes you at the cafeteria-style counter, leads you through the day's menu and spins around to work the kitchen. A charismatic Amazon of a woman, she'll let you know what's worth ordering today ("I made every bit of it, and it's ALL good"), chat about the café's history ("I've been here twenty-seven years, and I still love it") and explain her cooking techniques (to a point).

From the looks of things, the lunch crowd has more than its share of elderly, very prim Uptown ladies that favor pastel-toned Chanel suits on grocery day. These are women who probably shopped Canal Street at its heyday, and the same ones who just might buy a love seat after a mid-week luncheon.

Though the sandwich options are most likely offered every day, the rest of the menu rotates according to Miss Gloria's mood. On any given day, the menu plays both ends of the fussy spectrum: you might catch a crunchy, claw-meat crab cake sitting on a molded mound of rice and *macque choux* (pepper-smothered corn smothered) or a simple crunchy-skinned baked chicken served with soft peas and potato salad. As the lady says, it's ALL good, so choose according to your mood.

Pushing back from the fetching marble-topped dinette table ("This is nice . . .

CLASSIC

Red Beans and Rice

With two days of leisure behind us and a long workweek stretching ahead, New Orleans celebrates Monday with a bowl of red beans.

This simple riff on the universal "beans and rice" tradition includes aromatics known as the "Holy Trinity" (onion, bell pepper and celery) and is most often flavored with a bit of the pig (a ham hock, andouille sausage, smoky tasso or pickled pork). Nearly every restaurant in town does some variation on the dish, from creamy, long-stewed beans ladled from steam tables of downtown lunch joints to the puréed "red bean soup du jour" at the fancier restaurants.

The "beginning of the week" custom started in the days before indoor plumbing, when laundry was a scrub-with-your-hands all-day affair. Monday was the traditional laundry day, and cooks needed a dish that could sit on a low fire as they tended to their laundering tasks. The dish also made the most of the hambone that was often left over from Sunday dinner.

Some restaurants put red beans on the menu all week—even in the modern kitchen it's still a low-maintenance dish—but die-hard traditionalists usually wait until Monday to get their proper weekly fix.

wonder where they got this?"), you'll do well to head back to the counter and consider dessert. The cellophane-wrapped samples look like homemade bake-sale portions and are every bit as tasty. The deep chocolate blackout cake practically oozes fudge, and the lemon meringue pies have the telltale scalloped edges that indicate a Nilla Wafer crust. The Bananas Foster cheesecake—a substantial wedge of subtly flavored richness topped with a layer of dark caramel—is a swoon in every forkful.

Asked for a printed to-go menu, Miss Gloria replied that she doesn't believe in the practice. "I don't print anything out," she said with a quick grin and sweet sense of absolute control, "You come in. I want to *see* you."

Jacques-Imo's Café
8324 Oak St. (at Dante)
504-861-0886

zone: Uptown
website: www.jacquesimoscafe.com
reservations: parties of 5 or more only

meals: dinner Mon–Sat, closed Sun
specialty: eclectic Louisiana
fancy factor: low-middlebrow
price range: $15–20

caveats: dinner only, long waits, loud rooms, slammed during Jazzfest, limited reservations
bonus points: roadhouse portions, complimentary salad course, two hefty side dishes, always-festive atmosphere

There are restaurants where patrons absolutely refuse to wait. ("Fifteen minutes? Hmmmm. Thanks anyway . . .")

There are places where patrons might tolerate a half hour at the bar. Given that hunger makes people cranky and restaurant patrons aren't a particularly patient lot, only a few establishments have would-be customers that are happy—joyous, even—to wait over an hour before being seated. But go into Jacques-Imo's Café on any given evening and you'll see the most festive (and well-attended) extended wait in town. Dedicated fans fill the list early, grab a cocktail and join the party.

The whole Stepford-smiley scene would completely defy real-life logic if it weren't for Jacques-Imo's bulletproof and long-standing reputation. Street-level buzz consistently rates Jacques-Imo's high for over-the-top takes on Louisiana classics, huge family-style portions and bang for the proverbial buck. In its eight storied years of operation, frenetic owner/chef Jack Leonardi and his hard-working kitchen crew have made this tiny eatery into one of New Orleans' most-recommended neighborhood dining experiences.

Located inside a tiny Oak Street storefront, Jacques-Imo's seems to thrive on its close quarters. After waiting up in the front bar or at the nearby Maple Leaf Bar, diners pass straight through the bright bustling kitchen to the small dining rooms toward the rear. To keep up with demand, vinyl-clothed tables are pushed close together, leaving just enough space for waitstaff to operate without major incident.

Jacques-Imo's menu reflects the old-school Creole standards of Chez Hélène veteran chef Austin Leslie and the inventive bent of Leonardi. A split menu—standards and specials on facing pages—shows the two kitchen minds at work. The standards show a deference to home-style classics—stuffed pork chops, grilled duck, and Leslie's renowned fried chicken—as well as a deep stable of vegetable sides from mashed sweet potatoes to stewed cabbage with alligator sausage. On the specials side, Jacques-Imo's specials show the kitchen's experimental side with more far-reaching techniques and ingredients with offerings such as tender pork "osso buco" and whole flounder stuffed with crabmeat dressing. No matter what the mood, all bases are covered.

A standard starter, the shrimp and alligator sausage cheesecake, demonstrates the kitchen's well-balanced creative streak. This savory take on the dessert course standby is rich without being heavy and effectively plays a warm, spicy cream against chunks of shrimp and sausage. Less traditional is a starter-sized roast beef poboy: gravy-soaked, fully dressed, batter dipped, and lovingly deep fried. Somehow, Leonardi can make this dish seem perfectly normal.

In a long list of notable entrées, the "Cajun bouillabaisse" stands out for its multilayered flavor and outstanding presentation. A roasted, sawtooth-cut acorn squash is filled with chunks of red snapper, shrimp and a scattering of mussels in the shell. This mélange floats in a curried cream sauce thinned by the seafood's residual juices. The result is a brothy, delicately-spiced sauce that accentuates the squash's sweetness (scrape the sides) and complements the assorted fishflesh without obscuring the dish's individual flavors. And the good news is that it's on the "always available" side of the menu. Boisterous surroundings and borderline anarchy are part and parcel of the whole Jacques-Imo's experience, and there are nights when chaos can rule the kitchen, the dining room or both. As a high-traffic establishment, sometimes the kitchen

isn't quite as attentive to details as they should be; in the dining rooms, extremely close quarters often make for conversation-killing volume levels. It's all part of the package—a good natured brawl that always seems to work out, provided you go in with somewhat happy-go-lucky expectations.

The usual "first come, first served" routine is waived for tables of five or more, which cuts the wait for large groups. Otherwise, the only way to snag a quick seat is to show up at opening time (6:00 PM, no later) and hope that other early birds haven't packed the joint. During Jazzfest (their busiest weekends)—you can bank on longer-than-usual waits as Leonardi's scads of admirers show up and happily wait their turn for dinner.

Mother's
401 Poydras St (at Magazine)
504-523-9656

zone: CBD/Warehouse
reservations: none

meals: breakfast, lunch and dinner daily
specialty: Creole food, poboys
fancy factor: low-middlebrow
price range: $5–21

caveats: long lines, tour bus destination
bonus points: baked ham

In business since 1938, Mother's is an aging breakfast and lunch joint that's *exactly* what many tourists expect from a simple New Orleans eatery. It's got the requisite patina of local history, a funky brick and concrete "hole in the wall" ambience, and a long list of familiar

Louisiana specialties (gumbo, jambalaya, poboys, etc.) on the menu. Match that with a location that's a manageable hike from the Quarter or a cakewalk from the CBD hotels and you've got the makings of a high-traffic New Orleans legend.

Whether they come as part of a package tour or at the recommendation of a friendly concierge, most first-time visitors clock at least one meal at Mother's. On any given day, you can see the telltale sign of Mother's spreading popularity—empty tour busses waiting at the curb, diesel engines thrumming along to prevent vapor lock. During peak tourist sea-sons, lines of hungry travelers snake onto Poydras Street's sidewalk and lick their chops as they ponder the restaurant's house specialty-turned-tagline "World's Best Baked Ham."

And though the pork gets primary billing on signage and menus, Mother's local claims to fame comes from another slow-roasted specialty—the chunky beef specialty known as "debris" gravy. In concept, debris is a simple by-product of a straightforward cooking process: as a roast reaches the "fall-apart tender" phase of cooking, chunks of beef tumble into the roasting pan and mingle with the

INGREDIENT

Gulf Shrimp

Whether they're packed into an overstuffed poboy sautéed to buttery perfection or butterflied and lovingly stuffed with lump crabmeat dressing, these tasty and familiar crustaceans find their way onto just about every menu in Louisiana. To the uninitiated, they're not much to look at—beady eyes, long whipping "whiskers," and a thin, translucent shell—but to Louisiana cooks, they're a fresh-caught treasure that appears from late spring until mid-December.

In a time when most shrimp are farm-raised, quick-frozen and pre-peeled halfway around the globe, Louisiana shrimp are still wild things—starting their lives in saline marshes on the coast and growing to maturity in the shallow bays and saltwater lakes along the Gulf. The state is the largest domestic producer of shrimp with two bona fide shrimp seasons per year—brown shrimp from May to July and white shrimp from August to December. In season, most markets proudly display their shrimp with head and whiskers still attached—a sure sign of fresh product.

Louisiana seafood nationalists (chefs and diners alike) are justifiably proud of the native shrimp's superior texture and flavor and protective of coastal fishing communities that have suffered in recent years. Farm-raised imports from countries like Thailand and India—shelled, pre-frozen and as tasty as silicone caulk—have been dumped on the domestic seafood market, driving down prices as the economic invisible hand puts a stranglehold on Louisiana's shrimpers. The local seafood industry has started to fight back with education—alerting diners and chefs to the difference between local product and the farm-raised imports.

rich caramelized meat juices. Ladle a serving of this chunky concoction onto a roast beef and ham sandwich and you've got a "Ferdi"—a nickname that's been picked up by other poboy shops around town.

Hardcore gravy aficionados may expect debris to be a thick, full-bodied beef sauce, but at Mother's it's more of a thin-bodied jus with a scoop of pot-roast shreds on top. Some people swear by it, but this school o' gravy has a distinct downside: the poboy's bottom bread tends to get waterlogged, leading to French loaf disintegration and bite-to-bite chaos. The jus is somehow reminiscent of beef consommé: nice in a bowl, but not so much on a sandwich.

Mother's keeps the kitchen going from morning 'till night, serving up everything from sizable biscuits (topped with your choice of ten different meats) to grits with debris to gumbo, jambalaya and plenty of combination platters. Customers order at the stand-up counter, but most of the dishes are brought to your table after paying. Prices are also a couple of dollars higher than they ought to be, but just about what you'd expect for a high-profile tourist joint.

Which brings us back to the lines: Mother's has the feel of a local joint and the pedigree of a local classic, which is exactly why many New Orleanians can't seem to get near the place. If you're competing with normal-sized groups for seating, that's one thing—but waiting behind a 30-minute line of diners trucked in by the busload can take a sizable chunk out of a leisurely morning or standard-issue lunch hour. City-based regulars often avoid the rush by dining off-cycle and hitting the counter early or late.

Uglesich's Restaurant and Bar

1238 Baronne St. (at Erato)
504-523-8571

zone: Garden District
website: www.uglesich.com
reservations: none

meals: lunch Mon–Fri, closed Sat-Sun
specialty: creative Louisiana seafood
fancy factor: low-middlebrow
price range: $10–18

caveats: lunch only, closed during summer, long waits, pricy for lunch
bonus points: great raw bar, close to streetcar line, good wine and beer selection, late lunch

Call it a "fine dining dive." Call it a hidden gem. Call it an endangered species.

Uglesich's—a ramshackle, 10-table eatery in a dicey industrial section of Central City—routinely garners as much national press as the city's most revered white-linen establishments and enthusiastic accolades from celebrity chefs and legions of loyal foodies.

From its humble beginnings as a neighborhood bar and oyster house in the 1920s, Uglesich's has become one of the city's most-recommended restaurants, thanks in part to a famous fan base that includes respected restaurateurs like Emeril Lagasse, Susan Spicer and Frank Brigtsen as well as lifestyle maven Martha Stewart and just about every travel journalist writing about the city. Its semi-secluded location provides a little adventure for Quarter-bound travelers, and the creativity of the cuisine makes people feel as if they've discovered the essential New Orleans "diamond in the rough," even if their midday meal comes with a bottle of Belgian Trappist ale and sets them back $30 to $40 a person.

For nearly thirty years, diners have been drawn to Uglesich's for a menu that balances deep-fried New Orleans classics and distinctive dishes developed by Anthony and Gail, a self-taught husband-and-wife team. Hungry travelers line up to indulge in succulent shrimp stuffed with herbed lump crabmeat and delicate sautéed oyster "shooters" drenched in a cane syrup/sun-dried tomato vinaigrette. They wait for hours in the midday sun for a taste of the kitchen's peerless grilled speckled trout or their deep-fried interpretation of shrimp and grits.

And with each passing year as owner Anthony Uglesich inches closer to retirement, they wonder if this will be their last chance to taste the dishes he and his wife Gail made famous.

So if you're wont to get the classic Uglesich's experience while you still can, it helps to know the drill.

Once you wedge yourself inside the door, you'll find a tiny room packed with lunchtime loyalists waiting patiently for seats at the ten-table dining area. Grab a menu, decipher the tiny print, and when you're ready, Anthony Uglesich will give you the inside line on the day's catch.

Uglesich's menu is heavy on New Orleans seafood classics and surprisingly sophisticated for a seemingly simple lunch joint. On the first reading, you'll notice decidedly nonstandard dishes like Firecracker Shrimp (barbecue shrimp topped with horseradish cream sauce) and oyster brie soup.

That's why it's best to make a few preliminary picks, then ask Mr. Anthony for his recommendations. On any given day,

there will probably be one ingredient that's particularly fresh or another that's not quite up to his exacting standards. Hunkering over his order pad, he might talk a little about the weather—but mostly about how storm systems or today's climate are affecting his local seafood suppliers. He's also been known to steer enthusiastic patrons away from one of his simple specialties (fresh-cut French fries) because the day's potato shipment didn't pass muster.

Whatever you choose, you'll usually be in for a bit of a wait. As one of the least-kept lunchtime secrets in town, Uglesich's packs early for their daily one-meal serving schedule. Get there early (11:00–11:15 is safe) and you've got a pretty good shot at a quick table.

But even the near-inevitable delay has its benefits, in this case fresh-shucked oysters from the joint's tiny live bar. The nimble oystermen make small talk as their blunt knives flash. "Yeah, these are good today, but not like they were yesterday. When they're that good . . . they just GO."

In between trays of fresh dozens, they shuck for the kitchen—a rare practice—ensuring that the poboy oysters are nestled safely in their shell minutes before hitting the fryer.

If you brave the crowds, you'll also be privy to quality local eavesdropping and easy conviviality around the oyster bar. Doctors, local chefs, lawyers and a few better-informed tourists keep you company as you contemplate your starters—marinated shrimp and a cup of seafood gumbo. Tender shrimp are topped with a tart vinaigrette, served on crunchy rounds of toasted French bread and topped with a mix of finely minced parsley, shallot and celery. The layers of flavor make for a good balance of rich and clean, and the portion size is just big enough to whet the appetite for the entrées to come. The gumbo, thick with okra, tender oysters and shrimp, is almost filling enough to be a meal in itself.

Paul's Fantasy, one of Uglesich's wide list of house specials, shows Anthony's way with local seafood. In this dish, a thick filet of pan-fried speckled trout is covered with coastal home-style favorites—tender grilled shrimp (also huge) and crispy griddle-fried new potatoes—with LOTS of butter thrown in for good measure. There are many reasons why local chefs revere Mr. Uglesich as a god, and these simple dishes rank high on the list.

Of course, after (over)indulging in one of the classic New Orleans lunch experiences, you'll be faced with an old-school payment plan—cash only, no exceptions. So be sure to stock up on folding money and you'll be rewarded by a definitive New Orleans lunchtime experience you can lord over future generations of traveling foodies.

Ye Olde College Inn

3016 S Carrollton Ave. (at Fig)
504-866-3683

zone: Uptown
reservations: yes

meals: lunch daily; dinner Mon.–Sat,
    brunch Sunday°
specialty: neighborhood seafood and
    diner specialties
fancy factor: low-middlebrow
price range: $9–25

bonus points: zydeco brunch Sunday

In a town where historic architecture borders on the commonplace, Ye Olde College Inn has a distinct "welcome to the suburbs" vibe to it. With mottled beige bricks and tacked-on Revival columns, the building seems like it could be plopped down about anywhere in Central Suburbia—southern New Jersey, the strip- mall stretches of old Colorado Springs, anywhere called "the Tri-State Area."

But the peeling billboard overlooking the Inn's side parking lot betrays its local roots—"Special OYSTER LOAVES" blaring in script and block letters. In between faded illustrations of half and full poboys—a bit of a boast: "Almost Actual Size."

In business since 1933, Ye Olde College Inn is Uptown's epitome of the non-retro neighborhood diner. It's the kind of businessman's lunch joint that's comfortably stuck in time circa 1953 and waiting for Elvis to come—the first time. Instead of self-conscious drive-in graphics or sparkly vinyl booths, the Inn sports wooden chairs and grained Formica tables—and if it seems like your grandmother's favorite restaurant, look around. She's probably sitting with her friends in the back room or catching an afternoon beer in the bar.

Fried seafood and other straightforward fare have been the Inn's hallmarks since the Depression, but its 2003 purchase by Rock N' Bowl impresario John Blancher has brought a few subtle changes. The dining room's wooden telephone became a makeshift wine rack. A few updated dishes snuck onto the entrée list—green onion Dijon chicken, for one—but it's not enough to detract from the joint's workaday momentum.

On the whole, the menu plays to comforting traditional tastes, at times bordering on the bland. The mayo-heavy pink remoulade sauce is absent any kind of spicy kick and could easily be mistaken for pickle-free Thousand Island dressing. It's no doubt that the kitchen pays due respect to the deep-frying process—the fried green tomatoes that act as base for the dish are crunchy and cooked to perfection.

Monday lunch red beans are silky and comforting, served with a sizable link of smoked sausage and a bit of flavoring meat in the beans themselves. Long cooking gently poaches the sausage and makes it tender enough to cut with a spoon.

Keep a sharp eye out for the plates on OTHER people's tables—the Inn sports a list of daily specials seemingly designed to keep diners guessing. Southern-style "meat and three" aficionados can put together a respectable vegetable plate from the long list of sides. And if you're a fried onion fan, order a plate full of the crispy "secret recipe" rings before your butt hits the chair. You won't regret it.

One final word of encouragement and caution to poboy fans: it helps to know your terms when ordering a sandwich at Ye Olde College Inn. A standard-sized poboy is listed as "on French" and clocks in at well under $10. Order an "oyster loaf" like the one on the sign and you'll get a gargantuan sandwich that requires ample upper body strength to heft and can easily be a quick lunch for the Saints' entire offensive line.

The billboard, it turns out, wasn't kidding at all.

HOUSE bistros

I n the 1980s, not long after Paul Prudhomme combined city and country traditions into a new Louisiana food, a new restaurant type was born in New Orleans.

Ambitious young chefs, many of them veterans of Prudhomme's kitchen with local roots, turned old houses into more casual restaurants and brought fine dining to the residential areas of Uptown and Midcity. In the kitchen, the young upstarts continued their own experiments with the local ingredients, respected traditions and new flavors. The new bistros drew curious diners from the French Quarter and expanded New Orleans' reputation as an up-and-coming culinary destination, especially among annual Jazzfest pilgrims. More than twenty years later, house bistros have become their own recognizable category in the city's restaurant scene.

In terms of ambience, these restaurants exude a kind of easy comfort—casual, approachable and likable. If you ask locals to list their favorite meals, they'll probably mention at least one of these restaurants.

Most of the older house bistros have survived for decades as independent chef-owned enterprises—no small feat in such a competitive restaurant town. Though they're rarely considered among the city's cutting-edge eateries, the bistros draw their own steady loyal crowds who watched these award-winning chefs contribute to the city's culinary evolution.

Brigtsen's

723 Dante St. (at River)
504-861-7610

zone: Uptown
website: www.brigtsens.com
reservations: recommended

meals: dinner Tues–Sat, closed Sun–Mon
specialty: updated Louisiana seafood
fancy factor: high-middlebrow
price range: $18–24

bonus points: weekday early bird

Chef Frank Brigtsen's little bistro tops my personal list of restaurant recommendations—especially for first-time travelers to the city. The food and the atmosphere are both perfectly balanced between formal and homey. The menu has a great selec-tion of Louisiana standards (a pitch perfect rabbit and andouille gumbo, oysters *en brochette* reinterpreted as a spinach salad) that deftly unite Cajun and Creole in ways that teach you about the possibilities of Louisiana cuisine.

Nestled in formerly residential corner of the Riverbend, the renovated side-hall shotgun is unassuming and casual—there doesn't seem to be a lot going on inside. But in that way, it's got the feel of a culinary speakeasy: a hidden garden indoors, with happy diners chattering away, peals of laughter and smiles all around. The dining area meanders through the cottage's three main rooms, each small enough to be intimate without feeling cramped.

Frank's wife, Marna, and her two sisters (welcome refugees from the Dakotas all) run the front of the house with a familiar grace that makes first-timers feel like friends of friends.

As a kid in suburban New Orleans, Frank Brigtsen grew up fishing the shallow-water bays and marshes along the Gulf coast. He learned how to cast for redfish in grassy marshes, which abandoned oil rigs draw the most speckled trout and why sheepshead congregate around shell reefs. Then as no, he spent as much time on the water as he could, heading for open water with a boatload of fishing tackle. Later in life, he learned about flavor working in Commander's Palace and K-Paul's kitchens under Paul Prudhomme.

Brigtsen's love of the Louisiana coast gives him a heightened appreciation for local seafood, and that understanding shows when he steps behind the stove. He wraps a delicate filet of sheepshead crabmeat in parmesan crust. He drizzles a Worcestershire-spiked meunière sauce over perfectly pan-fried flounder or a sautéed soft-shell crab. He loves the lesser-known fish that swim in Gulf waters, such as the tender triggerfish that he pairs with a crunchy potato pancake and red pepper sour cream.

The chef also does as well with game dishes as he does with fish. His signature roasted duck is a seemingly simple dish that bridges the gap between the rustic Cajun and French bistro traditions. The ducks are slow-roasted, deboned, diced and arranged on a bed of sage-hinted cornbread dressing. The entire assembly is covered with a layer of crispy broiled duck skin and served with a honey-pecan pan gravy. If you're a fan of the fowl, don't miss this dish.

Clancy's
6100 Annunciation St. (at Webster)
504-895-1111

zone: Uptown
reservations: recommended

meals: lunch Tues–Fri, dinner Mon–Sat, closed Sun
specialty: contemporary Creole
fancy factor: high-middlebrow
price range: $19–29

caveats: insider crowd (if you're out)
bonus points: insider crowd (if you're in)

The maître d' at Clancy's doesn't seem to meet a lot of strangers. Every time the door at this former corner store swings wide, he seems to open with the appropriate first-name greeting and a familiar, ingratiating tone. The more standard salutation—"Welcome to Clancy's"— isn't nearly as common at this out-of-the-way house bistro, which for years has catered to a core of well-heeled regulars. Buried in the maze of Uptown's side streets, Clancy's is one of the more unassuming restaurants in the city, which seems to suit its loyalists just fine. It's another of the "secret clubhouse" restaurants that locals often keep to themselves—and on any given night, the older crowd reflects a genteel Uptown vibe. Most of the gentlemen (doctors, lawyers, captains of industry) are clad in suits or sports coats, "dressing for dinner" though it's no longer expected. Ladies are dressed a bit fancier than everyday and gussied up with a fresh coat of lipstick.

Few travelers end up at Clancy's, but when they do, they invariably make a meal of the kitchen's signature dishes. The fried oyster starter with melted brie would be considered rich by any standards, but the addition of lemon beurre blanc puts it over the top. A shrimp and grits appetizer plays a sweet sauce against smoky tasso and caramelized onions.

Blue Crabs

Huge claws, menacing spikes, six pointy legs—the blue crab needs all the protection it can get. That's because inside its hard protective shell, this bulletproof crustacean stashes away some of the most sought-after meat in the sea.

The crab known as *callinectes sapidus* (Latin for "savory beautiful swimmer") plays a special part in seafood-centric cuisines from Texas' Gulf coast all the way around the tip of Florida and up the Atlantic coast as far as New York. Maryland's much-ballyhooed Chesapeake Bay crabs and South Carolina's prized she-crabs are the same species that Louisiana watermen pick out of traps all along the state's coastline. In fact, due to its warm water and ideal salt-to-freshwater ratio, the Louisiana Gulf coast leads the nation in blue crab export and crabmeat production. In certain seasons, the crabs they're crackin' in Baltimore might have grown up in Louisiana waters.

If you've ever worked your way through a whole boiled crab, you probably know that getting to the meaty bits is anything but simple. Bits of shell and cartilage are always a problem, and the deeper you get into a crab, the more delicate handwork it requires.

Jumbo lump crabmeat, found just behind the crab's rounded swimming legs, is the most delicate, and richest in terms of flavor, texture and cost. This is the flawless, addictive meat you'll find in crabmeat salads and many Creole butter-sauce dishes. If a waitress draws out her syllables while saying "topped with jummmbo lummmmp crabmmmmeat sautéed in butter," she's seducing you with shellfish. If you can handle the price, succumb to the pleasure. You won't be disappointed.

Backfin meat comes next; a bit less pristine than the lump variety, but still possessing a fine, clean flavor and preferred for marquee dishes like crab and corn bisque, stuffed crab or crab cakes. **Flake** crabmeat (also called "special") is less costly and comes in smaller shreds than the more expensive grades. Last comes the **claw meat**, which doesn't have the pure white color of the body meats, but instead leans toward the grayish hues with a nuttier flavor and texture similar to lobster tail.

You also might see another swimmer-related term at local seafood markets: **gumbo crabs**. These are smaller specimens, usually cut in half and frozen for stocks and seafood gumbos.

The soft-shell crab entrée looks simple enough—sautéed and topped with lump crabmeat—until the first bite reveals another layer of subtle flavor. Before hitting the pan, the crab spent time in a smoker adding to the dish's savory complexity. There's always a slice of the house "ice-box pie" for dessert—a tart wedge of creamy frozen custard that never fails to trigger a tang-induced wince on the first bite.

For the uninitiated, the lack of atmospheric polish might seem strange. Indeed, the former dry goods store is a bit rougher around the edges than your usual fine dining establishment. Clearly popular before the advent of restaurant design specialists, the room is decked out in worn gray indoor/outdoor carpet, aging ceiling fans and a few framed prints. On the first encounter, Clancy's feels like a downmarket lunch joint that renovated by buying a set of white tablecloths.

But the regulars will tell you that the lack of polish only contributes to the charm. They look past the décor to the special treatment and favorite dishes that, in their minds, make this hidden clubhouse their favorite. And if you don't understand the appeal, then it's to be expected. Maybe one day, if you get to be a regular, you'll understand.

Dante's Kitchen

736 Dante St. (at River)
504-861-3121

zone: Uptown
website: www.danteskitchen.com
reservations: recommended

meals: lunch and dinner daily, brunch Sun
specialty: contemporary Louisiana

fancy factor: middlebrow
price range: $16–20

bonus points: outdoor seating, open nightly, brunch

After years of working for the Brennan family's Garden District flagship, Emmanuel Loubier left the bustling kitchen at Commander's Palace to follow his own path. Loubier (called "E-man" by friends and customers) took over an Uptown sandwich shop and remade it into the newest of the city's house bistros.

E-man's new enterprise fits nicely into the Riverbend's restaurant scene, which also includes noted neighbors such as Brigtsen's (across the street) and Mat & Naddie's (just up the River Road). A pristine little shotgun house forms the core of the restaurant, but structural additions—most notably a slope-roofed bar/dining area and multitiered outdoor terrace—add versatile seating space to the cozy eatery.

Loubier's cooking style—contemporary takes on Louisiana and regional standards—also fits the neighborhood quite nicely. Diners familiar with the Commander's repertoire will recognize some of his tasty adaptations—grilled

Gulf fish "on the half shell" (served as a "skin-on" filet) topped with crabmeat, an outstanding crab and sweet corn soup, house-made pâtes and sausages—while other offerings show a more experimental streak. His signature falafel-encrusted Gulf fish and "wild boar cookout" (grilled chop and braised leg served as upscale barbecue) show his penchant for bold flavors, while his version of shrimp and grits (rich and creamy served with an almost rustic red-eye gravy) shows off his sense of balance.

The restaurant was quick to build a loyal following by playing to the strengths of its location (near the Uptown universities) and filling the lunchtime voids in the neighborhood scene. Dante's does brisk weekday lunch business and weekend brunches on Saturdays and Sundays. During the dinner rush, the crowd skews young, showing E-man's popularity with the students.

Dick and Jenny's
4501 Tchoupitoulas St. (at Jena)
504-894-9880

zone: Uptown
reservations: none

meals: dinner Tues–Sat, Closed Sun–Mon
specialty: eclectic regional homestyle
fancy factor: middlebrow
price range: $15–21

caveats: no reservations
bonus points: parking lot across street, kids menu

Rustic, homey and pleasingly rough around the edges, Dick and Jenny's has a distinctly handmade feel. Hand-painted plates line the wall, mason jars serve as water glasses and floral-pattern oil-cloth table coverings stand in for white linen. Arrive during a rush and you'll be shuffled to the back porch to bide your time—a practical lesson in "first come, first served" that matches this Uptown standard's almost family-casual vibe.

Simultaneously casual and upscale, it's a favorite of locals, Tulane students dining on Daddy's tab, and loyal fans of chef Richard Benz. Its location a half-block from Tipitina's also draws a consistent pre-gig music crowd.

Keeping with a grandma-comfortable ambience, Benz—a veteran of Upperline, Gautreau's and Commander's— freely mixes rustic Louisiana classics with contemporary flavors and techniques. The resulting dishes are soothing and comforting, true to local tradition while providing stylistic surprises. He's been known to pan-fry sweetbreads to crispy tender perfection, then serve them with chunky roast-beef "debris" gravy, or give garlicky barbecue shrimp a distinctive Asian turn by replacing tangy Worcestershire sauce with an eye-opening shot of chili paste.

Benz shines with home-style interpretations on the hearty end of the spectrum: his nearly spoon-tender braised lamb shank with cassoulet and rich (yet nonstandard) goose and andouille gumbo can chase away the worst winter chill. The sweet list also reflects a home-style sensibility—a fresh-fried cake donut topped with maple-stewed apples or spicy persimmon pudding are perfect finishers.

Scan the hundreds of hand-painted ceramic plates and you'll notice names of regulars, renowned local chefs and friends of Benz and his wife, Jenny, who runs the front of the house with charm and grace. Hoping to offset renovation costs for the aging former grocery, the couple raised operating cash by selling customized plates—each painted and fired by the chef himself and marked with the patron's name as a visible sign of support.

Though most nights this Uptown standard qualifies as a locals-only hideaway, the dining room is quick to pack on weekends, especially during the bigger citywide celebrations. The strict no-reservations policy definitely benefits the early birds, who know to line up for the 5:00 opening time. On these nights, it's great to belly up to the main-room bar (if there's space) and take a mental roll call of the chef's friends and admirers—plate by hand-painted plate.

Gabrielle
3201 Esplanade Ave. (at Mystery)
504-948-6233

zone: Midcity
website: www.gabriellerestaurant.com
reservations: recommended

meals: lunch Fri, dinner Tues–Sat, closed Sun–Mon

specialty: contemporary Louisiana
fancy factor: high-middlebrow
price range: $14–32

bonus points: Friday lunch

For the last twelve years, chef Greg Sonnier has been held hostage by a duck—a signature dish that Sonnier has kept on his menu since opening his Midcity bistro in 1992.

An ample portion of boneless slow-roasted duck meat sits atop a bed of crunchy/tender French fries, sauced with rich pan gravy and studded with butter-browned crimini mushrooms and roasted red pepper strips. Hearty, almost impossibly tender meat falls to moist shreds at the slightest touch and is topped with a crunchy square of flash-fried duck skin. Cajuns would call it a duck *graton*, or cracklin'—a crispy pork rind for poultry lovers.

Bite by bite, the texture of the dish changes, as the savory reduction sauce—with concentrated layers of flavor (orange, dry sherry, aromatic vegetables)—soaks into the shoestring-cut fries. Over time, the potatoes absorb the savory gravy, providing perfect counterpart for the forkfuls of duck fragrant with the earthy scent of caramelized onion and rosemary.

The dish can claim at least three links to local tradition: the original gravy-soaked fried potato poboy, the classic French preparation duck l'orange and an improvised staff meal at K-Paul's Louisiana kitchen, where Sonnier started ed his culinary career. The chef's earthy yet refined duck pays homage to the early days of Louisiana cuisine, and has been a house standard with a well-earned fierce following. At this point, Sonnier couldn't take if off the menu if he tried. A local boy with family ties to rural Acadiana, Sonnier chose restaurant work

on the list. Sometimes Sonnier mixes it up a bit and substitutes vermicelli for the potatoes. If that's the case, respectfully request the fries. You won't be disappointed.

Gautreau's
1728 Soniat St.
504-899-7397

zone: Uptown
reservations: recommended

meals: dinner Mon–Sat, closed Sun
specialty: modern Louisiana
fancy factor: high-middlebrow
price range: $19–32

caveats: tough to find

over a career in law enforcement, and found a home at K-Paul's in the early years before setting up shop on scenic Esplanade Avenue, a stone's throw from the New Orleans fairgrounds. A 1994 "Best New Chef" honor from *Food and Wine* generated plenty of national buzz as he built a solid reputation among locals and Jazzfest regulars alike. His wife Mary (also a K-Paul's alumnus) runs the front of the house, making it yet another New Orleans family affair.

Sonnier's menus reflect his strong Louisiana lineage—he's never too far from a riff on barbecue shrimp, stuffed flounder, or shrimp remoulade. He's also adept at playing with lesser-known Cajun classics, such as a *oreilles de cochon* (pig ears); a crispy fried pastry that the chef stuffs with seared foie gras and drizzles with Louisiana blueberry demi-glace.

But for duck devotees or fans of the French fry, there's really only one choice

Precious, charming and all but invisible from the street, Gautreau's is the secret clubhouse of Uptown's white-linen restaurant scene. If you're going to find it, a street map and solid sense of direction won't do you much good; a vine-covered portico and a jungle of potted plants shield the entrance from view. No sign, no parking lot, no visible signs of business. Enlist the help of a native guide or knowledgeable taxi driver—first-time visitors would have an easier time stumbling on the secret entrance to Bruce Wayne's Batcave.

Gautreau's caters to an almost exclusively local crowd, in a tiny room that makes you feel . . . well . . . exclusive. In a previous life, the historic building was a neighborhood drugstore; the renovation to upscale eatery suits the building well with its patterned tin ceiling and deep jewel-toned walls. Glass-front apothecary cabinets are now an elaborate liquor cabinet. Early evenings, the dining area is quiet and romantic, but as the dozen or so tables fill, the room takes on the convivial energy of a culinary speakeasy. This private-club ambience, combined with solid bistro-style menu make Gautreau's a dependable getaway for upscale residents yearning for sophisticated, tourist-free environs.

The kitchen tends to have a relatively high chef turnover rate—especially in recent years—but it has played host to such local luminaries as Richard Benz (now of Dick and Jenny's) and John Harris of Lilette. Chef Mat Wolf currently runs the kitchen with a menu that updates the French bistro fare without significant Creole influence. A native of Seattle and Commander's Palace veteran, this 30-year-old has garnered plenty of national press with precise execution of dishes like seared scallops on truffled black pepper linguine or Gulf wahoo atop asparagus risotto paired with a tangy/earthy turnip vinaigrette. Not exactly New Orleans fare, but a welcome departure for locals who want a little distance from New Orleans cuisine in elegant clubhouse surroundings.

Mat & Naddie's Cafe

937 Leonidas St. (at the Levee)
504-861-9600

zone: Uptown
reservations: recommended

meals: lunch Tues–Fri, dinner Tues–Sat, closed Sun-Mon
specialty: contemporary Louisiana
fancy factor: high-middlebrow
price range: $19–28

Mat & Naddie's is a charming little shotgun house quite literally on the edge of town—overlooking the levee and Uptown's River Road. The restaurant's

Wild in the Water

With tourism a year-round market and many Gulf fisheries only seasonal, many chefs turn to farm-raised seafood for consistency of supply and lower food costs.

The problem is that the domesticated product—whether it's catfish, crawfish, redfish or shrimp—often doesn't have the same distinctive taste as the animals netted from the Gulf or other natural waterways. Their diet and activities aren't controlled but they are also susceptible to natural environmental variation. To differentiate these seafoods from the controlled aquacultural varieties, cooks and fishermen have started using the term "wild" to describe ocean-caught seafood.

"Seafood is the last wild food we have. Everything else is from a farm," says chef Frank Brigtsen of Brigtsen's Restaurant (see page 71). "Wild shrimp are more difficult because there's flux in size from day to day and catch to catch. But you bite into a farmed shrimp and the flavor's just not there. Even if you call it something with caché like 'tiger prawn,' it's just another bland farm-raised shrimp."

Shrimpers and shrimp distributors from eight Gulf Coast states (including Louisiana) have launched a campaign to raise awareness of the industry and the advantages of ocean-caught shrimp. For more information, visit www.wildamerican-shrimp.com.

atmosphere is simultaneously funky and well preserved—cypress floors meticulously restored, the original brick chimney standing in the room's center, colorful folk art hanging on the outside patio. The cuisine at Mat & Naddie's matches its ambience perfectly, with eclectic takes on Louisiana classics prepared with creativity and precision. Their grilled oysters, a riff on Drago's trademark dish, avoid the dreaded rubbery, overcooked texture, instead arriving plump and moist on the inside and topped with a thin layer of browned Romano cheese and garlic. The entrée list shows that the chef isn't afraid to hit the road in search of new flavor combinations, from smothered hen "tandoor-style" to Japanese-style fried shrimp served with red chili sauce. Local standbys also get welcome updates—crispy pan-roasted grouper filets are accompanied by a slightly tart, light-bodied version of *sauce piquante* over rice. The addition of perfectly cooked baby eggplant to the sauce makes you realize the thin line between the Cajun classic and Mediterranean ratatouille.

If you've got a weakness for sweets, you might just want to flip the traditional meal order and eat dessert first. If you see so many compelling sugary choices on a full stomach, it might break your heart. It's hard to resist a rich caramel cheesecake, but the real standout is their pannéed bread pudding—a perfect disk of velvety rich pudding pan-fried to golden-brown crunch, surrounded by a pool of rum caramel sauce and bananas caramelized "brûlée-style." Never has a bread pudding had so many layers of satisfying crunch.

Upperline
1413 Upperline St. (at Prytania)
504-891-9822

zone: Uptown
website: www.upperline.com
reservations: recommended

meals: dinner Wed–Sun, closed Mon–Tues
specialty: updated Louisiana classics
fancy factor: high-middlebrow
price range: $17–25

At most restaurants, the word "hostess" describes a front-of-house function rather than a person. Oftentimes, it's a nattily-dressed coed responsible for "front-door duty"—greeting guests, juggling misplaced reservations, playing air traffic control, and occasionally keeping impatient diners at bay with a whip and a chair.

At Upperline, JoAnn Clevinger takes a more traditional approach to the role—personally welcoming her guests as she patrols the dining room of her Uptown bistro. If you've eaten at this bright yellow townhouse-turned-restaurant, you've probably met Clevinger—Upperline's energetic owner and one of the city's most enthusiastic ambassadors. A native of north Louisiana, Ms. Clevinger has lived in New Orleans for nearly fifty years and still maintains a new transplant's zeal for her adopted home.

Since opening Upperline in 1983,

Clevinger has built a reputation for mixing heartfelt hospitality with well-executed updates of Creole and Southern favorites. One of the now-classic combinations of contemporary New Orleans—fried green tomatoes and shrimp remoulade—originated in Upperline's kitchen. Until his death 1994, chef Tom Cowman wowed locals with his trademark dishes (roast duck, liver à l'orange, lamb curry) as well as tried-and-true New Orleans standards.

Hometown favorite Ken Smith currently heads the kitchen and balances the menu with nods to Upperline's legacy dishes (duck with ginger-peach or garlic-port sauce, corn cakes with smothered duck and andouille) and well-executed samples from the Creole canon (an outstanding duck gumbo, oyster stew flavored with a touch of Herbsaint, veal grillades with cheese grits). Warm pecan pie—a nod to Clevinger's north Louisiana upbringing—is a dessert list standout.

Smith doesn't necessarily push the culinary envelope with his everyday menu, but rather pours a significant amount of energy into Upperline's many special-event menus that celebrate annual "happenings" ranging from Christmas-season Réveillon feasts to the restaurant's summertime garlic festival. Chef Ken puts his considerable cookbook library and research skills to good use for event menus like Thomas Jefferson's favorite dishes for a Louisiana Purchase wine dinner, foods mentioned in Tennessee Williams's plays or dishes prepared for the food-themed Danish movie *Babette's Feast.*

The various dining rooms at Upperline are lined with JoAnn's considerable collection of New Orleans–themed art. In the main room, paintings cover every

CLASSIC

Shrimp Remoulade

Shrimp remoulade is one of those New Orleans dishes that just about everyone can appreciate. Boiled shrimp are peeled and chilled, then served with a tangy tomato-based dressing flavored with coarse-grained Creole mustard, horseradish and spices. Many first-timers consider it an amped-up version of a familiar shrimp cocktail, usually served on a bed of lettuce.

As the local gift to the salad course, the seafood concoction has the advantages of using fresh Gulf shellfish, being served cold (great for hot weather lunches) and not being deep fried (a boon for the diet conscious and fat phobic). Nearly every restaurant that specializes in Louisiana cuisine will have some variation of remoulade on its menu, be it an entrée-sized salad or appetizer portion served atop crispy fried green tomato slices.

Fans of continental French cuisine might be a bit confused by most Louisiana remoulade recipes, since most Euro-versions call for a mayonnaise base spiked with mustard and capers. You'll occasionally see this type in New Orleans restaurants—referred to as a "white remoulade" or ravigote sauce—but in most of the city, red remoulade reigns supreme.

inch of wall space while folksy sculptures sprout from nearly every horizontal surface. Even the building's exterior sports a striking mural-sized triptych from local artist Martin Laborde ("Love Each Other. Love Your Pets. Love Yourself.").

At some point during your meal, Clevinger will stop by for a quick hostess chat. She'll probably start out asking about your meal, but might well end up asking where else you've eaten, and suggesting her favorite New Orleans culinary and cultural experiences. (She keeps a list of them on the restaurant's website for easy reference.)

As JoAnn makes her way across the room, her generosity of spirit shines through—the consummate hostess and contributing to her guests' New Orleans experience even after they've left for the night.

celebrity SITES

ost people can spot the TV chefs a mile away. Since Paul Prudhomme took to the airwaves of TV morning shows in the 1980s, working chefs have emerged from behind their stoves and taken their turn on the stage and small screen. Single restaurants become media-fueled empires, complete with spin-off shows, kitchen product lines and crowds of hungry, star-struck viewers.

New Orleans has its share of instantly recognizable celebrity chefs, but the Crescent City is also home to a cadre of chefs who enjoy a similar superstar status among the city's dining public and traveling foodies as well.

One side note: if you're looking for Mr. Prudhomme (the city's original celebrity chef), check out the Cajun Imports section (page 113).

Bayona
430 Dauphine St. (at Conti)
504-525-4455

zone: French Quarter
website: www.bayona.com
reservations: required

meals: lunch Mon–Fri, dinner Mon–Sat, closed Sunday
specialty: French Mediterranean
fancy factor: highbrow
price range: $18–28

bonus points: validated parking, patio seating

Think that you've got a busy schedule? Chef Susan Spicer can relate.

Not so long ago, Spicer split her time among three local restaurants and a few food-related side projects. In addition to her duties at her famed French Quarter flagship restaurant, she launched a shared kitchen partnership with Donald Link at Herbsaint, held down a consulting chef gig at the newly launched Cobalt and ran a specialty food market. Though her roles differed at each, it wasn't uncommon for her to work the lunch at Bayona, then shuttle over to Herbsaint to oversee the dinner shift.

After a few years of heavy-duty multi-tasking, the Beard Award–winning chef has pared her schedule and now focuses on the little Creole cottage on Dauphine that made her a local celebrity.

A New Orleans native, Spicer opened up Bayona in 1990 after years working in kitchens around the city and a few travel stints to California and Europe. She had previously made a name for herself at the Bistro at Maison de Ville (page 121) by deftly combining light and bold flavors in her Mediterranean-influenced dishes. In 1989, she snagged a "Best New

Chef" honor from *Food & Wine*, and at the helm of Bayona continued to win both national and local awards.

Over the years, Spicer has developed a strong repertoire of signature dishes, and Bayona's split-menu setup—trademark offerings on one page, seasonal specials on the other—ensure that the chef's most-requested dishes are consistently available. It would be a shame for game lovers to miss out on her salad with crispy smoked quail, for example, or Francophiles to miss her creamy sweetbreads sautéed with earthy mushrooms and topped with tangy sherry mustard. On the other hand, lucky winter diners will be able to catch an outstanding roasted breast of pheasant teamed with a cherry/fig compote and a rich pinot noir reduction. It's unlikely that such a cold-weather dish would make the permanent roster, but we can always hope. The dessert creations of pastry chef Meagan Roen (another local returned from culinary travels in New York) rank among the best in town.

The prim little Creole cottage also reflects a sense of the city's history with the Mediterranean influences that permeate Spicer's cuisine. The main room is painted a shade of terra-cotta brown that softens evening light perfectly and manages to be formal without crossing the line to stuffy. In the spring and autumn months, a lush courtyard is a perfect place for relaxed, romantic al fresco dining. And that's something that even the most harried diner (or chef) can slow down to appreciate.

Emeril's

800 Tchoupitoulas St. (at Julia)
504-528-9393

zone: CBD/Warehouse
website: www.emerils.com
reservations: required (good luck)

meals: lunch Mon–Fri, dinner nightly
specialty: "New" New Orleans
fancy factor: highbrow
price range: $26–39

caveats: reserve early
bonus points: valet parking

Before the cooking shows, before the nationwide restaurant empire, before the cookbooks, appearances on *Good Morning America* and call-and-response chants of BAM!—there was Emeril's.

After leaving his post at Commander's Palace, Emeril Lagasse opened his eponymous restaurant in the still-transitional Warehouse District and worked the kitchen 15 shifts a week. His reputation for "new New Orleans food" took root and spread through the city, attracting the attention of the national food press and eventually a media star was born.

Open since 1990, Lagasse's flagship restaurant consistently attracts a steady flow of the dedicated, the curious and locals who remember when the charismatic chef was running things on Tchoupitoulas. Since Emeril's ever-widening duties take him away from the city, chef de cuisine Chris Wilson currently oversees the kitchen on a nightly basis and shows comparative restraint given Emeril's over-the-top reputation.

Dish descriptions still lean toward hyper-description—Butter Lettuce Wedge Drizzled with a Warm Bacon–Black Eyed Pea Vinaigrette with Balsamic-Braised Onions, Spiced Walnuts & Pears Topped with Roquefort Bleu Cheese, for example—but on the plate, the dishes aren't lacking in subtlety or understatement. A savory tea-glazed duck gets a hint of tang from an orange glaze and earthy counterpoint of bread pudding flavored with caramelized onions. A thick "beef marmalade"—a hyper-reduced version of debris gravy—tops a seared petit filet and, when paired with truffled stone-ground grits, makes for exceptional beef-on-beef action.

Lagasse loyalists will still find a few of Emeril's trademark dishes—the deconstructed BBQ shrimp, monstrously large double-cut pork chop, banana cream pie—sprinkled amongst the new stuff. If you're there for Emeril's greatest hits, there will always be a few from which to choose.

The restaurant underwent a full-scale renovation in 2000, and the changes (including a secondary dining room and swanky bar area) also do quite a bit to take the edge off the traditionally noisy room. There's still a lot of action and excitement regardless of the night, but intimate conversations got a bit easier.

Thousands of Emeril's devotees book well in advance of their pilgrimage meals, and you should as well. When any large-scale group packs local hotels, it's the

Emeril's Empire

The current international representative of Louisiana cuisine is neither a Cajun come to the city or a revered Creole chef, but an energetic, media-savvy import from the Portuguese side of Fall River, Massachusetts.

Emeril Legasse, ever-present icon of Food TV Network, came to prominence as executive chef of Commander's Palace, a Garden District mainstay that launched the career of fellow star chef Paul Prudhomme. Throughout the 1990s, Emeril developed a distinctive, often "over the top" culinary style with roots in Louisiana classics and built an enthusiastic fan base whose cries of "BAM!" signaled the reentry of men into home kitchens nationwide.

Of the nine restaurants that bear the chef's distinctive name, three of them are located in New Orleans—the original Emeril's in the Warehouse District (see page 83), the French Quarter's NOLA (see page 86), and the revived classic Emeril's Delmonico (see below) on St. Charles Avenue. His legions of loyal fans gravitate to these local outposts of Emeril's empire to experience their hero's globetrotting approach to Louisiana cuisine, where any international technique or ingredient is fair game as long as it appeals to a bold, experimental palate.

While you'll be able to taste many of the chef's trademark dishes, the odds of catching His Bamness behind the stove are slim. With nine restaurants, two television shows, an expanding product line and countless takes promotional appearances to juggle, Lagasse holds the post of Executive Chef and trusts the day-to-day operations and menu development to his trusty *chefs de cuisine*. These capable chefs (Chris Wilson at Emeril's, NOLA's Michael Ruoss, Shane Prichett of Delmonico) interpret Lagasse's culinary vision with their own dishes while executing Emeril's signature preparations.

---

toughest reservation in town, even if the concierge is your brother-in-law. Fallback strategies fall into the "brinkmanship" category—call at 2:30 the same day to nab any cancellations, show up early to scoop the evening's first no-show or stake out a seat at the bar.

Emeril's Delmonico

1300 St. Charles Ave. (at Erato)
504-525-4937

zone: Garden District
website: www.emerils.com
reservations: required

meals: lunch Mon–Fri, dinner nightly, brunch Sunday
specialty: traditional/contemporary Creole
fancy factor: highbrow
price range: $18–35

caveats: reserve ahead, formal dress code
bonus points: valet parking, on streetcar line

When Emeril revived this staid eatery—his third in town—it already had a century of history under its belt. Long considered a mid-level Creole standard, it filled a niche somewhere between the formal polish of Antoine's and the blue-collar simplicity of Mandina's.

In 1997, Emeril gave it a modern facelift (bamboo wall coverings upstairs, grand piano in the bar) while restoring the original's old-world polish. Lagasse has definitely drawn a new crowd to the St. Charles Avenue favorite, which now plays host to a bustling, almost trendy scene most nights.

Not surprisingly, Lagasse's eclectic style is definitely the draw here, with a bit of homage to Delmonico tradition. Expect layer upon layer of powerful flavor—crunchy sweet-and-sour calamari, earthy roast duck with rich grits and sweet dried cherry sauce—but don't forget the simple standouts. The dry-aged rib eye—perfectly seared and nearly spoon-tender—is considered among the best in town. Tableside baked Alaska is heavier on flash than flavor; the nutty double-chocolate pie packs more punch for a more fulfilling finish.

With a high-traffic kitchen and high-roller clientele, expect plenty of action, an often-claustrophobic bar scene and very few tables for walk-in customers.

NOLA
534 St. Louis (at Decatur)
504-522-6652

zone: French Quarter
website: www.emerils.com
reservations: recommended

meals: lunch Mon–Sat, dinner nightly
specialty: eclectic
fancy factor: middlebrow
price range: $27–36

caveats: loud downstairs
bonus points: validated parking

NOLA was originally envisioned as a casual alternative to the original Emeril's and a place for locals to experience the chef's rapidly evolving cuisine unrestrained by the "new New Orleans" label.

The unassuming building, tucked away on narrow Rue St. Louis, has since become a pilgrimage spot for diners unable to get reservations across town or diehard fans hoping to score an Emeril-themed hat trick by dining at all three of the chef's restaurants in a single trip.

Lagasse's culinary vision involves intense, no-holds-barred tastes, and NOLA seems to have the boldest (and least consistent) kitchen of the three Emeril's properties. It's not uncommon for menu descriptions to be twenty or more words and run the cultural gamut, as in NOLA's "Hickory-roasted duck with whiskey-caramel glaze, buttermilk-cornbread pudding, *haricot vert*–fire roasted corn salad, natural jus and candied pecans." Emeril's interpretation of Creole meunière sauce is a dark brown reduction heady with Worcestershire and spice rather than a clearish, nutty butter sauce. Ladled over a nut-crusted flounder filet, the sauce is paired with a flurry of flavors—broiled sections of sweet ruby grapefruit, butter-sautéed asparagus and a thick aioli fragrant with terragon.

This level of complexity is present throughout the menu, from the starter options (almond-crusted local oysters with bacon–brown sugar glaze, melting brie and rosemary-fennel apple slaw) to the dessert menu (flourless chocolate torte with bittersweet chocolate mousse, brandied apricots and chocolate ganache).

Fans hoping to get close to the kitchen are in luck—a "chef's tasting bar" brings you within feet of NOLA's busy cooks. Rotating tasting menus offer the chance to sample seasonal dishes and specially paired wines while watching the action from a ringside seat.

Peristyle
1041 Dumaine St. (at N. Rampart)
504-593-9535

zone: French Quarter
reservations: recommended

meals: dinner Tues-Sat, closed Sun-Mon
specialty: contemporary French
fancy factor: highbrow
price range: $24–28

bonus points: valet parking

If you're heading to this renowned French Quarter restaurant to taste the culinary stylings of Anne Kearney, you're in for a bit of bad news: you just missed her.

The esteemed Ms. Kearney, a James Beard Award–winning chef and culinary wunderkind, kept her outstanding little bistro humming through all kinds of tur-moil—a four-alarm fire and career-altering health crises among them—but always managed to bounce back once the smoke (literal and figurative) had cleared. In the summer of 2004, Kearney made the surprising announcement that she'd sold Peristyle to colleague Tom Wolfe, a local chef responsible for Wolfe's of New Orleans near Lake Pontchartrain. Kearney, having overcome a 9-year run marked with trials and tribulations, passed the torch while cooking at her best: effectively taking a break at the top of her game.

In 1995, Kearney bought the restaurant from the estate of John Neal, Peristyle's original chef/owner and one of her culinary mentors. At the young age of 28, she garnered a near-bulletproof reputation for skillful execution of dishes anchored firmly in classical French technique while giving the occasional nod to local Creole traditions. One signature salad featured nuggets of Louisiana lump crab dressed with a creamy, aromatic horseradish emulsion and served on slices of earthy roasted beets. The typical menu listed familiar bistro offerings such as house-made charcuterie platters and aioli-topped mussels steamed in Provençal-style shellfish broth. Even Ms. Kearney's nods to local classics exuded sophistication and simplicity—her oysters Rockefeller poached in an anise-scented velouté sauce instead of baked in the shell, seared squab played a savory rice dressing against a flawless port/foie gras reduction.

The transition of chef/owners marks a new era in the kitchen, but returning guests would be hard-pressed to see many differences in the atmosphere of the Dumaine Street eatery. The updated grocery and oyster bar retains its casual, romantic feel—deep brown leather banquettes and wraparound mirrors providing just the right balance of comfort and formality. Regulars have noticed mostly familiar faces among waitstaff and bartenders.

At press time, Wolfe is currently making an admittedly tricky transition—taking over another chef's concept while asserting his own style and identity. Wolfe, a New Orleans native who met Kearney while working with her at Emeril's, has a markedly different style—elaborate and contemporary compared to Kearney's classical leanings. A few months into the changeover, Wolfe has gradually replaced Kearney's signature dishes with his own—duck breast with juniper and foie gras served over sweet potato/duck crackling hash—and will launch his own menu after the traditional August vacation of 2004.

No matter how you look at it, Kearney's departure is a loss for the city's dining community, but it's hard not to wish the young chef well. After a stellar run, she'll be returning to her roots in native Ohio, having added another entry to the "You Shoulda Been There" hall of fame.

Restaurant August
301 Tchoupitoulas St. (at Gravier)
504-299-9777

zone: CBD/Warehouse
website: www.rest-august.com/
reservations: recommended

meals: lunch Mon–Fri , dinner Mon–Sat, closed Sun
specialty: contemporary French
fancy factor: highbrow
price range: $27–32

caveats: competitive reservations
bonus points: valet parking

In the age of New Orleans celebrity chefs, John Besh is the very model of a modern culinarian. With a winning trifecta of local pedigree, photogenic good looks and precise, thoughtful cooking style, Besh developed a steady following at his Warehouse District flagship and somehow still finds time to run an upscale steakhouse in the nearby Harrah's casino complex.

Restaurant August took a renovated warehouse space and turned it into the city's fine-dining hot spot with an eclectic aesthetic that plays bare brick against muted French provincial furnishings and crystal chandeliers. Its three dining areas project distinctly different, though consistently swanky, moods: a comfortably plush main room; a spare, split-level wine cellar rendered in Scandinavian blond woods; and a clubby back room.

Though Besh describes the basis of his work as "contemporary French," he isn't shy about incorporating wide-ranging influences into his seasonal dishes: stellar Moroccan-spiced duck with crunchy/creamy seared foie gras and dates fried in Japanese tempura, crispy pheasant with tangy sweet *choucroute* and roasted apples. But hailing from nearby Slidell, the chef also has a penchant for local ingredients, especially seafood. A signature pasta starter tops meltingly tender house-made gnocchi with aromatic truffle cream, a healthy shaving of Parmigiano Reggiano and a huge, flawless nugget of jumbo lump crabmeat; a perfectly cut diamond on an equally stunning setting. He also teams Gulf escolar with lobster-whipped potatoes, encrusts delicate flounder filets with black truffle shavings and tops a slab of *pain perdu*

(French toast) with buster crab, lettuce and tomato for a lighthearted BLT.

An alumnus of the prestigious Culinary Institute of America and veteran of Windsor Court's Grill Room, Besh has a penchant for exquisitely composed dishes. And Besh does some of his best experimental work when he presents three tasting-portion variations on a single ingredient. An example is his "lamb three ways": marinated loin meat wrapped in rice paper and flash fried, then cut into savory, perfectly rare medallions; shoulder cuts braised to amazing savory shreds; and a single double-cut chop rounds out the trio with simplicity and perfect execution.

Ruth's Chris Steak House
711 N. Broad St. (at Orleans Ave.)
504-486-0810

zone: Midcity
website: www.ruthschris.com
reservations: recommended

meals: lunch Sun–Fri, dinner nightly
specialty: steaks
fancy factor: high-middlebrow
price range: $18–36

bonus points: valet parking

Before this familiar steakhouse chain opened franchises in Tampa, Toronto and Taipei, local restaurateur Ruth Fertel perfected her formula on Broad Street in New Orleans.

In 1965, Fertel was a working mother of two and a lab technician at Tulane Medical School. Looking for a business that would allow her to send her children to college, she bought a restaurant she saw in a newspaper ad and added her name to the existing moniker, making it Ruth's Chris Steak House.

The premise was pretty simple—fine beef at reasonable prices at a time when "fine dining" meant steak. Ruth's trademark became a symbol of carnivorous excess—every grill-seared cut arrived at the table sizzling in a pool of melted butter. The drama of the presentation made steak lovers swoon, and Fertel did the old advertising adage one better—she sold the steak AND the sizzle.

By the mid-1970s, Ruth opened up a couple of other locations in Louisiana, perfecting a restaurant concept and slightly New Orleans–influenced menu. Before long, she'd hit on a winning formula—a beef-centric menu served in a clubby atmosphere that's one notch fancier than casual. Out-of-state franchises followed, and the chain now stands at over eighty locations in five countries.

Though she could have moved her local operation to the traffic-heavy French Quarter, Ruth stayed loyal to the Broad Street mothership location—a stone's throw from the original Chris' building and an important hangout for local politicos and other New Orleans power brokers.

Before her death in 2002, Ruth sold the company to a corporate group, but it doesn't seem to have influenced the original too much. Because of supply chain standardization, the steaks are pretty much the same as those you'd have in your local Ruth's, so there's no real gain to dining at the original on a visit to the city.

THE brennans

*I*t's hard to discuss New Orleans' contemporary food scene without mentioning this prolific restaurant family. Starting at a single French restaurant in the French Quarter, the relations of Owen Brennan created a far-flung empire since well before their celebrity chefs even started in the kitchen. The dynasty started at the Royal Street Brennan's, then spread to the Garden District's Commander's Palace before splintering into two factions—let's call them the Royal Street Gang and the Commander's Crew. The former—made up of the sons of the late Owen—consolidated their territory to the single Royal Street property that gained national attention for its extravagant brunches and breakfasts.

The Commander's Crew—led by Owen's sister Ella and her children along with Ella's surviving siblings (John and their kids)—built an empire from their bright blue Victorian headquarters on Washington Street. As years passed, they honed an admirable front-of-house system and a reputation for progressive Louisiana cuisine without ignoring the old-line Creole classics.

The various members of the Commander's Crew currently own and operate nine different restaurants in New Orleans, five of which are included in this collection. An intricate set of multiproperty partnerships in most of the restaurants keep the family working together as a unit, and make sure that new additions to the empire maintain their family resemblance.

Brennan's Restaurant
417 Royal St. (at Conti)
504-525-9711

zone: French Quarter
website: www.brennansrestaurant.com
reservations: recommended

meals: breakfast, lunch and dinner daily
specialty: extravagant Creole brunch
fancy factor: high-middlebrow
price range: $15–36

caveats: crowded on weekends

bonus points: validated parking, prix fixe evenings, exceptional wine list

"Breakfast at Brennan's" is the trademark meal at this Royal Street landmark, but it's not the kind of light day-starter you might expect. The phrase might imply a garden-variety "bacon and eggs" day-starter, but the elaborate morning menu features dishes that go well beyond traditional breakfast fare with all the excess you'd expect from a renovated eighteenth-century mansion. Imagine the most decadent brunch you've ever had, then double it.

First, there's the long list of Brennan's trademark "Eye Openers" (see page

98)—morning-compliant cocktails that go well beyond the usual mimosa and Bloody Mary options. Even if you show up 8 AM for the first seating, your waiter will *always* ask if you'd like a cocktail to start. Consider it a sign that you should yield to temptation rather than striving for virtue. Passing up a brandy milk punch at Brennan's would be a sadly wasted opportunity.

The house standard is a three-course prix fixe menu with a dozen entrée options, most of them local variations on the Eggs Benedict motif. Over the years, Brennan's developed a whole stable of dishes based on the poached egg and hollandaise sauce combination, many of which incorporate the region's distinctive ingredients into the menu. Eggs Sardou features tender artichoke bottoms and creamed spinach in place of Benedict's Canadian bacon and English muffin (here called a "Holland Rusk"). Other dishes such as Eggs Hussarde and Eggs Owen (named for the late patriarch) are topped with *marchands de vin* sauce (a rich reduction of wine, veal stock and shallots). The dish that stands out most, though, is the Eggs Nouvelle Orleans, where the eggs are simply an excuse to indulge in a decadent heap of sautéed lump crabmeat and brandy cream sauce. For dessert, there's a choice of two pyrotechnic presentations, Bananas Foster (see page 94) and Crepes Fitzgerald (creamy crepes with flambéed strawberries). If you've never seen a tableside Bananas Foster show, this is the place to catch the whole "end of meal" performance. Brennan's is, after all, where the dish was invented, and they take the whole affair—five-foot flames and all—very seriously.

On weekends, getting a table can be tough, as tourists and locals pack the bar in anticipation of their leisurely, possibly coma-inducing breakfast. Travelers walking in from French Quarter hotels have a distinct advantage, since their beds are conveniently close.

Tip to tail—after cocktails, wine and a cab home—the experience will definitely cost a pretty penny, but it's worth doing once even for locals. It might seem to be a lot to pay for a few eggs, but add in plenty of history and a fiery finish, and you've got the makings of "breakfast AND a show."

Commander's Palace
1403 Washington Ave. (at Prytania)
504-899-8221

zone: Garden District
website: www.commanderspalace.com
reservations: required

meals: lunch Mon–Fri, dinner nightly, brunch Sat–Sun
specialty: contemporary Creole classics
fancy factor: highbrow
price range: $26–39

bonus points: great lunch specials, jazz brunch weekends, near streetcar line

If you want to see the kitchen that launched both Paul Prudhomme and Emeril Lagasse to stardom, you'll need to give the Commander's folks a little advance notice—generally about six months' worth.

This level of advance planning will get you a reservation for four at a Commander's Palace chef's table and an insider's view of this Garden District landmark. While many chef's tables resemble private formal dining spaces, the coveted seats at Commander's are inside the kitchen itself. A four-seat banquette, set with formal linen and silver, faces the perpetually humming hot line, giving diners a full view of the evening's action. For the same price as a normal tasting menu ($115 per person at press time), your party is served approximately five appetizer-sized courses, each paired with an appropriate wine and a swirling dessert "storm" (one of everything from the after-dinner sweets menu) to cap off the evening. As dining experiences go, it's not particularly quiet, intimate or romantic, but for the fanatical foodie, it's a hell of a show.

Admittedly, snagging the appropriate reservation is a bit of a long shot, but it's an exceptional night of culinary theatre in a restaurant known for creating exceptional dining events. Their Sunday jazz brunch in the verdant courtyard or sun-drenched "Garden Room" is considered by many to be a required part of any weekend in New Orleans. The weekday lunch special—reasonably priced two-course meals and twenty-five-cent martinis—ranks among the best midday deals in town.

In the modern era, Commander's Palace is easily one of New Orleans' most influential restaurants. Bought by the Brennan family in 1974, this Garden District standby straddles the line between old-line classic and progressive culinary launching pad. Two of Louisiana's dominant celebrity chefs—Prudhomme and Lagasse—rose to prominence at the helm of Commander's kitchen; countless other chefs of local renown gained valuable experience working there. The chefs consistently credit matriarch Ella Brennan for teaching them important business lessons and providing on-the-job lessons in consistent customer service.

Culinary specifics shift from chef to chef—Washington native Tory McPhail currently heads the kitchen—but certain aspects of the menu are all but written in stone. Creole gumbo and sherry-spiked turtle soup are always available, as is a soup sampler (termed the 1-1-1) that serves small cups of each and the kitchen's soup du jour. A pecan-crusted Gulf fish makes for a suitably traditional Creole entrée, while the tomato-based seafood courtbouillion can take a meal in a decidedly Cajun direction. The signature dessert is a spicy bread pudding done soufflé-style, then punctured and filled with a sugary whiskey sauce. These house favorites have achieved a near-

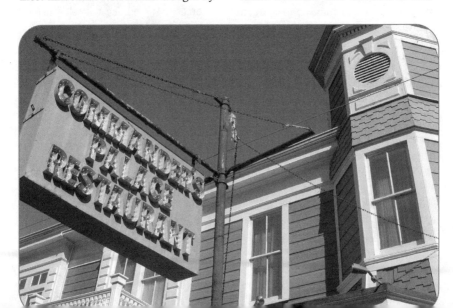

sacred status. As one former employee jokes, "If they took those dishes away, the Uptown ladies would absolutely riot."

Commander's service is consistently prompt, amazingly well-choreographed and almost always a group affair. When a course is about to be served, a small swarm of waitstaff appear tableside, present the dishes in a single motion and vanish as quickly as they appeared. Some of Commander's service-related finesse points have become trademarks at the other Brennans' properties, most notably the soup presentation. Soups and gumbos arrive at the table in small steel pitchers and are poured onto formal soup plates with a bit of understated flourish. It's a nice touch that all but eliminates the "cold soup" conundrum.

The ambience owes a lot to the old school of interior design so popular in the 1950s. The décor is flowery and a bit precious, with that level of formality that would appeal to *anybody's* grandmother. But just when you feel your spine stiffen a bit, your always well-pressed server will suggest "a cocktail, perhaps?" with just a hint of a mischievous grin. If you quickly scan the dining room, you'll see that the Uptown ladies are midway through their lunchtime tipples. You'd do well to follow suit.

Bourbon House

144 Bourbon (at Iberville)
504-522-0111

zone: French Quarter
website: www.bourbonhouse.com
reservations: recommended

meals: lunch Mon–Fri, dinner nightly, brunch Sat–Sun

specialty: updated Creole classics
fancy factor: middlebrow
price range: $17–31

caveats: no parking or garage
bonus points: great oyster bar

Even if you love the Bourbon Street scene, sometimes it's good to see the good-natured, boozy chaos through a nice thick sheet of plate glass. Preferably if you're sipping a nice cocktail and slurping down a few dozen cold, salty oysters at this, Dickie Brennan's latest French Quarter eatery.

Tacked on to the Iberville side of the Astor Crowne Plaza hotel, the Bourbon House has the trademark Brennan's formula down pat. The built-from-scratch space takes all the classic New Orleans architectural cues (clubby dark wood, tiny white hex tiles in the bathroom, intricate iron work on a spacious indoor mezzanine) and some that mark the restaurant as a descendent of Commander's Palace (brass NO and YES direction markers on the kitchen doors). The menu features well-executed Creole standards (shrimp Creole, Gulf fish amandine, seafood gumbo, baked oysters

Bananas Foster

Most white-linen restaurants in the Crescent City offer some version of this sweet after-dinner ritual—the tableside preparation of sautéed bananas in a sugary butter sauce spiked with liqueur and fragrant spices.

Usually performed atop a rolling cart-turned-stovetop, the simple sauté-and-stir process climaxes with a fiery WHOOSH, thanks to the last-minute addition of high-octane rum. It's a pyrotechnic flourish that borders on dangerous magic as a five-foot blue flame shoots toward the ceiling, then settles down as a hot, mahogany-colored syrup reduces in the pan. After a few minutes of stirring, the waiter ladles the soft bananas and rich sauce onto scoops of bean-flecked vanilla ice cream—a decadent sweet treat worthy of the show.

In a way, the flashy show makes Bananas Foster so distinctive, but its flavors and textures make it a New Orleans classic. Hot, soft fruit with bubbling syrup balanced against cold ice cream. Caramelized brown sugar and rich butter spiced with cinnamon and a hint of an aftertaste of rum. Prepared correctly, the bananas soften a bit in the sauce while maintaining a bit of their natural firmness. And since these complimentary flavors lend themselves to experimentation, there are countless variations on the Bananas Foster theme—from crispy pastry Napoleons to creamy tarts to morning *pan perdu* (lost bread, or French toast).

Unlike many other modern New Orleans classics, Bananas Foster can be easily traced to its source—Brennan's Restaurant on Royal Street. Originally prepared by chef Paul Blangé and named for regular customer Richard Foster, the dish became a Brennan's trademark, and soon spread to the kitchens (and tableside carts) of other local restaurants. Before long, Bananas Foster became a standard dessert offering and required post-meal performance in most fancy eateries.

served on fragrant herbed rock salt) along with a few contemporary updates (simple skin-on grilled redfish with wine-sauced lump crabmeat, Cobb salad with shrimp and crabmeat). The details are nice enough, but on the whole, the main room seems a bit contrived—a well-executed New Orleans-*style* atmosphere that could thrive in just about any American resort complex. If it was Bourbon House Las Vegas or Bourbon House Orlando, it would be an impressive establishment; it's somehow less remarkable located in the cradle of historic Crescent City culture.

That said, the spacious cocktail/oyster bar practically begs you to kill an afternoon there, sipping beer after beer and ordering yet another "what the hell" dozen on the half shell. The window tables provide ringside seats for the city's constant flow of Bourbon-bound traffic, from high-school brass bands playing for tips to the sorority girls wrapped in five-dollar feather boas. The sizable circular oyster bar seems more contemporary than traditional (Scandinavian wood instead of durable marble) as does the presentation (complex French brasserie-style seafood *plateaux* with boiled shrimp, crab claws and lobster joining the usual fresh-shucked oysters). A chalkboard behind the shuckers shows the home waters of today's catch, described by coastal area—a visual that never fails to spark discussions about the local oyster trade.

Farther from the bar and closer to the streetside windows, the cocktail portion of the bar suffers from an unwanted modern intrusion—state-of-the-art plasma TVs and a huge wall-sized projection screen provide way to much distraction on the average visit. If it's game day, that's one thing, but the flickering images tend to detract from the beauty of the room and its prime location as well.

Whatever the weather, you should order at least one glass of their Bourbon milk punch, a signature drink that might well be the best use of frozen cocktail technology in the city. The first sip of the smooth, creamy drink might trigger distinct taste memories for those familiar with other Brennan's establishments: the flavor smacks of the vanilla-bean ice cream that accompanies the original Bananas Foster, mixed with a little whiskey and topped with an aromatic dusting of nutmeg. Sweet, rich and absolutely addictive, it's a wonderful riff on this traditional Louisiana Christmastime cocktail; a perfect choice whether it's blustery or sultry out on the street.

Even if you never make it inside the building, it's possible to pick up a go-cupful of the drink at the restaurant's street food concession—a brightly lit stall that cooks fresh crepes for the Bourbon Street crowds. The plastic cup, convenient though it may be, steals a little bit of the drink's creamy texture, but when it's 2 AM in the Neon Zone and you find yourself munching a steaming, fresh-cooked crepe, chasing it with a sweet milk punch—there's *very* little reason to complain.

CLASSIC

Bloody Mary

Being a hard-drinking lot, the bartenders of New Orleans take their "morning after" remedies quite seriously, and nowhere is this more evident than in local Bloody Mary variations. Some days, a morning cocktail isn't optional, but rather a matter of (perceived) life and death.

Instead of starting with stomach-soothing tomato juice, most Crescent City Bloodies start with a spicy cocktail mix spiked with enough pepper sauce to induce a healthy case of the morning sweats. Bartenders employ a wide range of additional ingredients for flavor and effect—pickled green beans or okra pods, prepared horseradish, lime, black pepper, beef stock, various other "clear liquors"—with near-endless possibilities.

A healthy double shot of vodka is *de rigueur* in most bar or brunch Bloody Marys—not so much a gentle trickle to ease your aching head, but another heavy shot designed to induce a nice long morning nap.

Mr. B's Bistro

201 Royal St. (at Iberville)
504-523-2078

zone: French Quarter
website: www.mrbsbistro.com
reservations: recommended

meals: lunch Mon–Sat, dinner nightly,
  brunch Sun
specialty: contemporary Creole
fancy factor: middlebrow
price range: $18–29

bonus points: Saturday lunch, validated
  parking

My first lasting impression of Mr. B's is one of my favorite New Orleans restaurant scenes: entering the clubby French Quarter dining room and finding it filled with local executives clad in disposable plastic bibs. It was Friday afternoon, so the crowd was likely on its third cocktail; the better to

offset the richness of the near-universal entrée—a bowl of barbecued shrimp soaking in a pool of spicy butter sauce.

Scanning table to table, the power-lunch crowd seemed to be locked in mid-deal mode without a hint of self-consciousness. Serious talk of mergers or simmering palace intrigue creased the faces of the silver-haired captains of industry as they twisted heads off the pink-tinged crustaceans or waved a butter-soaked morsel of French bread for conversational emphasis. Smaller side dishes held mounds of transparent shells, a natural byproduct of a properly made barbecued shrimp. Draped in a thin layer of protective plastic, the executives might feel vaguely ridiculous in any other city—wearing a bib to negotiate the Rabinowitz deal?—but at Mr. B's, the overgarment is a required midday uniform. To go without is to risk fat-splattered lapels or a garlic-buttered necktie.

Housed in a former grocery and lunch counter, Mr. B's opened in the late 1970s and has been a solid French Quarter performer ever since. The bustling atmosphere retains part of the 1980s "fern bar" ambience while working the "dark wood and tiny tile" aesthetic. Part of the restaurant's appeal is location—a block off Canal and across from the landmark Hotel Monteleone—while culinary accessibility also plays its part with the tourist crowd.

The menu reads like a meticulous cross-breeding of traditional Louisiana and New American Bistro schools of cooking. There are always a couple of gumbos on the menu—including an exceptional chicken and andouille variation they call "Gumbo Ya Ya." Familiar preparations from the casual French school get the appropriate American or local twist: jambalaya interpreted with pasta instead of rice, roasted garlic chicken, Niçoise salad topped with a blackened Gulf tuna. The years have also added a few trendy turns in the form of vaguely Asian-influenced appetizers (confit-stuffed duck spring rolls, coconut-battered shrimp).

The barbecued shrimp—cooked in the shell and peeled by bib-clad diners—are a hit with local purists as well as tourists who aren't afraid of a little butter spatter. The primary flavor is the trademark garlic, but the dark sauce also has its share of piquant black pepper, Worcestershire sauce and a hint of lemon. The sweet shrimp are cooked to the point of tenderness, and once they're polished off, it's tradition to clean the bowl with hand-torn chunks of bread or slabs of ersatz crostini that arrive in the bowl.

If it's your reflex to order the shrimp but balk at the bib, take a quick look around and check the other tables. You'll probably see a fair share of obvious tourist types laughing at their overgrown toddler attire, but odds are you'll also see lifelong residents wearing the same protective coating. And unless you're particularly adept at manual shrimp peeling, remember this: when it comes to barbecued shrimp, misplaced pride can result in astronomical dry-cleaning bills.

Palace Cafe

605 Canal St. (at Chartres)
504-523-1661

zone: French Quarter
website: www.palacecafe.com
reservations: recommended

meals: lunch Mon–Fri, dinner nightly, brunch Sat–Sun

specialty: eclectic Louisiana
fancy factor: middlebrow
price range: $18–33

bonus points: weekend jazz brunch, late lunch

If there's a perfect lunch spot on modern-day Canal Street, it's gotta be the front corner banquette at the Palace Cafe. From this cozy vantage point, you look out onto the Palace's soaring, split-level dining space and peek out onto downtown's grand boulevard.

Before the advent of suburban shopping malls, Canal Street was the city's premier shopping district, with marquee department stores drawing huge crowds dressed up for a trip downtown.

Housed in the former Werlien's music-store building, the Palace created a sense of old-school grandeur with an ambitious renovation in 1991. The architects opened up the second floor as a soaring gallery, connecting it to the main dining room with an ornate Art Nouveau staircase. Intricate trompe l'oeil accents give the upper floor the feel of a Parisian opera house; ochre walls balance the clubby feel of the first floor. In the reflected light of huge windows, the Palace is the ideal place to while away a leisurely afternoon, lingering over contemporary Creole specialties and people-watching in between bites.

Owner Dickie Brennan (of Redfish Grill, Bourbon House and eponymous steakhouse fame) runs the house with the family's usual panache, and stocks the menu with dishes that wouldn't be markedly out of place at any of his other outposts. French-Creole standards are either played straight (turtle soup, seafood gumbo, tableside Bananas Foster) or deconstructed just enough to modernize them (sautéed shrimp with mushrooms and meunière, pannéed rabbit with mustard cream sauce, a light barely sweet brioche bread pudding served with white chocolate ganache).

As you'd expect, the Palace draws a mix of local businessmen and upscale tourists attracted by the room and the food, both well-executed updates on New Orleans classics. But the suits usually have set time frame—multihour lunches becoming less common even in New Orleans—leaving the early afternoon for the tourist crowd and other folks with time to kill. If you're lucky enough to score that front banquette, you might just settle in, idly watching the sidewalk spectacle as the Palace slowly becomes your own private dining room.

CLASSIC

Milk Punch and Morning Shots: The Eye Openers

The early morning cocktail is a local tradition on lazy weekend days that all but demand an extravagant breakfast. In the 1950s, Owen Brennan made his "Eye Openers" a brunchtime food group by creating an event tailored to the flavorful adult beverages, which include such concoctions as the Ramos Gin Fizz (see page 220), anise-flavored Ojen Frappe (essentially an Herbsaint on crushed ice) and Absinthe Suissesse (milk, Herbsaint and egg white sweetened with almond syrup). Then there's the milk punch, a morning standard and holiday treat. Essentially an egg-free nog, the basic milk punch is made with light cream (half-and-half), dark liquor (usually bourbon or brandy) and various grace notes that fine-tune the concoction's flavor (sugar for sweetness, vanilla, and a pinch of grated nutmeg). At full strength, the rich cream masks the liquor's warm kick and makes it a perfect brunchtime alternative to Bloody Marys. The final product can be mixed in punchbowl batches to satisfy an evening's worth of revelers or blended to a rich slush-like consistency for a quick internal freeze.

The Bourbon House (see page 93) makes a particularly good bourbon version with a modern twist—it's pumped out of a standard margarita machine, so it's perfectly blended and crystallized. With a dusting of nutmeg, it's a treat whatever the weather.

The Commander's Crew: Four More

Though *Eating New Orleans* contains stories about five of the Commander's Crew restaurants, it only seemed fitting to provide thumbnail sketches of the other four.

Bacco

310 Chartres St. (at Bienville)
504-522-2426
website: www.bacco.com
Upscale Italian in a French Quarter setting.

Café Adelaide

300 Poydras St. (at S. Peters)
504-595-3305
website: www.cafeadelaide.com
A new arrival in the CBD's Loew's New Orleans Hotel and named for a beloved, quirky Aunt Adelaide. Chef Keven Vizard, formerly of Restaurant Indigo, offers "boosted New Orleans bistro" cuisine.

Dickie Brennan's Steakhouse

716 Iberville St. (at Royal)
504-522-2467
website: www.dickiebrennanssteakhouse.com
Straightforward steakhouse fare with a few Louisiana twists a half a block off Bourbon Street.

Redfish Grill

115 Bourbon St. (at Bienvillle)
504-598-1200
website: www.redfishgrill.com
Hard-to-miss casual seafood restaurant on the Bourbon Street strip.

Ralph's on the Park

900 City Park Ave. (at Dumaine St.)
504-488-1000

zone: Midcity
website: www.ralphsonthepark.com
reservations: recommended

meals: lunch Mon–Sat, dinner nightly, brunch Sun

specialty: Louisiana French
fancy factor: high-middlebrow
price range: $16–30

bonus points: jazz brunch

This restaurant's tag line "For locals, by locals" seems appropriate for this Brennan's property, mostly due to its semi-secluded Midcity location. Though this impressive restoration sits right across the road from the live oaks of City Park, it's a view that few tourists normally see. By the time you arrive at Ralph's you're halfway to the suburban cemeteries; past the parks biggest tourist draw (the New Orleans Museum of Art) and well off the mental map of most visitors. Locals are more apt to find the place, but travelers might consider seeking out this isolated eatery, especially those inclined to fancy weekend meals.

Originally constructed in the 1860s as a coffeehouse, the building had its own storied history as a restaurant, tavern and nightclub before Ralph Brennan (also of the French Quarter's Bacco and the Redfish Grill) renovated the space. The resulting eatery, like many of the other Brennan's establishments, has a well-balanced ambiance—formal parlor-like dining room and "upscale casual" bar on the ground floor, private dining rooms upstairs—decorated with all manner of City Park memorabilia.

To head the kitchen, Brennan recruited Gerard Maras, a veteran of Mr. B's Bistro and the much-mourned Gerard's Downtown. The resulting menu shows Maras doing splendid work within the Brennan's framework—an eponymous baked oyster dish (bacon, spinach and jalapeño cream) replacing the usual Rockefeller, housemade charcuterie platters changing daily, entrées reflecting bold flavors (braised smoked sausage, pork and sauerkraut) and restraint when appropriate (flawlessly subtle baby drum filets baked with buttery bread crumbs). A big promoter of the local farmer's markets, Maras usually offers well-considered meatless options on a separate vegetarian menu.

True to the owner's tag, the crowd tends to be mostly locals—after all, it's just about midway between the Quarter and the suburbs, and seems to be a default meeting place for groups willing to split the difference on distance. As for the parkside view, catch it during one of their daytime meals (breakfast and lunch Saturdays, brunch Sundays, lunch weekdays) to see the oaks in all their quiet glory.

contemporary

Even in a town with long-standing culinary traditions, there's always room for experimentation. Just because we have the traditions doesn't mean that chefs are always bound to them. New Orleans has an active community of chefs who, while respecting the ways of the city, bring a broad range of other influences into their work, with exceptionally tasty results.

Cobalt

333 St. Charles Ave. (at Perdido)
504-565-5595

zone: CBD/Warehouse
website: www.cobaltrestaurant.com
reservations: recommended

meals: breakfast Mon–Fri, lunch Mon–Fri,
    dinner nightly, brunch Sat–Sun
specialty: upscale Southern regional
fancy factor: high-middlebrow
price range: $16–29

As *Eating New Orleans* goes to press, Cobalt is in a bit of a precarious position: it's a chef-driven restaurant without a chef.

As the house restaurant of the quirky/swanky Hotel Monaco, Cobalt started life as Susan Spicer's third New Orleans eatery after her successes at Bayona and Herbsaint. Spicer brought much-needed star power to the project as she interpreted various American regional dishes (house-made sausages, Chinatown five-spice duck, velvety butterscotch pudding) in the ground floor of

CLASSIC

Bread Pudding

Vanilla-bean crème brûlée. New York–style cheesecake. Flourless chocolate cake drizzled with raspberry puree. Long before these offerings became national dessert standards, bread pudding ruled the New Orleans sweet scene. Like Mexican *flan* or Greek *baklava*, New Orleans bread pudding is a default sweet that occupies a slot on nearly every dessert menu, from downscale lunch counters to the trendiest upscale eateries.

As a former colony with a distinctive French-influenced cuisine, New Orleans has a logical affinity for pillowy French bread. In the days before cellophane bags or convenient shrink-wrap packaging, fresh-from the-oven loaves toughened to hard-tack in a matter of days. But with a little ingenuity and a few simple ingredients, yesterday's dried-out baguettes could be recast as a perfect way to end any meal.

In its most basic form, bread pudding is straightforward culinary recycling—stale bread brought back to life with fridge and pantry staples. A quick-mix custard of eggs, cream, butter and sugar transforms loaf-sized croutons into a rich, decadent treat. An hour in the oven sets the mixture, resulting in a moist, cakelike texture and bits of crunchy, butter-drenched crust. These few simple steps turn dried bread into pure, comforting goodness.

This simple formula practically begs for experimentation, and Louisiana cooks have developed countless versions over the years. Poboy shops serve raisin-studded squares of firm pudding spiced with cinnamon and topped with a sugary whiskey sauce. Pastry chefs in upscale establishments use the dish as a blank canvas, then integrate complimentary flavors—chocolate chunks, crunchy roasted pecans, fresh seasonal fruits—into the batter.

Herbsaint: Crescent City Absinthe

Another product of New Orleans' French connections, the translucent *liqueur d'anis* Herbsaint has been made in New Orleans since the mid 1930s.

Produced by local distillers Legendre & Company, the yellow-green liqueur was developed as a substitute for absinthe, the notorious anise-flavored drink that enjoyed immense popularity in Europe and New Orleans during the eighteenth and nineteenth centuries. French Quarter landmarks such as the Old Absinthe House speak to the popularity of the drink in the Francophilic city.

After a largely sensationalized French murder trial in 1905, absinthe was out-lawed in Europe because of alleged links between potentially poisonous wormwood (one of absinthe's prominent components) and erratic behavior among its habitu-al drinkers. The U.S. followed suit and absinthe proper remains illegal today.

The post-Prohibition introduction of Herbsaint brought a wormwood-free facsimi-le of the licorice liqueur to New Orleans, where it figures prominently in local spe-cialties such as oysters Rockefeller and "Eye Opener" cocktails including the Absinthe Suissesse and Absinthe Frappe.

Present-day Herbsaint is distilled and sold, fittingly enough, by New Orleans' own Sazerac Company.

---

the CBD's Art Deco Masonic temple. But as the chef's responsibility grew and her consulting contract expired, it was time for a new chef at the helm.

Enter Brack May—a well-traveled California boy who took the existing concept and put a more focused region-al twist on it, dubbing his style "Big Fat Southern Food." May was known for having plenty of fun with his dishes, many of which showed both creativity and playfulness. He made a decadent downscale dish—creamy baked maca-roni and cheese—much more interesting by cutting it in firm blocks and deep-fry-ing it until crisp. His turn on barbecue ribs involved a delicate rack of lamb and a spicy ancho chile rub. Of course, the chef included plenty of Louisiana food in the category, including an earthy

braised pork shank ("Osso Boudreaux") with a spicy tomato-based gravy over a meaty dollop of rice dressing.

But Chef Brack's tenure at the hotel ended in summer 2004, both sides claim-ing an amicable breakup for "creative dif-ferences," or some such. So for the time being, Cobalt's kitchen keeps chugging along, working May's last menu without covering any new ground culinarily. When a new chef takes the helm, she'll steer it into the next era.

One of the dishes that Brack brought to the city remains, for now at least, one of the restaurant's most popular Thurs-day lunch specials: an updated riff on chicken and waffles.

The combination of crispy bird and breakfast pastry is most commonly asso-ciated with a Los Angeles eatery

(Roscoe's Chicken and Waffles) but May adapted it to suit his more buttoned-down lunch crowd. Instead of whole pieces of poultry, he started off with a boneless chicken breast, then marinated it in a mixture of tangy buttermilk, a sweet *gastrique* (a reduced blend of sugar, vinegar and lemon juice), rosemary and a little hot sauce. The overnight soak imparts its component flavors to the chicken meat while keeping it moist and tender throughout the breading and frying process. For added savor, the crispy chicken is served with a dollop of chunky pan gravy made with browned chicken bits, shallots, a light roux, heavy cream and just a hint of bourbon.

The other half of the ampersand—a standard malted waffle—is a semicircle of slightly sweetened starch topped with maple cinnamon butter and studded with toasted pecan bits. A tiny creamer filled with amber maple syrup completes the set and allows diners to tailor each bite to their liking.

With any luck at all, May's replacement will leave this one well enough alone. After all, one could do worse than inherit a deep-fried cult favorite.

Cuvee
322 Magazine St. (at Gravier)
504-587-9001

zone: CBD/Warehouse
website: www.restaurantcuvee.com
reservations: recommended

meals: lunch Mon–Fri, dinner Mon–Sat, closed Sun
specialty: Creole Continental
fancy factor: high-middlebrow
price range: $20–30

bonus points: exceptional wine list and staff, valet parking

When Cuvee's waitstaff starts talking about wine, they can barely contain their excitement. Forget the image of the stuffy, condescending wine steward; these people are so into their wines that they practically bubble over with enthusiasm leading you through the restaurant's sophisticated wine-centric menu.

The waiters are likely to be, as ours were on several occasions, wine geeks with an energetic schoolkid's sensibility. Whatever your level of viticultural knowledge, they'll lead you through an impressive list based on your menu choices.

Chef Robert Iacovone deftly mixes genres, textures and traditions in a style that he terms "Creole Continental," a style that draws from traditional French and now-trendy Spanish cuisines while still maintaining nods to Louisiana roots. The Gulf fish is served with fresh local ingredients (Louisiana crawfish tails, tender baby lima beans) and accented with salty Serrano ham and saffron rouille. Fat charbroiled oysters take an upscale turn with Parmigiano-Reggiano and a hint of aromatic truffle oil.

Your food preferences will often lead to unexpected discoveries on the wine list. Often, there are a few outstanding off-list choices—uncorked vintages from a high-dollar tasting or new shipments from an outstanding yet unknown micro-vineyard—that your waiter will suggest like a kid showing off a hidden fishing hole. The waiter's suggestion of a sparkling rosé proved to be a bubbling epiphany in a flute glass with flavors perfectly matched with the delicate crepe stuffed with rabbit confit.

One dessert—an incredible triple chocolate cake—stands the test of time after several visits and has luckily survived at least one change in the pastry chef department. A four-layer exercise in chocolaty richness—cake with a texture that makes it seem fudge infused, light ganache in between layers—lends itself to different variations but is always the star of the sweet course. One time it might be accompanied by peppermint cream, another might team it with a shot-sized banana milkshake. But the midnight-dark ultra-decadent treat, barely visible in Cuvee's muted cellarlike atmosphere, always takes the cake.

GW Fins
808 Bienville St. (at Dauphine)
504-581-3467

zone: French Quarter
website: ww.gwfins.com
reservations: recommended

meals: dinner nightly
specialty: modern seafood
fancy factor: high-middlebrow
price range: $20–29

bonus points: great bar, validated parking

It's a billboard that makes you think.

Two human-scale, apparently content fish strapped into airline seats: one staring out the window clutching a smart martini glass, the other peering through eyeglasses at the day's newspaper. Above them, the sign indicates that these are no normal fish, but in fact, they're flying in front of the first-class curtain, happily awaiting their arrival at GW Fins down in the French Quarter.

Now putting aside the obvious opposable-thumb issue and "fish have no asses" conundrum, questions arise about Fins' supply chain. Why on earth would you fly in fish when you're so close to the productive fisheries of the Gulf? The image would make sense in just about any landlocked municipality (Kansas City? Fine. Dubuque? OK. Scottsdale? You betcha)—but in New Orleans? In this neck of the woods, fish packing thumbs could just hitch a quick ride up from the docks at Grand Isle.

And just about anywhere else in the city, a mostly foreign fish list would be considered suspect, but chef Tenney Flynn works his way around such suspicions. A former high muckety-muck (Director of Culinary) with the Ruth's Chris Steakhouse chain, Flynn takes a different approach to fresh fish in a

seafood-saturated town—expand your vision beyond the Gulf, but make damned sure the raw materials are worth the airfare.

Flynn changes and prints his menu daily, a sign that pretty much every option is the catch of the day somewhere. A summer menu might include scallops from New Bedford, Chesapeake Bay rockfish alongside scamp grouper and escolar from local fisheries.

The common theme to Fins' ever-morphing menu is seafood, but preparation techniques and flavor profiles can run the gamut from indigenous (red snapper teamed with crawfish étouffée) to new American (local mahi with crab crusted) to Asian variations (quick-seared yellowfin tuna served sushi style, whole-roasted bass with grilled banana and curried rice). Meat maniacs will, of course, find a few non-aquatic options hiding among the fishy bits.

Flynn's range of cooking methods seems as focused as his palate is expansive. The sauté station gets its share of specialties (scamp grouper with crabmeat *macque choux*, rockfish with Merlot sauce), as does the wood grill, which churns out splendidly simple plates that let the fish speak for itself. During its peak summer season, Fins' grilled pompano might be the best way to experience the rich flavor and delicate texture of this coveted Gulf specialty.

Fins' dining room is a spacious, split-level affair that plays contemporary design (semi-circular rows of raised booth seating) against exposed warehouse brickwork. Dinner-shift popularity often translates to high ambient volume—especially on floor level—so request one of the booths to cut the noise.

Even during slower nights, there tends to be plenty of action, as staff roam the floor carrying tongs and mysterious cloth-lined baskets that contain the kitchen's distinctive bread course—flavorful, impossibly light drop biscuits served piping hot from the oven. After an initial crunch, these lard-based beauties dissolve on the tongue and usually inspire a common diner command "Leave 'em all."

The biscuit factor tends to make desserts a moot point, which is probably why the fresh-baked apple pie (topped with a salty/rich cheese pastry crust) comes with a 20-minute advance ordering policy. Go ahead and order it, though—it's worth every bite and makes for great morning-after leftovers.

Herbsaint

701 St. Charles Ave. (at Girod)
504-524-4114

zone: CBD/Warehouse
website: www.herbsaint.com
reservations: recommended

meals: lunch Mon–Fri, dinner Mon-Sat, closed Sun
specialty: contemporary French-American
fancy factor: high-middlebrow
price range: $14–22

caveats: small bar
bonus points: great bar, on streetcar line, good for large parties

For the first few years of its history, Herbsaint built its reputation by trading on a big name in its kitchen: co-owner Susan Spicer.

Those were the days when Spicer bounced among three different restaurants—Bayona in the French Quarter, Cobalt in the CBD and this sophisticated, minimalist bistro in the Warehouse District.

These days, Herbsaint's stellar reputation belongs to the lesser-known chef in the kitchen: co-owner Donald Link.

Link was raised in Acadiana—Lake Charles to be exact—and worked as a journeyman chef on the west coast before returning to New Orleans. This combination of local sensibility and contemporary style show in Link's well-balanced menus—collections of contemporary dishes that skillfully blend Louisiana classics with eclectic New American influences. He has clearly done his share of traveling, soaking up inspiration all along the way.

Link is particularly strong with earthy

flavors and standards from the American bistro songbook. His riff on spaghetti carbonara shows Link's considerable skill and creativity in action. Fresh pasta is coated in a thick, peppery cream sauce, tossed with chunks of salty pancetta and topped with a deep-fried poached egg. The egg yolk, still liquid despite the double-cooking process, adds eye-rolling richness to the dish. And in a move that would make Alice Waters proud, both the pasta and pancetta are made in house.

His spoon-tender beef short ribs get a rich, creamy kick from a heady sauce of mustard and horseradish. Link glazes a fatty pork belly with spicy sweet chile and serves it with lentils and aromatic

INGREDIENT

Soft-Shell Crabs

The soft-shell crab is a regular blue crab caught in an embarrassing state of exoskeletal undress.

Like a schoolkid in mid-puberty, the crab routinely outgrows its shell and needs to get rid of its confining duds. The biological routine is to binge-eat like a monster, absorb as much water as possible, and shed the shell like a gluttonous Homer Simpson doing his impersonation of the Incredible Hulk. A crab in this pre-molting mode is called a "buster crab" (insert old Flash Gordon joke here). As the covering breaks, the crab scampers off with a larger, softer shell, which starts to harden in about twelve hours.

Unfortunately for the crabs, this stage of development makes them vulnerable, tasty and popular with diners. With no hard shell to crack, soft-shell crabs require very little cleaning and can be eaten—claws, legs and all—without a nutcracker in sight. The most common preparations are sautéed in butter, lightly pannéed or deep fried and crammed legs-up in a Jazzfest poboy.

These days very little is left to nature and even less to chance. Though the seasons for live soft-shells are still spring (March-June) and early fall (September–October), crab processors have elaborate "cage and tank" setups to monitor and manage the crabs' change of clothing. During the peak seasons, you can find soft-shells live and kicking; other times you're most likely getting frozen busters.

mint. And in case you were wondering, the addictive fries and hangar steak are equally strong.

Link and his kitchen folk also have their fun with the usual suspects of Louisiana cuisine—both city and country variations. Another fresh pasta—a rustic pappardelle—acts as a base for savory fricasseed rabbit and wild mushrooms. Dirty rice makes its way alongside duck confit; delicately fried oysters with slaw and hot sauce couldn't be a more simple local adaptation. His warm chocolate beignets, though sometimes dry, are moistened with juice from brandied cherries.

Situated on St. Charles halfway between Canal and Lee Circle, Herbsaint is a modern, almost minimalist room decorated with oversized historic photos and artsy, soft-focus photos. References to the eponymous liqueur (see page 102) abound—close-ups of antique absinthe rigs decorate the bar, the walls of the main room match the hue of slightly diluted Herbsaint. Unfortunately, the recent paint job—the new minty green instead of the cream it replaced— comes on a bit strong and gives the room a slight, seasick cast. The more private back room is done in striking red hues and features a mural by local artist Amy McKinnon.

Closer to the street, the small bar remains one of the best in the city when it comes to cocktails. The bartenders can whip up any of the trendy cocktails imported from other cities while doing justice to New Orleans' native concoctions. Their "traditional Sazerac" hearkens back to the cocktail's early days— before rye whiskey ruled the city—and is a smooth, refreshing variation on the classic.

La Petite Grocery

4238 Magazine St. (at General Taylor)
504-891-3377

zone: Uptown
website: www.lapetitegrocery.com
reservations: recommended

meals: dinner Mon–Sat
specialty: American bistro, local
  ingredients
fancy factor: high-middlebrow
price range: $17–24

caveats: loud room

Just about the time that Anne Kearney sold her landmark French Quarter restaurant, Peristyle veteran Anton Schulte made his way Uptown and opened his own place on a rapidly gentrifying stretch of upper Magazine Street. Schulte and various business partners turned a rundown florist shop into a simple, sophisticated restaurant that's the spiritual successor to Kearney's Peristyle.

Playing off the building's history as a neighborhood store, La Petite Grocery is an elegant room that borders on minimalist—walls and pressed tin ceilings painted a soothing off-white with burgundy banquettes and an atmosphere that's stylish yet comforting.

Though he's the new kid on the block—the restaurant opened in early 2004—Schulte showcases the skills he perfected at Peristyle. Flawless saucework is one of those trademarks, and dishes like a Riesling-and-cider reduction over grilled pork loin show that Schulte is still at the top of his game. Other dishes artfully blend Mediterranean influences—from saffron-steamed mussels with basil aioli to a hearty duck breast pan-roasted with fragrant thyme and fig preserves. He also brings local ingredients into the mix with standouts such as a free-form crawfish ravioli and a delicate blue crab and artichoke salad.

Schulte's wife Diane oversees the front of the house and has gotten accustomed to crowds. In its first year of business, La Petite Grocery has done a steady business as one of the hot new places on the local scene. The room has plenty of romantic potential but when it's filled to capacity, the volume borders on deafening. This can be a drag if you're planning a tête-à-tête, but just about perfect for a larger, more convivial table of friends.

Lulu's in the Garden

2203 St. Charles (at St. Ann)
504-568-1885

zone: Garden District
website: www.lulusinthegarden.com
reservations: accepted

meals: breakfast, lunch and dinner
   Wed–Sun, brunch Sun
specialty: farmer's market contemporary
fancy factor: middlebrow
price range: $17–23

caveats: closed Tues
bonus points: valet parking, weekend
   brunch

Finding chef Corbin Evans usually takes a bit of work, but it's always worth the effort.

This Ohio native and Philadelphia transplant made his name in New Orleans in the most unlikely of venues— a tiny lunch-only sandwich counter with a cramped kitchen and about ten tables spilling onto pedestrian-only Exchange Alley. On rainy days, his table count was cut to five. He named the place Lulu's and churned out a simple menu that blended the market-fresh and short-order traditions. Huge salads and creative sandwich options always had a seasonal twist with modern sensibility—roasted vegetables with local farmer's cheese, herbed béchamel sauce on the ham and cheese instead of slap-dash mayonnaise. His simple yet insanely rich brownie was what most molten-chocolate concoctions aspire to—free-form fudgy goodness in a cellophane wrapper.

A few years later, Evans opened up this relaxed, casual eatery in a somewhat hidden Garden District hotel and expanded his menus to fit his considerable skills. He trained at the prestigious Culinary Institute of America, but keeps his preparations simple, sophisticated and, most importantly, seasonal.

"I'm not trying so much to cook New Orleans food so much—my influences are from the Midwest, Philly, New York and my love of Southern food. I use the market like I would in other places and I cook for myself—the way that I like to eat."

Evans spends a lot of time at the local farmer's market, and it shows on his menus. Creole tomatoes become the early summer salad, spicy gazpacho, and tomato tartar for crab and rice croquettes. In winter, local citrus and root vegetables play a prominent role.

On most restaurant menus, the most predictable entrée on the list is likely to be the chicken. For fat-free fanatics and the low-carb crusaders alike, the skinless/boneless breast is a comforting (if often unimaginative) common ground.

Evans manages to make his nightly poultry offering—the Farmer's Market Chicken—into a statement of edible philosophy. The dish starts with a straightforward preparation—crispy roasted breast of chicken with a savory herbed "pan gravy"—but it's Evans' choice of supporting ingredients that gives the dish its seasonal magic.

During the summertime, the chicken might be teamed with golden yellow summer squash, creamy Silver Queen corn-off-the-cob and freshly roasted Gypsy Gold sweet peppers. Weeks before, the same menu item might have featured slices of tender roasted sweet potato and baby okra smothered with tangy tomatoes. When temperatures drop, intensely flavored baby beets or garlicky wilted collard greens might take their place on the plate.

There's really no way to lock down Evans' chicken—a nightly special at his restaurant Lulu's in the Garden—because it features the best offerings of local organic farms in rural Louisiana and nearby Mississippi. The usually lackluster bird becomes a showcase for the best of the region's seasonal produce: month to month, week to week, market to market.

Evans talks about approaching food from "field to table," and has recently put this philosophy into action by becoming a part-time farmer. After selling the original lunch joint, he became a partner in a farm in Tylertown, Mississippi, an hour outside the city. So on his days off, he's likely working the fields that will eventually supply his Garden District kitchen. He's still kinda tough to find, but always worth it.

Muriel's
801 Chartres St. (at St. Ann)
504-568-1885

zone: French Quarter
website: www.muriels.com
reservations: recommended

meals: lunch and dinner daily
specialty: contemporary Creole
fancy factor: high-middlebrow
price range: $15–32

bonus points: great balcony and bar, validated parking

From a cocktail table on Muriel's second-story balcony, you get a perspective of Jackson Square that puts the postcards to shame. Above the iron fence and broad pedestrian promenade, you see the street musicians and tarot readers ply their trades. The sun sets; the crowds gradually thin and St. Louis Cathedral lights up in dramatic profile. As dusk deepens, the few straggling fortune-tellers hope for one last performance and after-dark tour groups float by, led by ersatz pirate kings or appropriately vampiric goth girls.

Veteran travelers might remember this particular prime location as the old

From the Fields: Louisiana Vegetables

The fertile lands of Louisiana provide a wide variety of distinctive produce and with no harsh winters to worry about, local farmers like to stay busy.

Here are a few of the crops that are associated with Creole and Cajun cuisine. You'll see many of these products on menus year 'round, but when they're in season, nothing tastes better.

Creole Tomatoes—Ask ten different locals for a definition of Creole tomato and you'll likely get twelve different responses. Though the meaning of *Creole* in this context is often debated, the quality of the deep, red fruit is not. The juicy, tangy tomatoes peak in the late spring and early summer (roughly mid-May through June). Most of New Orleans' precious Creoles come from farms in the river country south of the city (St. Bernard and Plaquemines Parishes).

Mirliton—(pronounced *MEL-lee-towhn)* Known elsewhere as *chayote* or vegetable squash. Often stuffed with ham and shrimp dressing, pickled or added to salads. Peak season runs from October to November.

Okra—Tender, green and delicious, this summer vegetable appears in local markets in the heat of the summer (usually July) and flourishes until the first winter frost.

Sweet Corn—Another fleeting crop that locals pine for most of the year. Early summer brings the sweetest, plumpest corn, (late May–June), just in time to coincide with crab season. NEVER pass up a chance to try summertime corn and crab bisque.

Greens (mustard, collard, turnip, et al.)— These regenerating winter vegetables can be long-stewed with pork, quick-sautéed with garlic or turned into the Holy Thursday classic *gumbo z'herbes* (green gumbo). The peak season runs through deep winter until early March.

Sweet Potatoes—Oftentimes mistakenly called "Louisiana yams" (go pick that fight with a botanist), this tuber is picked fresh in the summer and dried until October, when they hit the markets just in time for autumn dishes. The most renowned examples hail from the Cajun prairie town of Opelousas.

Chart House restaurant, by most accounts best known for its ornate carved wood bar and stunning balcony view. Again, the realtor's mantra proves true: location, location, location.

In 2001, the historic 18th-century property—former grand mansion, saloon, grocery and pasta factory—became its current restaurant incarnation. Eclectic in menu and décor, Muriel's is an elaborate showplace specializing in intricate, innovative turns on New Orleans classic dishes.

After a few quick chef changes, local Erik Venéy took charge of the kitchen and showed his deft touch with indigenous ingredients and trademark Creole flavor combinations. Modernized Creole dishes are consistently well executed, especially grilled offerings like a flame-kissed quail starter paired with tender sweet potato cubes and roasted pecans. Sautéed redfish amandine is layered with insanely rich "sweet pea mashed potatoes" and meticulously trimmed baby carrots. Steak lovers should be impressed by the filet medallions drizzled with flawless cabernet demi-glace and pleasingly funky blue cheese wontons. The signature dessert is an outstanding peanut/chocolate bombe filled with delicate mousse and caramel—an architectural treat that's almost too pretty to eat. The formal/funky downstairs rooms sport ambitiously eclectic décor: deep red walls covered with newspaper collage work evoke a playful Parisian feel, aging brick and antique photos provide a more historic plantation vibe. Heavy on gold-leaf opulence, the second story contains a few ornate event rooms, including the Séance Room—a magnet for Anne Rice fans if ever there was one.

If you tire of the outdoor balcony, or just want a little bistro-style table service,

retire to Muriel's outstanding interior courtyard. The hulking "Chart Room bar"—an impressive bit of architecture in its own right—sits at the back of the room filled with iron and marble café tables and the atmosphere of an "Old New Orleans" stage set.

Riomar

800 S. Peters St. (at Julia)
504-525-3474

zone: CBD/Warehouse
website: www.riomarseafood.com
reservations: accepted

meals: lunch Mon–Fri, dinner Mon–Sat, closed Sun
specialty: Spanish and Latin-inspired seafood
fancy factor: high-middlebrow
price range: $15–22

caveats: street parking only
bonus points: tapas lunch, near Convention Center

In a historical sense, the Spanish never seem to get full credit for their contributions to New Orleans. As administrators during the tail end of the 18th century, they rebuilt the French Quarter (twice), offered the exiled proto-Cajuns safe haven and laid the foundation for modern-day Uptown. Then Napoleon waltzed back in after thirty-five years, made a quick real estate flip to the Americans and adds to his immortality.

In a modern culinary sense, it's the Spanish influence—or to be more accurate, the pan-Latino sensibility—that shines at this Warehouse District seafood spot. RioMar bills itself as a "seafood destination" and more than lives up to its billing—no mean feat in America's Creole capital city.

Chef Aldolfo Garcia, a local native with Panamanian ties, does a great job interpreting fresh Gulf seafood using a wide range of cooking traditions—from the South American ceviche of Ecuador and Peru to the Spanish dishes that freely mix seafood with chunks of chorizo sausage and salty Serrano ham.

From the cozy open dining room, diners can watch Chef Garcia go through the paces in his tiny open kitchen. The relatively small space, as comfortable as a beachside tapas joint in Cadiz, echoes with delicious sizzles and clanks from the kitchen; the ambient light changes every so often with a dramatic flare from the stove.

The periodic flashes from the kitchen are an atmospheric sign of what's obvious on most of the chef's plates: Garcia has a way with direct flame. Any of his grilled dishes benefit from a light touch and uncomplicated approach: let the fish speak for itself with a few well-chosen supporting ingredients put in for harmony's sake. A seared tripletail filet is accented with an aromatic anise-infused olive oil; crunchy caper berries and salty Kalamatas play off the rich flavor of grilled Gulf escolar.

Garcia seems equally comfortable working with Old and New World cuisines, all the while keeping an eye on local fisheries. Salt cod, a staple in much of Spanish cooking, is a staple on the menu as tasty *bacalaitos*—crispy fritters with a soft, pillowy interior. Two-bite *empanadas de atun* (fried pies stuffed with tuna and olives) can make the most generous diner instantly and rabidly territorial.

Other specialties are equally strong: starchy Valencian rice cooked with garlicky, carmelized chorizo and tender littleneck clams might make you reconsider Spain's jambalaya connections; a saffron-rich *zarzuela de mariscos* (seafood stew) is a soothing sinus-opener from the *sauce piquante* school; the generous portion of perfectly seared hanger steak, blood rare and beefier than any tenderloin cut, does its Argentinean co-owner proud.

The compact yet welcoming bar area seems perfect for exploring the small-plate lunch menu, especially when the wall-height front doors open to the sidewalk, turning the room into an urban tapas café. And with a deep wine list—heavy on the Spanish vintages, most of them available by the glass—it seems only natural to offer a toast to the Spanish, and the delicious legacy they left behind.

Low-Key Cajun

There are plenty of tourist restaurants that advertise "authentic Cajun specialties," but it's what's on the plate that really matters. Here are a few *actual* Cajun specialties hidden on non-Cajun menus around town.

- Brigtsen's—Rabbit and Andouille Gumbo
- Coop's Place—Jambalaya
- Franky and Johnny's—Boiled Crawfish
- Mr. B's—Gumbo Ya Ya (Chicken and Sausage Gumbo)
- R&O's—Boiled Crawfish
- Slim Goodie's—Crawfish Étouffée
- Ye Olde College Inn—Boiled Crawfish

cajun IMPORTS

*W*ell-established marketing shtick aside, authentic Cajun food isn't readily available inside the limits of Orleans Parish—at least not in the restaurants that tend to splash "REAL CAJUN" all over their menus. In New Orleans, hybrid Louisiana cuisine may be the norm, but true Cajun food is an imported ethnic cuisine.

If you want to taste real Cajun cuisine, your best bet is to head west for an Acadiana day trip (see page 226). If you want to stay in the city, here are a few Cajun restaurants that are worthy of the name.

K-Paul's Louisiana Kitchen
416 Chartres St. (at St. Louis)
504-524-7394

zone: French Quarter
website: www.kpauls.com
reservations: recommended

meals: lunch Fri–Mon, dinner Mon–Sat, closed Sun
specialty: contemporary Louisiana cuisine
fancy factor: high-middlebrow
price range: $30–36

caveats: pricy
bonus points: piece of history

In the early 1980s when Paul Prudhomme took the American food world by storm, K-Paul's was a tiny 60-seat restaurant with communal tables, no reservations, and with lines routinely reaching around the Conti Street corner, plenty of waiting. Prudhomme's goals for the tiny restaurant were initially quite modest. "The idea was to do lunch Monday through Friday, have fun, serve good food, have a lot of locals come," he says, "and take a lot of vacations."

Things didn't quite work out according to plan, though. K-Paul's became the epicenter of a modern-day culinary revolution that forever changed the way outsiders view both Cajun and Creole cuisines; and in the process increased New Orleans' stock as a culinary destination.

If you were a fan of K-Paul's in the early days, you might be surprised by its current-day incarnation. The original ground-floor dining room is filled with smaller linen-clad tables; exposed brick and shiny cypress floors provide a balance of sophistication and earthiness. Though more formal than in earlier days, the ambience retains a casual sensibility and a hint of the family vibe that reigned before the renovation. If you call ahead for a reservation, you'll likely be seated in the new upstairs area—an additional 100-seat space that merits its own second-floor kitchen.

Cajun 101

Cajun food is rustic cuisine that developed in the rural areas of south Louisiana. Much of Cajun cooking is typified by slow-cooked one-pot dishes such as crawfish étouffée (crawfish tails smothered in a buttery sauce), fish-based courtboullion (a seafood dish similar to the French *bouillabaisse*) and snappy sauce piquante (meat or seafood stewed in a spicy tomato sauce).

The originators of this unique and diverse cuisine were the Acadians, French refugees from maritime Canada who arrived in Louisiana during the late 1700s. The Acadians (whose group name eventually Anglicized to "Cajuns") adapted their elemental one-pot dishes to the swamps, prairies and waterways of coastal Louisiana.

Though the Acadians settled in small, mostly French-speaking communities and lived in relative isolation, other ethnic groups had a significant impact on the evolution of the communities and their cuisine. Smaller ethnic populations settled among the Acadians, and eventually blended into the communities.

The simpler cuisine of the Cajuns featured bolder spices than their Creole counterparts, and also made use of readily available ingredients: the freshwater seafood (including the trademark crawfish) in bayou country, Gulf seafood along the coast or barnyard favorites (pork, smoked sausages, chicken) in the flat coastal prairie. (For a more complete discussion, see page 229.)

For many first-timers, K-Paul's is a destination restaurant; a chance to taste the food of the familiar celebrity chef, the personable man who brought Cajun food to restaurants across the country and laid media groundwork for future celebrity chefs.

Though Prudhomme no longer works the kitchen—having moved on to other business pursuits—the place is now in the able hands of another Opelousas native, Paul Miller. At the helm of a modern landmark, Miller has to pull off a delicate balancing act, providing the classics that pilgrims expect while developing other dishes of his own. You'll still find the blackened fish here—though it's more likely to be Gulf-caught black drum or yellowfin tuna than redfish. (The Cajun craze decimated Louisiana's redfish population, effectively shutting down the commercial redfish industry. The only sources now are farm-raised redfish, by most accounts a less tasty variation.) All the standards are here—jambalaya, a deep chicken and andouille gumbo, fried "duck boudin" patties and beef tenderloin smothered in debris sauce.

As you might expect, dining at the historical landmark adds a significant premium to the cost—but the regulars and occasional visitors who remember what the place used to be won't be too concerned. After all, not having to fight the lines might be reward enough for the faithful.

Bon Ton Cafe
401 Magazine St. (at Poydras)
504-524-3386

zone: CBD/Warehouse
reservations: recommended

meals: lunch and dinner Mon–Fri
specialty: traditional Cajun/Creole
fancy factor: middlebrow
price range: $18–33

caveats: closed on weekends

Not long after this downtown restaurant reopened in the early 1950s, the Bon Ton became known for serving menu items you just didn't see much in New Orleans. The owners, Al and Alzina Pierce, served the foods of rural Terrebonne and Lafourche Parishes, such as crawfish étouffée and jambalaya without tomato. It was food that you'd recognize if you spent time in the country, but nothing that city people were used to tasting. The kitchen would serve up the more com-

≡ CLASSIC ≡

Blackened Redfish

Never underestimate the power of a celebrity chef. A dish gets trendy and next thing you know, whole species can teeter on the brink of extinction.

In the mid-1970s, Chef Paul Prudhomme developed his trademark "blackening" technique and restaurants across the country went crazy for it. He rubbed fish filets with a spicy seasoning mixture and quick-seared the fish in a cast-iron skillet heated to supernova temperatures. It was a smoky, messy cooking method, but nonetheless swept the country as the most visible dish of the 1980s Cajun craze. Though the technique wasn't traditionally Cajun or species-specific, Prudhomme's "blackened redfish" dramatically increased demand for the saltwater fish.

It took less than ten years for the flourishing redfish (also known as red drum) population to be dangerously depleted. Since 1988, it's been illegal for commercial fishermen to catch redfish off the Louisiana coast.

So if you see redfish on any New Orleans menu, it's probably been shipped in from one of the two remaining wild fisheries (Mississippi and North Carolina) or raised in saltwater aquaculture operations.

If you're picky about the taste, it's best to ask if the fish is farm-raised. Many chefs steer clear of the domesticated redfish because of its sub-par texture and taste, opting instead to substitute another species (usually black drum) for blackened dishes.

Jambalaya

Jambalaya is Louisiana's most flexible rice dish—a savory mix of meat, poultry, aromatic vegetables and spices combined in a brothy mix, then simmered gently with raw rice. The rice absorbs the flavors if the various morsels (usually any combination of chicken, sausage, shrimp or crawfish) and the result is a chunky composed rice dish similar to *paella* or the near-universal Latino dish *arroz con pollo*. Many say that this chunky, *paella*-like rice dish is the most visible Spanish contribution to New Orleans cuisine and point to the root of the word as *jamón*, the Spanish word for ham.

In general, Louisiana's city and country cooks take a different approach to this popular dish. New Orleans cooks are more likely to add tomatoes or sauce to their recipes, making for a Creole or red jambalaya. Cajun traditionalists use deeply browned onions as their base, making for a more earthy brown jambalaya.

mon Creole dishes, to be sure, but early on the Bon Ton got the reputation as the first Cajun restaurant in New Orleans.

Nowadays, of course, the Bon Ton doesn't have a lock on the Cajun food market, but it's an interesting eatery nonetheless. Sometime in the 1970s, they moved a block closer to the Federal Courthouse and are now a midday hangout for most of the New Orleans legal profession. With exposed brick walls and Audubon prints, the dining room seems like a lawyer's office, but the red-and-white-checkered vinyl tablecloths add a somewhat jarring sense of informality.

During any weekday lunch rush, you can see power brokers discussing cases, making deals, and munching on dishes like Redfish Bon Ton (butter-seared black drum topped with sautéed crabmeat and a few onion rings), rich crabmeat au gratin or steak (for dedicated meat-and-potato eaters). On Mondays, most diners dig into a bowl of red beans served with a split link of smoked sausage and a slab of tender pickled pork—two pigs for the price of one. If you're trying to cut down on your whiskey intake, you should exercise caution around the bread pudding, which is simultaneously super-sweet and borderline flammable.

Coop's Place
1109 Decatur St. (at Ursulines)
504-525-9053

zone: French Quarter
website: www.coopsplace.net
reservations: none

meals: lunch and dinner daily
specialty: Cajun bar food
fancy factor: lowbrow
price range: $6–15

caveats: smoky bar
bonus points: kitchen open after hours

On the downriver side of Decatur where the foot traffic slows to a trickle, the doorway of Coop's Place sits in the darkness facing the block's primary tourist attraction, Jimmy Buffet's franchise bar. Coop's might seem outclassed when it comes to curb appeal—no neon, no blaring Floribbean party tunes, no visible light—just an ovoid sign with a toque-clad alligator licking its chops.

What this downmarket bar and grill lacks in visual flash, it makes up in street buzz. For more than twenty years, the kitchen here has been pumping out respectable versions of Cajun classics along with the usual suspects from the New Orleans culinary lineup. You've got your poboys, your burgers, your gumbo and red beans; fried chicken and a few boneless breast options for the birdfolk.

But the one thing that regulars know is that somewhere in the back of this 19th-century structure, Coop's fine kitchen folks spend a little extra time to smoke 'em when they got 'em; in this case meaning they spice and smoke their own tasso for use in dishes like the popular jambalaya and cream sauce for their Chicken Tchoupitoulas. The jambalaya supreme rabbit and sausage version of the chunky rice dish with a tomato base and the smoky pork dish thrown in for added savor. (The tomato is a strange call for a Cajun-inspired version, but whaddaya gonna do?)

Coop's ambience—smoky, jukebox blaring, barflies singing along at times—lets you know that the bar business takes precedence over the restaurant trade; a fact which turns into an advantage after the witching hour, when many restaurant kitchens have shut down for the night. As an added bonus, the kitchen serves two shifts of their breakfast menu: first from 11 AM to 4 PM, then again from midnight to 3 AM. Good news if you're looking for a substantial meal and a few off-key jukebox harmonies.

Mulate's New Orleans
201 Julia St. (at Fulton)
504-522-1492

zone: CBD/Warehouse
website: www.mulatesrestaurant.com
reservations: recommended

meals: lunch and dinner daily
specialty: Cajun food
fancy factor: middlebrow
price range: $14–22

caveats: cavernous
bonus points: near Convention Center,
    Cajun dancing, large-group friendly

As the urban outpost of a renowned Acadiana restaurant and dance hall, Mulate's came to the city with street cred and landed one of the sweetest locations in town—a cavernous renovated warehouse space about 200 feet from the Convention Center's main entrance. Of course,

Crawfish

With all due respect, we don't really care what you call them back home. In Louisiana, they're called crawfish (or *écrevisses* to French speakers) and they occupy an esteemed place in our collective food culture.

The scientific name for the delicious little beastie is *procambarus clarkii* (the red swamp crawfish), and originally that's still their preferred habitat. In the wild, crawfish thrive in standing water and burrow into any kind of soggy ground—swamp floors, riverbanks, ditches, waterlogged cattle pastures—creating telltale chimneys with the excavated mud. With such a high water-to-land ratio, swampy south Louisiana is a crawfish wonderland.

Some European cooks, including French and Scandinavian chefs, use the little crawlers for food, but it was Cajun cooks who took the little critters into the big time. As a plentiful resource with a reputation for scavenging, crawfish have traditionally been a food of last resort for denizens of rural Louisiana. Up until the 1950s or so, eating crawfish was a sign of poverty and backwardness. Even now, some older Cajuns have a hard time eating crawfish on the grounds that it "tastes like hard times." Over time, boiling points and seafood patios brought the local specialty to more diners, and family crawfish boils became more commonplace across the social spectrum. By the 1970s, crawfish had shed their stigma of "poor man's food" and were embraced as a symbol of south Louisiana.

With the exception of rich, labor-intensive crawfish bisque, dishes starring the beady-eyed beast were comparatively rare in New Orleans cooking until the Cajun incursions of the 1980s. When Prudhomme came to the city, he brought the crawfish with him and added the meat to a wide variety of now-standard Louisiana dishes.

Wild crawfish—especially those caught in the Atchafalaya Basin swamp west of Henderson—have traditionally been considered a springtime food. The crawfish lie low during the cold winter and emerge into waiting traps as the water warms up. The omnivorous crawfish feed on the bounty of the swamp and develop a distinctive flavor that varies with the animal's diet. In Acadiana, "Basin crawfish" are the most prized springtime specimens. With the advent of modern aquaculture methods, large-scale crawfish farms have developed throughout the state, especially in the rice farming country of the Cajun prairie near Lafayette.

Since they're cooked while still alive, crawfish don't travel well and are best consumed near the source, especially in their boiled form. Many of the standard dishes of the Cajun/Creole repertoire—crawfish étouffée, crawfish stew, crawfish pies—only require peeled tail meat, which can be purchased in one-pound bags from a variety of seafood processors.

it's also across the street from the River-walk shopping mall, surrounded by Warehouse District hotels, and visible from the new cruise ship docking complex. The business plan must have seemed like a license to print money.

Billed as "the original Cajun restaurant," Mulate's plays to its core audiences—conventioneers and tourists—with a menu of easily recognizable dishes from the country and city songbooks. The lunch menu is mostly poboys (fried seafood, country sausage, the obligatory grilled chicken) along with a few salads thrown in for good measure. The specialties of the house include a couple of not-terribly-spicy blackened fish options, hamburger steaks, gumbo and the other usual suspects. The étouffée, sadly, can be gummy in texture and light on the crawfish. The rich brown jambalaya—chunky with well-browned sausage and chicken but available only as a side dish—would make an Acadiana home cook proud.

As conventioneers spill out onto the streets after a long day, they'll hear the sounds of soaring fiddle and accordion music emanating from Mulate's—recorded in the daytime and live at night. In true Cajun tradition, the huge open room has a stage at one end and a well-worn wooden dance floor for evening festivities.

Zydeque Bayou Barbecue
808 Iberville St. (at Bourbon)
504-565-5520

zone: French Quarter
website: www.zydeque.com
reservations: none

meals: lunch and dinner nightly
specialty: barbecue and Cajun specialties
fancy factor: low-middlebrow
price range: $5–13

caveats: draws Bourbon Street crowd
bonus points: late-night on weekends

Barbecue just isn't the cult phenomenon that it is in other regions (Texas, Kansas City, the various Carolinas), but that doesn't mean that Louisiana is lacking its own indigenous smoked meat traditions. Given that, it was only a matter of time before someone tried to turn the Cajun *boucherie* traditions into a mainstream restaurant concept.

CLASSIC

Andouille

When it comes to gumbo, red beans or jambalaya, a Cajun cook's sausage of choice is usually a thick link of *andouille* (ahn-DOO-wee). Made from coarsely ground chunks of lean pork shoulder, this garlicky smokehouse specialty is simply spiced (salt, red pepper, black pepper) and slowly smoked over pecan-wood fires.

Though sausage-making is notorious for its use of "mystery meats," Cajun andouille is about 95 percent lean with a flavor close to its "on the leg" counterpart—ham. Browned in a skillet, andouille fills the kitchen with the aroma of well-smoked bacon. In a gumbo, the chunky pork product imparts an amazing depth of flavor to chicken- or game-based varieties.

Other Cajun Standbys

These dishes might not have the high profile of gumbo or jambalaya, but they're integral parts of south Louisiana's food culture nonetheless. They're far more common on home tables outside New Orleans, especially when there's a hunter or a fisherman in the house.

étouffée (crawfish or shrimp)—Cajun cooks look for any excuse to serve foods "étouffée" (or smothered in a rich, buttery sauce). Crawfish étouffée, made with the tender tail meat of the noble critter, is one of the treasured dishes of Acadiana and commonly seen in New Orleans restaurants. When cooks use the term to describe other meats, they're describing what southerners would commonly call "smothered chicken" or "smothered steak." Either way, the resulting dish is served on a bed of white rice.

courtbouillon (prounounced KOO-bee-yahwn)—The Cajun version of this tomato-based fish stew is thickened with a dark roux and can be made with just about any firm-fleshed fish (such as snapper, grouper or catfish). This Louisiana usage is not to be mistaken for the classical French cooking term (an aromatic poaching liquid).

maque choux—This simple vegetable dish is made with sweet corn and bell pepper, usually cooked with a little bit of milk for a smooth texture. In many New Orleans restaurants, it's referred to as "corn maque choux" to pre-answer the inevitable question: "What's in it?"

sauce piquante—Another tomato-heavy stew that's a first cousin to the Cajun courtboullion, but with a more pronounced peppery kick. While courtboullion is primarily a fish dish, a sauce piquante can be made with just about any kind of meat or wild game, including chicken, turtle, venison, rabbit or alligator.

The owners of GW Fins, a nearby upscale seafood restaurant, tapped south Louisiana's various traditions to create their own "bayou barbecue" joint that fits into its Bourbon Street surroundings. The room is decorated with colorful, playful mix of south Louisiana memorabilia and folk art including rainbow-hued zydeco posters and a menacing sheet metal garfish. The split-level dining area is separated by metal NOPD crowd barricades familiar to any Mardi Gras veteran.

Zydecue does a good job of sticking to its Louisiana roots: smoked specialtiies include andouille and smoked boudin as well as pork ribs and chicken; brisket and *cochon de lait* (a smoked version of the traditional pit-roasted suckling pig) fill out the plate and sandwich offerings. They also dip into the festival-food repertoire for a double-cooked turkey leg (smoked, then deep fried) if you're in a Henry VIII kinda mood. The house standard sauce is pretty close to the Opelousas/ Ville Platte style—sweet and tangy with chunks of minced onion. Plates are served on paper-lined beer trays and come with a pleasingly greasy round of crunchy skillet cornbread.

Purists will probably bemoan the lack of a seriously smoky punch to the meat, but they probably haven't come to the Crescent City because of its sterling reputation as a barbecue town. But if you're burned out on poboys and jonesing for a meatgut experience halfway through a Neon Zone drinking jag, it's safer than an impromptu road trip to Rocky Mount.

french CONNECTIONS

*S*ometimes it's not enough for a restaurant to be "French influenced," "French inspired," or "prepared according classical French technique." Sometimes you crave flavors and experiences that are straight-ahead continental French without American or Creole affectations of any kind.

Here are a few of New Orleans' outstanding French bistros—one contemporary, three traditional, and one whose atmosphere demands it be included in this category.

Bistro at Maison de Ville

727 Toulouse St. (at Bourbon)
504-528-9206

zone: French Quarter
website: www.maisondeville.com
reservations: recommended

meals: lunch Mon–Sat, dinner nightly
specialty: contemporary Creole
fancy factor: high-middlebrow
price range: $24–30

bonus points: romantic as all get-out, patio dining

From the cordovan banquettes at this too-prim-to-believe French Quarter bistro, it's hard to believe that you're half a block from where the Bourbon Street "soup" flows freely.

Approaching the Bistro from Toulouse, you can hear the perpetual thump of the Neon Zone's cover clubs, but step across the threshold and the hushed atmosphere recalls a backstreet on Paris' *rive gauche*.

The kitchen of this tiny hotel restaurant produced a long string of notable New Orleans chefs—Susan Spicer in her early years, Peristyle's original chef John Neal, his protégé-turned-star Anne Kearney and Dominique Macquet.

New Orleans native Greg Picolo has been at the helm for a few years now, showcasing his own complex take on a crossbred bistro/Creole cuisine. An apparent disciple of the "more is better" school, Picolo's menus are long on description and tend to read like a French novelette. Oftentimes, the chef starts off with a simple riff—a panned filet of Gulf drum, wrapped in a cylinder for example—and proceeds to add flavors, textures and degrees of difficulty as he goes. By the end of the description, the fish is stuffed with barbecue oysters and eggplant pasta spirals, then drizzled with a chervil beurre blanc. As is often the case with ambitious "concept cuisine," Picolo's reflex for complexity doesn't always benefit the final dish.

Price limits imposed by the lunch trade can often handcuff a chef, but here the constraints actually work to the kitchen's advantage. At midday the menu shifts toward most straightforward bistro fare (steak frites or Belgian-style mussels) and more restrained modern interpretations (a courtboullion of seared grouper with red sauce and crawfish/pecan risotto).

Wine geeks dote on the Bistro's devotion to high-level wine culture, which is apparent from a quick scan of the cozy, narrow room. Huge bottles of special-edition vintages are lined up along the banquette mirrors; the wine list reads like a viticultural encyclopedia. Patrick Van Hoorebeek, a charismatic whirlwind of a host, runs the front of the house as maître d' and sommelier—his proper yet infectious enthusiasm permeates the Bistro's wine program, but at a price. Though diners are encouraged to ask about "Patrick's best-kept secrets," they're also presented with dessert wine pairings that suggest a sixteen-dollar glass of ice wine to accompany a six-dollar chocolate crème brûlée.

La Crepe Nanou

1410 Robert St. (at Prytania)
504-899-2670

zone: **Uptown**
website: www.lacrepenanou.com
reservations: none

meals: dinner nightly
specialty: crepes and traditional bistro fare
fancy factor: middlebrow
price range: $8–18

caveats: no reservations
bonus points: sidewalk seating, open nightly

With its deep burgundy paint job and art nouveau–style glass canopy, Crepe Nanou pulls off a convincing Paris Metro vibe, despite the fact that it faces a parking lot in Uptown New Orleans. Pass by on any balmy night and you'll find sidewalk café culture in full bloom—clusters of prospective patrons sipping wine as they wait for a table inside the popular neighborhood bistro.

La Crepe Nanou has been an Uptown favorite since before the latest wave of aspiring restaurateurs put their twists on the now-trendy genre. While shying away from the haute cuisine aspirations, Crepe Nanou presents everyday fare with impeccable substance and casual style. The simple listings showcase simple French dishes—from soft, hot-off-the-griddle crepes to more substantial dishes such as grilled salmon with a flavorful béarnaise sauce.

The starters here are simple but top-notch, including the brothy mussels *marinière*—a bowl of steamed mussels in a garlic/wine sauce perfectly complimented by a mound of salty fries. The crabmeat/crawfish coquilles put a local spin on the creamy-rich variation French scallop dish; crepes stuffed with earthy beef *bourguignon* are also moan-worthy. Sweet crepes—filled with various ice-cream combinations or a brandy-spiked stewed apple filling—understandably dominate the dessert menu.

The crowd runs toward Uptown regulars and the down-on-the-wallet student crowd looking for a dependable night out without white-linen sticker shock. Crepe Nanou's two adjacent rooms have markedly different vibes: the cushy red-

velvet feel near the bar makes for a more romantic feel, the glassed-in garden room makes for a more energetic (if sometimes deafening) atmosphere.

The "wine and wait" is often the result of the restaurant's "no reservations" policy, except on Mondays, when much of the city's kitchens take a well-deserved night off. Expect higher traffic and a more active sidewalk scene when most other restaurants take their traditional early-week break.

Lilette Restaurant

3637 Magazine St. (at Antonine)
504-895-1636

zone: Uptown
website: www.lilletterestaurant.com
reservations: recommended, required Fri–Sat

meals: lunch Tues–Sat, dinner Tues–Sat, closed Sun–Mon
specialty: contemporary French
fancy factor: high-middlebrow

price range: $19–23
bonus points: Saturday lunch, outdoor dining

It's not surprising that in the boutique-heavy stretch of Magazine Street, Lilette stands out as an appealing little jewel-box of a bistro. In a section of Uptown where the shotgun houses have all become art galleries, jewelry shops and antique brokers, chef/owner John Harris runs a casual, sophisticated room and interprets French country classics with a distinctly American sensibility.

Harris is one of the current crop of New Orleans' young Turks—a veteran of Bayona and Gautreau's, *Food & Wine* best new chef—and a specialist in updated takes on French bistro specialties that consistently demonstrate creativity, precision and a fondness for nonnative ingredients. On any given night, the menu is likely to feature raw oysters imported from Alaska or sturgeon pulled from Washington State's Columbia River.

Harris' cuisine has a warmth and simplicity that gives the simply renovated corner drugstore an Parisian neighborhood feel with nods to the local traditions as well as other Mediterranean influences—saucy rolled beef *braciola* with creamy polenta, sautéed halibut with brightly flavored gremolata and saffron aioli. But that's not to say he brushes off the bistro standards: house-made *boudin noir* (blood sausage) is a consistent charcuterie option; his *steak frites* features the classic hangar cut seared perfectly rare and topped with a rich, marrow-enriched bordelaise sauce. For a subtle sweet course, he plays creamy chevre/crème fraiche quenelles against poached pears drizzled with lavender honey.

Lilette serves lunch and dinner from Tuesday through Saturday—a comfort for the ladies who lunch but a godsend for the day-job contingent. Inside the sleek but historic dining room or outside on the patio tables, Lilette has a pronounced sense of offhand romance; a perfect place to linger over a bottle of wine and consider the night's possibilities.

Martinique Bistro
5908 Magazine St. (at Eleonore)
504-891-8495

zone: Uptown
reservations: recommended

meals: dinner nightly
specialty: French bistro
fancy factor: high-middlebrow
price range: $17–22

caveats: weather-dependent, street parking tight
bonus points: courtyard dining, kids menu, bargain plat du jour

Before the owners of Martinique Bistro hung up their new oversized sign, most drivers on upper Magazine Street had a single thought on their way past the building—"Nice hedge." Pedestrians had a little more time to peer in two streetside windows; one revealing a cute little bistro dining room, the other a cramped, active restaurant kitchen in full swing. Despite the fact that the bistro sat directly on the sidewalk, Martinique was all but invisible.

The sign draws more attention to the mango-colored building, but inside, this little bistro maintains the romantic, somewhat clandestine feel that's made it a neighborhood favorite for Uptown regulars and Tulane students in search of a casual yet memorable date spot.

Martinique's dining area is split between two equally charming spaces—a note-perfect French-style bistro room with about eight tables and a much larger outdoor patio ringed by a fifteen-foot wall of tropical vegetation and climbing vines. At duskfall, guests unwind in the secret garden, concealed from the whoosh and clatter of street traffic as the sundown turns to night sky—al fresco dining interpreted by Magritte.

A former owner hailed from the Caribbean island that gave the eatery its name, so the menu plays to the traditional French with a bit of the islands thrown in for old time's sake. The kitchen is particularly fond of fruit and savory combinations as they riff on classic provincial dishes. A savory French toast starter combines shreds of hearty lamb confit and mushroom with a palate-teasing herbed blueberry reduction. A well-executed yet simple simple sauté of curried Gulf shrimp with dried mango continues the well-executed sweet/spicy theme. The sautéed pork medallions—accented with plums, shitake and walnuts, then drizzled with a fragrant Armagnac sauce—are a masterful homage to the flavors of southwestern France.

A few other details add to Martinique's welcoming, homey feel. A daily children's menu plays well with new families and a reasonably priced plat du jour attracts young professionals and students alike, even on nights when Daddy's not picking up the tab.

René Bistrot

817 Common St. (at Carondelet)
504-412-2580

zone: CBD/Warehouse
website: www.renebistrot.com
reservations: recommended

meals: lunch and dinner daily, brunch
  Sunday
specialty: contemporary French bistro
fancy factor: high-middlebrow
price range: $15–23

bonus points: great lunch specials, table d'hôte nightly, valet parking

Take one look around this modern-gone-retro room and it's easy to assume that Chef René Bajeaux chose the term "bistro" for its contemporary American sensibility. The muted, 70s-era color palette—orange, browns, golds and greens—looks like it hopped out of a trendy interior design magazine. Metallic mosaics, Eames-inspired chairs, copper planters—René is an elegant, post-postmodern supper club that would be at home anywhere on the west coast.

But look over the menu and you'll realize that the man in the kitchen is perfectly comfortable playing the posh appearance against rustic flavors. You can tell by the preponderance of traditional dishes—a savory onion and bacon tart, house-made pâté, grilled sardines with herbs and garlic, and roasted *poulet grand mére* (Grandmother's Chicken)— and two categories of reasonably priced daily specials: a rotating *plat du jour* and multi-course *table d'hôte*.

Alsatian native René Bajeaux rose to local prominence at the helm of the Winsdor's Court Hotel's swanky Grill Room, where he wowed upper-tier diners with complex, sculptural dishes and delicate flavor combinations. His follow-up bistrot (to use the less common French spelling) focuses on comparatively simple fare while maintaining a culinary precision and a sense of casual sophistication. One of his trademark starters, a smoked salmon galette, shows his ability to blend simple flavors and textures with flawless presentation. A crispy puck of potato is topped with a layer of savory smoked salmon arranged in a perfect, almost botanical, rosette. A tiny drizzle of crème fraiche and a scattering of micro-minced chives provide appropriate accent flavors and an artistic flourish. Not that the earthy onion soup (with a velvety Gruyere custard) is any less notable, but the galette is a dish that even die-hard Gulf fish lovers have after-meal dreams about.

OYSTER bars

When it comes to "take it/leave it" preferences, raw oysters tend to inspire extremes. Cut from the center of a sharp, rocky shell, the slick and sensuous meat of a Gulf oyster is reputed to be an aphrodisiac, and New Orleans' oyster bars have trafficked in this *au natural* seafood tradition since well before sushi made it to American shores.

The city is packed with "raw bars" that shuck their way through countless sacks of Louisiana oysters every year. With insanely productive coastal reefs within easy shipping distance, it's only natural that this Gulf seafood tradition should thrive in New Orleans, a town where you're never too far from a quick "dozen raw" chased with a nice cold beer.

Acme Oyster & Seafood House

724 Iberville St.
504-522-5973

zone: French Quarter
website: www.acmeoyster.com
reservations: accepted

meals: lunch and dinner daily
specialty: fried oysters, poboys
fancy factor: low-middlebrow
price range: $6–15

caveats: long lines common

A line in front of the Acme—it's one of those French Quarter sights that seems to be present just about any time of year. Easy striking distance from both Bourbon and Canal Streets, the Acme has managed to parlay its central location into a tourist-friendly gold mine—a casual general-purpose seafood experience that's accessible to rawbar fans and oyster-phobes alike. The Acme's fast-moving lines serve a dual purpose—to indicate a hot spot and to keep potential customers from developing a nasty heatstrokes.

The Acme has been plying its trade at his location since the 20s, and from the looks of things, they've adjusted to the modern traffic patterns of the Neon Zone just fine. Even on off nights, the Acme packs 'em in with an authentic "old saloon" atmosphere that's updated just enough to appeal to the T.G.I.Friday's set.

In fact, the Acme in its present form feels like the primeval Friday's—checkerboard vinyl tablecloths, approachable poboy list, veggie burgers for the squeamish and white zinfandel by the glass. Middle American approachability seems to be king at the Acme—gumbo and red beans are available in a "poopa" (hollow bread bowl), raw oysters and fried seafood on pressed rice become "Cajun sushi." The reasonably priced sampler platters have tasty smoked sausage and jambalaya, but fall short on the gumbo and red beans

fronts (the chicken/andouille lacking flavor, the beans a bit too bland).

At the raw bar, the high-traffic atmosphere can occasionally get the best of the shuckers, who keep the charm going even under pressure. Sometimes instant gratification isn't such a good thing— especially in the form of a pre-shucked dozen that's been sitting around awhile. And in the "give 'em what they want" hall of fame, boiled crawfish are on the menu well into the off-season summer months— even if it means they're tiny and shipped in

INGREDIENT

Gulf Oysters

Like blue crabs and various shrimp species, the American oyster (*crassostrea virginica*) thrives in the mixed-water environment of Louisiana's coastal wetlands. Raised in reefs where salty ocean water and sweet river waters mingle, these tasty mollusks are a valuable part of the state's food culture and modern-day economic base.

Among shellfish, oysters are most similar to mussels. At a certain point in their early life cycle, free-swimming larvae cement themselves to coastal reefs and settle in for the long haul, filtering out nutrients (mineral and micro-vegetation) from the surrounding waters. Oyster flavor varies naturally depending on the balance of fresh and salty water flowing by the oyster beds.

In earlier days, these collections of shellfish occurred naturally, but over time oystermen (many of them Croatians from the Adriatic coast) started hedging their bets with "seed oysters"—a management technique that assures fresh oysters in the city's raw bars year-round. With over a million acres of cultivated reefs, Louisiana is consistently one of the country's top oyster producers.

In a biological sense, peak season for these meaty treats occurs in the winter months, when the oysters are busy packing on fat (glycogen) in anticipation of an active summer spawning season. Then they're at their flavorful peak, with sweetness from the fat adding a savory dimension to the oyster's natural saltiness.

That's not to say that oysters won't be *available* during summer vacation—they'll just be more *flavorful* (plump and sweet) when the Gulf waters are coldest. All the more reason to hit town during Mardi Gras season.

(In recent years, there have been documented cases of poisoning occurring as a result of bacterial contamination. For a more in-depth discussion of this issue, refer to Seafood Safety (page 129).)

from farms in California. Thinking they're getting a taste of local culture, tourists will pay top dollar for crustaceans that probably traveled farther than they did.

In some ways, you could do worse on your first trip than a stop at the Acme, but hopefully it'll just whet your appetite for the great neighborhood joints that lay beyond the Neon Zone.

Casamento's

4330 Magazine St. (at Napoleon)
504-895-9761

zone: Uptown
reservations: none

meals: lunch Fri, dinner Tues–Sun, closed Mon
specialty: fried seafood, raw oysters
fancy factor: middlebrow
price range: $6–11

caveats: closed 1 June–30 August, all-lard frying
bonus points: all-lard frying, amazing tile work

In restaurant circles, the backhanded compliment of "It's so *clean . . .*" usually signals the kiss of culinary death. Joints that are renowned for their cleanliness are generally not feted for their food—especially in a funk-heavy town like New Orleans. Sterility is more often a signal of safety and control than creativity and good flavor.

But Casamento's, an oyster bar on the Uptown stretch of Magazine, is the exception that proves this particular rule. The walls and floor of this neighborhood institution are prime examples of mid-century tile work that has survived over half a century of daily wear and tear. The ridged yellow ceramic and decorative floral bouquet tiles give the divided room a sense of well-scrubbed funk, while the traditional stand-up oyster bar turns out some of the best oysters in town.

Located deep Uptown and near the western edge of the Garden District, Casamento's is one of the old-style oyster houses that favors local traffic over the tourist trade. (And ironically, that's what's led it to be listed in numerous travel guides. Ummm . . . like this one, for example.) Their fried oyster loaves and

INGREDIENT

Seafood Safety: R-Months and Shuck Talk

Most local residents were raised with the traditional wisdom that you should only eat raw oysters in the months containing the letter "R"—a scheme that rules out half-shell consumption in May, June, July and August. Any other time of year, you can shuck a sack to your stomach's content, but during the summer, it's better to stick with cooked oysters.

The old wives and modern scientists seem to agree on one thing—that warm waters in the Gulf bring increased risk of illness—but the scientists go one step more specific. They've traced the majority of raw shellfish sickness to specific bacteria—*vibrio vulnificus* and its cousin *vibrio parahaemolyticus*. These waterborne bacteria grow in warm water and concentrate in certain filter-feeding animals such as our precious Gulf oyster. At its worst, *vibrio* can trigger an intense, sometimes fatal, reaction among people with severely compromised immune systems. *Vibrio* poisoning is very rare, but the risk exists whenever you eat the raw shellfish.

For oyster eaters, the good news is that these microorganisms are pretty delicate—they're easily killed by high-temperature cooking and usually pose a danger to diners with existing liver damage or existing immune system problems. The bad news is that the *vibrio* threat doesn't go away when the Gulf waters get colder—a fact that all oyster restaurants announce on menus beside their raw bar offerings:

There may be a risk associated with consuming raw shellfish as is the case with other raw protein products. If you suffer from chronic illness of the liver, stomach or blood, or have other immune disorders, you should eat these products cooked.

So for the small segment of high-risk individuals (usually older folks, pregnant women and kids) there's really no safety zone. If you're in a high-risk group, it's better to play it safe and order them cooked.

Everyone else who bellies up to the bar should strike up a conversation with the hardworking shuckers—asking about current conditions in the Gulf, the shellfish's point of origin, and just about anything oyster related. You'll learn a lot and usually get an earful of good stories to boot.

---

fresh-shucked platters consistently show up on critics' lists and local readers' polls, as well as in the enthusiastic recommendations of food-savvy Yats.

The preparations and menu at Casamento's couldn't be more basic. Seafood dominates the list—oysters fried, stewed and on the half shell, trout, soft-shell crabs and fried shrimp—along with a scattering of short-order specialties including a few omelets, standard grilled sandwiches and a sweet-sauced spaghetti served with meatballs or slices of Creole-style roast beef (daube).

Simplicity has served Casamento's well—every lunch table seems to have at least one diner slurping from the half shell—as has the purist's practice of deep-frying in lard, the most flavorful but currently unfashionable cooking fat. The pro-lard policy rules out even the fallback French fries for hard-core vegetarians, who will probably also be disappointed with the trio of salad offerings (lettuce, tomato, and lettuce & tomato).

Contrary to the long-bread school of poboys, seafood sandwiches are built on triple-thick slabs of gooshy white "pan bread"—the precursor to budget steakhouse "Texas toast." Eating one of these sandwiches is an entirely different experience from the poboy norm as the bread molds itself around crispy seafood nuggets (flavorful shrimp, crisp/plump oysters) without contributing a crunch of its own. Different, to be sure, and well worth a try for students of New Orleans sandwich subculture.

Over at the raw bar, it's a traditional stand-up-and-slurp affair, with rocky shells served on the bar instead of iced platters. You can watch the masters at work while you sip a cold beer, pouncing on the plump Gulf beauties the instant they're cut free from the shell.

Summertime visitors in search of a Casamento's oyster fix are sadly set up for seasonal frustration. Since Casamento's opened its doors before the advent of cheap refrigeration, they still follow the tradition of closing down COMPLETELY during the hottest (and non-R) months of the year (June, July and August). Show up hungry during the off-school months and you'll be sorely disappointed.

Drago's Seafood Restaurant and Oyster Bar

3232 N Arnoult Rd. (at 17th)
Metairie, LA
504-888-9254

zone: Metairie
website: accepted

meals: lunch and dinner Mon–Sat
specialty: char-broiled oysters
fancy factor: low-middlebrow
price range: $13–40

caveats: packed at lunch, tough to find

Even though the cartoon mascot on Drago's sign is a happy-go-lucky Maine lobster (really, check the rounded claws), people seek out this casual suburban seafood house for another kind of shellfish: platters of garlicky char-broiled oysters.

Drago's house specialty is a cooked dish served on the half shell—shucked oysters topped with a potent mixture of garlic, butter, parsley and pecorino Romano cheese before being placed over a roaring gas flame. (A curious use of the prefix "char-", but who's to tell?) In minutes, the scorching hot shells poach the tender bivalves in the rich sauce, the delicate flesh sealed in a shell of crunchy browned cheese. Served by the dozen or half dozen, these little beauties come with plenty of French bread to soak up whatever flavorful sauce is left in the shells.

If you manage to find a seat at the bar, you can take a short imaginary trip to the place that inspired this dish—Croatia, in former Yugoslavia. It's the homeland of owner Drago Cvitanovich, and from the bar you can quite literally see the pristine Adriatic coast; a mural behind the bar lays out the blue waters and sun-drenched white houses of Drago's homeland, making you yearn for a trip as you scoop the shells clean with hand-torn morsels of bread. Off to the left, you can almost hear the waves breaking over the rocks, until you realize that it's the oyster grill loaded down with a fresh load of shells, water and garlic hissing over the flame.

As for the lobster—the tiny cousins of our mascot are certainly on the menu, but that's not really the point. Among some of the Metairie regulars, Drago's way with the fancy North Atlantic shellfish rivals the signature oyster dish and qualifies as the best reason for braving the labyrinth of suburban side streets.

Felix's Restaurant and Oyster Bar
739 Iberville St. (at Bourbon)
504-522-4440

zone: French Quarter
website: www.felixs.com
reservations: none

meals: lunch and dinner daily
specialty: seafood and oysters
fancy factor: low-middlebrow
price range: $10–19

caveats: kinda dowdy
bonus points: rarely a line at the oyster bar

CLASSIC

Sauce Yourself

Raw oysters are served with a simple squeeze of lemon or with various standard accoutrements—cellophane-wrapped- crackers (usually saltines) and a cold cocktail sauce spiked with horseradish or a vinegar-based cocktail sauce.

Mixing your own cocktail sauce is one of the prime survival skills at a proper New Orleans "raw bar." While the oyster shuckers are usually happy to help you concoct a passable version, you should know the basic ingredients involved so you can customize the traditional accompaniment to your personal palate. Build your own sauce from the following easily procured tabletop ingredients:

Tomato Ketchup—The sweet base of any successful cocktail sauce is this "King Condiment" from the time before salsa reigned supreme.
Prepared Horseradish—South Louisiana's version of wasabi, and every bit as powerful. This moist, fibrous Bloody Mary spice might seem foreign to you, but scoop with care. A little too much, and you're set for a painful sinus-to-brain WHOOSH.
Pepper Sauce—Usually Tabasco or Crystal. Used to add a little "on the tongue" heat. A couple of squirts should be plenty to balance the ketchup's sweetness.
Lemon Juice—Fresh squeezed into the sauce or straight onto the oyster, this citrus note provides tangy counterpoint for the bivalve's rich saltiness.

If you've ever paged through a family photo album in south Louisiana, you've seen this picture. Two happy couples in a classic "say cheese" tourist pose, grinning for the photographer or laughing out loud. From their attire—men in casual suits and slicked-back hair, ladies with white pocketbooks and the occasional pillbox hat—you can tell that it's a classic young parents' double date. Somebody's mama is watching the kids for the weekend and this group of friends is out on the town with no kids in tow and fewer plans for the evening. At their elbows, empty Jax bottles and spent oyster shells sit on the flecked marble bar. The colors on the old photo are faded to pastel shades, and around the scalloped yellow edges, a printed date says OCT 1961 or thereabouts.

Depending on their generation, these laughing people could be your parents, grandparents or even earlier incarnations of yourself—but if you grew up in French Louisiana, odds are the photo was snapped at "the Felix" on Iberville. This thoroughly unrenovated off-Bourbon oyster bar shows little sign of change since our photo was snapped: oysters in the front, seating mostly in the back, rocky shellfish unloaded by the sack into an ice-filled trough, a now-antique neon sign attracting walk-by customers with flashing red arrows. Its primary across-the-way competition ("the Acme") updated its image years back, but the

Felix just motors along. The menu for the sit-down trade has all the usual litany of seafood house dishes—fried plates, gumbo, poboys and the like. The newest thing in the place is probably the butcher-block Formica tops on the tables.

If the place is empty (as it often is) the shucker will motion you toward the front of the room as he slams the first oyster onto the soft metal anvil. It's an old trick of the trade: if the place seems full, then it might draw sidewalk gawkers or sweaty Acme customers inside for a quick dozen. The shucker slides the shells across to you one at a time, cold shell atop a cool marble surface. The barside banter will include the usual tourist inquisition—"Where y'all from? Here for work? See the game?" And so forth.

In early 2005, Felix's is slated to open another location Uptown, a couple of blocks off St. Charles and a world away from the pleasantly funky Neon Zone location. Will it be successful? Probably. But time will tell whether it will be as photogenic as the original.

Notable Restaurant Oyster Bars
- Arnaud's
- Bourbon House
- Bozo's
- Uglesich's
- Pascale's Manale

poboy SHOPS

*W*orkaday New Orleans is a city powered by the poboy. Hefty, flavorful and inexpensive, this cousin to other American "big sandwiches" (hoagies, subs, heros, grinders) is the Crescent City's native fast food, a dependable midday, evening or after-club meal wrapped in white butcher paper and packed with any of a million fillings—from sizzling fried shrimp to griddle-seared pork chops or hot sausage patties. Pound for pound, it's the best lunchtime deal in town.

Properly constructed, a Louisiana poboy is a hungry dockhand's dream—a substantial meal laid out on a foot-long chunk of pillowy French bread slathered with creamy mayonnaise and "dressed" with shreds of ice-cold iceberg lettuce, thin-sliced tomato and dill pickle chips. In a city where portion control borders on cardinal sin, the most-used descriptor for aspiring sandwich vendors is "overstuffed," a boast that results in two-pound sandwiches packed with garlicky meatballs, stacks of standard delicatessen ham and cheese or delicately fried soft-shell crabs. And though tourism has replaced shipping as the city's primary industry, New Orleans' modern-day desk workers can still shell out a few bucks and feast like hard-toiling stevedores.

In this city, good poboys lurk in the most unexpected of places. Lunch counters, corner groceries and after-hours barroom kitchens—it seems that any business with space for a meat slicer or deep-fryer also traffics in the sizable sandwiches.

A definitive list of New Orleans poboy joints would require its own book, so here's a short list of the great ones—establishments that serve up the kind of sandwiches that natives crave come lunchtime.

Café Maspero
601 Decatur St. (at Toulouse)
504-523-6250

zone: French Quarter

meals: lunch and dinner daily
specialty: sandwiches, simple New Orleans fare
fancy factor: lowbrow
price range: $5–10

caveats: cash only, sidewalk lines common
bonus points: cheap drinks, comfortable room

Another tourist institution to benefit from a prime Decatur Street location, Café Maspero always seems to have a line snaking down the sidewalk. Nothing will make a local avoid a restaurant more like the prospect of waiting outside on a superheated sidewalk—there are far too many comfortably dark bars within easy striking distance.

Warm and Cloudy: New Orleans–Style French Bread

In New Orleans, the simple phrase "French bread" implies a very specific set of flavors and textures—a thin, shatteringly crisp beige crust surrounding a pillowy soft interior. As the base of an overstuffed poboy or slathered with creamy butter, these airy loaves are the Louisiana baker's standard.

Compared to denser, hard-crusted baguettes, these loaves are mostly air and as such, don't age particularly well. Two days after baking, the inside crumb takes on its own crackly consistency, transforming it from table-ready to the active ingredient of a local dessert standard—bread pudding.

Daily shipments are key to the operations of New Orleans' many restaurants and poboy shops. This keeps fleets of trucks from the three remaining commercial bakers—Leidenheimer's, Alois Binder and Gendusa—on the road year-round.

Inside, though, it's pretty apparent why the novices seek out this historic room—the sandwiches are substantial, the beer is cold, and the whole menu is cheaper than you'd expect. The fact that its rustic front doors face the main entrance to the Jax Brewery mall doesn't hurt a bit either . . .

It's actually pretty amazing that this rustic, historic room hasn't been commandeered by the swanky restaurant development crowd. The bar itself is a hulking mahogany beauty; brick archways break up the space well. Indestructible wooden tables show the marks of graffiti-happy patrons and wooden chairs show wear marks from years of push and pull.

Strangely enough, the central location doesn't seem to have any inflationary effect on Maspero's menu—a solid sandwich with fries and draft beer will cost less than ten bucks, which counts as a minor miracle on this busy thoroughfare. The sandwiches themselves flaunt the elongated poboy model and are instead presented on slightly larger than Kaiser-size seeded Italian rolls. The effect works well for the single-serving muffuletta (served broiled with pastrami, salami and ham), but not so much for the lackluster roast beef variation.

Their version of Cajun jambalaya doesn't lack for pleasant meaty bits— small shrimp, chunks of grilled sausage, morsels of chicken—but a near-tasteless rice base makes the overall flavor more starchy than savory. Hot sauce lets people control their own heat level, but without a matching bottle of "chicken flavoring" on the table, the jambalaya lacks the required flavorings.

Maspero's owners seem to know their crowd's price/benefit priorities well—and offer dollar-a-glass options for beer, wine and frozen drink categories. In a pleasant convergence of economic flavor considerations, the Slurpee-style and significantly watered down strawberry daiquiri makes a great walking dessert—and at a dollar a cup, you can't beat the price.

Domilise's

5240 Annunciation St. (at Bellecastle)
504-899-9126

zone: Uptown
reservations: none

meals: lunch and dinner Mon–Sat
specialty: poboys
fancy factor: lowbrow
price range: $5–9

caveats: cash only, closes 7:00 PM

Stop by Domilise's any weekday for lunch and the neighborhood bar/poboy hums along at its regular pace. A single room split between tiny open kitchen, hand-built bar and open seating area. Enter from the corner door and you practically run into the kitchen—a few women cutting poboy bread, frying seafood, methodically laying out pickle chips on sandwiches. Nothing fancy, nothing hidden, nothing special.

But during Saturday afternoons—especially during football season—you see the

room as more than a hidden neighborhood barroom or classic poboy destination (though it's a great example of both). On Saturday afternoons, you can see Domilise's true nature—a family rec room that's inexplicably open to the public.

There are usually a few kids running around the clutch of Formica tables, maybe a baby carrier balanced on a wooden chair. Saturdays are a time that whole families drop in—an impromptu stop between errands or a steady weekend tradition. The kitchen ladies look up from their tickets long enough to visit a bit and coo over the infant in the carrier. Generations of babies—including the moppet doing laps around the tables and his parents as well—grow up to associate the smell of close-quarter deep-frying with the high-pitched cooing of strangers.

On Saturday, the kitchen serves up its special barbecue beef poboy—a thick concoction that's somewhere between a sloppy joe and Mexican *machaca* (shredded dried beef). Thick and pasty, sweet and meaty, it's got the taste and texture that let you know it's not competing for the acclaim of barbecue purists of any stripe—it's got "grandma's touch" written all over it.

Over by the bar, a line of neighborhood guys—some in their twenties, a few in the fiftyish range—hold court on whatever college game's on the tube. If you like to eavesdrop, it's easy to learn a few things about the game and little bits of neighborhood gossip without much effort at all.

The rough-hewn bar looks like a home improvement project launched with the surplus lumber from an unnamed garage project. A few coolers underneath, a few taps sticking through the top, and next thing you know, you've got a sports-friendly neighborhood hideaway. A collection of historic beer cans and trays makes perfect sense, but an old Falstaff sign never fails to raise an eyebrow:

Here's to the happiest days of my life, spent in the arms of another man's wife—my Mother.

Simultaneously wholesome, vaguely maudlin and disturbingly oedipal. Better to just order a draft or two, a bag of Zapp's. Maybe a root beer for dessert.

If you're very lucky, the raised door to the adjacent house opens wide, and the owner, Miss Dot Domilise, makes a stately appearance before heading out to afternoon mass.

Most other days, she'll be in the kitchen sweating her way through poboy duty, but on Saturday, she might be sporting a fresh beauty shop coif on her way to church. She'll float through the room, check in with the boys at the bar, wave to the girls in the kitchen and, with a quick smile, disappear back into her living room, then close the door behind her. Welcome to the neighborhood.

Guy's Poboys
5259 Magazine St. (at Valmont)
504-891-5025

zone: Uptown

meals: lunch Mon–Sat
specialty: poboys, plate lunches
fancy factor: lowbrow
price range: $6–10

caveats: closed Sun, full during lunch rush
bonus points: mystery sandwiches, good plate lunch specials

"Who told you about Da Bomb?"

From behind the low cashier's counter, Guy's owner Marvin Matherne shot me a semi-suspicious look after I ordered an off-menu (but nonetheless notorious) sandwich.

"We don't put it on the menu, but somebody wrote about it a few years ago," he said, turning to the kitchen. "People don't ask much about it anymore. You'll like it, it's a good sandwich."

The Poboy Known as Da Bomb isn't a variation that most customers would come up with on the spot—griddle-sautéed shrimp and catfish filets covered with a cheesy trifecta (American, Swiss and pepper jack). The result is a combination that most customers wouldn't exactly invent on the spot.

Guy's photocopied menu reads like just about any other New Orleans sandwich shop: fried seafood poboys, the usual deli meat options, hamburger permutations. Nothing fancy, nothing that requires explanation. Choose your filling, tell the cashier if you want it dressed or not, and sit at one of the neighborhood joint's five tables. If it's the weekday lunch rush, the tables are likely filled with clutches of construction workers, UPS drivers or policemen from the nearby 2nd District station.

The standard sandwich options usually suffice for most folks, but regulars at Guy's naturally gravitate to the daily specials board or the hidden code of the personalized poboy.

The half-wall blackboard gives an inside line on the daily plate lunch offerings (grilled pork chop with white beans or fries, a surprisingly flavorful baked potato stuffed with cheese and marinated grilled chicken) and sandwiches that make occasional appearances, such as an outstanding alligator sausage poboy. It's

not the addition of reptile meat that gives this mostly pork sausage its flavorful edge, but Matherne's cooking technique that makes it stand out. A single link is cut into 1/8 inch slices, then cooked on the flat-top griddle until each slice develops a layer of crunchy brown goodness. Once inside a finished poboy, these fairly dry layers of spiced meat mingle with the cool dressing components (creamy mayo, runaway juices from tomato, lettuce and pickle) to give the best BLT a run for its money.

Occasional diners might know the weekly specials routine, but ordering one of Guy's signature creations requires an additional layer of knowledge—a personal connection that turns this poboy shop into a gangster-era speakeasy.

The exchange is always fairly simple—"Hey, I was talking to [friend's name] and he told me to order his poboy."

Whether he's working the kitchen or the register, Matherne will search his memory, ask for a quick confirmation ("Lee . . . Big guy? Always wears a Saint's cap?") then rattle off the various ingredients ("Yeah . . . Lee gets a large roast turkey, bacon and Swiss with debris. Dressed, no pickles").

Some sandwiches remain the personal domain of their individual creators and others receive nicknames that achieve legendary status among regulars. Know the code, and you're in.

As for Da Bomb, it's pretty much like you'd expect from the description—a spicy mix of seafood held together by a trio of creamy Velveeta-like cheesefoods. The mayo mixes with the cheese to make a sauce something like a blue-collar Alfredo, while the edges, having spent time on the griddle, are bubbly, brown and crisp. Fans of coquille St. Jacques would definitely approve.

Why hasn't Matherne put Da Bomb on the regular menu?

"I haven't printed any in a while, and even then I'd have to explain it every time. It's better if people who know just ask. But you liked it, huh?"

Johnny's Po-boy Restaurant
511 St. Louis St. (at Decatur)
504-524-8129

zone: French Quarter

meals: breakfast and lunch daily
specialty: poboys, plate lunches
fancy factor: lowbrow
price range: $4–8

bonus points: free delivery

When you see a poboy listed as "Judge Bosetta" on the menu board, you're pretty much ordering on faith. With no explanation beyond the cryptic name, you might think it's some kind of Prohibition-era code phrase, or perhaps a homage to a well-fed regular. Or if you keep up on your arty French cinema, you might chalk it up to a cannibalistic conspiracy posing as a lunch special.

Make the leap, though, and you'll get one of the city's outstanding underground poboy options. The Judge is a hefty, apparently hand-molded oblong patty made of three different ground meats—ground beef, Italian sausage and hot sausage. The ovoid patty spends a good amount of time on Johnny's busy grill, getting crispy in all the right places and greasy in all the others.

It seems that hand-mushing the meats is more of an art than a science, resulting in a chameleon of a sandwich. On first bite, you might mistake it for a juicy burger; the next might have a heady burst of fennel from the Italian sausage; a subtle burn of cayenne might dominate a few mouthfuls later. In a way, it's like playing Name That Tune with pre-ground meaty treats.

The Judge is one of the few specialty poboys at this French Quarter landmark, a no-frills eatery that locals seem more than happy to share with visitors from out of town. Open since 1950, a half-block off the Decatur Street tourist zone, Johnny's is a classic short-order establishment that maintains a good balance of French Quarter regulars and fresh-off-the-bus tourists. The layout couldn't be simpler—stand in line, order from the board, and wait for the cooks to scream your number above the din. Twenty or so tables. White vinyl tablecloths. Autographed glossies of Hal Linden and weather hunk Willard Scott with "real hair." You get the picture.

The menu has a few other offerings—eggs for the breakfast crowds, seafood platters, blue plates from red beans to chicken tenders—but the wide range of poboys, even if you *could* resist ordering the Judge, would keep you busy for quite a while. Whether you order the standard shrimp or the somewhat puzzling boudin version, they're all served slightly toasted, crunchy and filling. Light eaters might be overwhelmed by the standard size, but could team up with a friend and still leave stuffed.

INGREDIENT

Hot Sausage and Chaurice

When it comes to ordering poboys in New Orleans, you need to be specific. Before stepping up to the counter, make sure you can answer the question "hot or smoked?" when the cook puts pen to pad.

Smoked sausage is familiar enough—a firm pork link that's spent sometime over smoldering wood—but the term *hot sausage* can cause a little bit of confusion for newcomers. In New Orleans, this smooth-textured fresh pork product can be formed into patties or stuffed into links. The flavor has a spicy red pepper edge to it, and when it's formed into patties and griddle-fried, makes one of the city's trademark poboys. The patties get crispy around the edges, adding crunch and texture to the soft poboy bread. Heat from the pepper and the bright red grease play well against pungent Creole mustard and mayonnaise.

Some butchers form the sausage into links and call it *chaurice,* an essential ingredient in Creole gumbo (see page 42). Other butchers have different recipes for each, spicing hot sausage with cayenne and chaurice with jalapeño and garlic.

The Roast Beef Poboy

In a city awash in fresh local seafood, the roast beef poboy seems an unlikely specialty, but this meaty version of the big sandwich is a worthy obsession for many New Orleanians. Unlike deli meat poboys (ham and cheese, turkey, etc.), roast beef poboys are often served hot—meaning, of course, covered with a healthy dose of savory brown gravy—and usually dressed in the usual manner. The resulting sandwich is a magical, hearty mess of a meal sauced by a mixture of gravy and cool, rich mayonnaise. If you're averse to a sloppy sandwich, you'll do well to order something a bit more straightforward, as successful roast beef poboys are measured in napkins: the higher the count, the better the experience. Sloppiness can indeed be a virtue. It goes without saying that the better the meat and gravy, the better the poboy; joints renowned for their roast beef tend to spike it with garlic, cook it slow, and make gravy with the drippings. Beware the shop that pours bland microwaved gravy over cold sliced beef.

Recommendations

R&O's Pizza Place (page 140), Parasol's (page 167), Parkway Bakery and Tavern (see listing below)

Parkway Bakery and Tavern

538 Hagan Ave. (at Toulouse)
504-482-3047

zone: Midcity
reservations: none

meals: lunch and dinner daily
specialty: poboys
fancy factor: lowbrow
price range: $4–7

bonus points: outdoor seating, Hubig's for dessert

The week that he bought this then-dilapidated Midcity bar, Jay Nix put up a big sign that read WE'RE SAVING PARKWAY.

A contractor by trade and neighbor by proximity, Nix purchased the property out of concern for the neighborhood and connection to the past. Generations of locals had cut their teeth on Parkway's specialties—bread from its ovens, poboys from its kitchen and beer from the bar—since the joint opened up sometime in the early 1900s. Word on the street was that the building might become a liquor store, so Nix decided on a preemptive purchase plan, hoping that he could find someone to renovate and reopen the Bayou St. John landmark.

"I came out here every morning for about eight years and just looked at it," Nix remembers. "I had this raggedy teardown and couldn't get anybody to take it over. So I decided to do it myself."

"Besides, people kept asking me about the sign. 'When you gonna open? When you gonna open?' for eight years."

After six months of cleanup and renovation, Nix reopened the Parkway as something it hadn't been for years—a clean, well-lighted place for poboys.

Nix converted the run-down building into a rose-colored memory of the old place, with improvements that hark back to the Parkway's previous life. His new saloon-style bar, a design inspired by some of the classic French Quarter bars, blends in like it's been here all along. The footrest at its base foregoes the brass rail tradition and instead consists of a double row of firebrick from the old bread ovens out back. The décor does a fair amount of historical "bait and switch"—bottles of now-defunct local brews (Jax, Falstaff, Regal) sit atop the current lineup, 70s-era signs advertise Bud longnecks for a quarter, and the chalkboard menu lists tongue as one of a dozen poboy options.

The sandwiches, wrapped in white butcher paper and hefty for their size, are no-frills overstuffed beauties from the old school. Fried shrimp spill out of the sides on the first crackly bite; hot roast beef steams the bread to a perfect sloppy softness without reducing the crust to watery mush. But the hot sausage poboy is a true standout—thick patties of the usually squishy meat product are perfectly grill-seared, with the cooling mayo and lettuce harmonizing with the sausage's potent cayenne afterburn.

Nix also turned the vacant lot between his house and the bar into a dual-purpose space—a comfortable patio seating area and a paved parking lot. As the Parkway gained its footing, he began experimenting with family-friendly weekend music shows. "I close the parking lot gate and people just spread out. It's looks like a daycare out there," he says with a smile. Nothing, it seems, is more traditional than a neighborhood bar that welcomes the kiddies as well as their parents.

After the renovation was complete, Nix altered the sign and hung it proudly near the bar door. After a bit of simple Marks-a-lot work, the sign now reflects the barroom's renaissance: WE SAVED PARKWAY.

R&O's Pizza Place
216 Old Hammond Hwy.
504-831-1248

zone: Bucktown
reservations: none

meals: lunch and dinner Wed–Mon, closed Tues
specialty: poboys, seafood, pizza
fancy factor: lowbrow
price range: $7–20

caveats: closed Tuesday

Even though the lakefront neighborhood of Bucktown is a solid fifteen minutes' drive from my house, R&O's Pizza Place is usually the first place I drag hungry houseguests.

R&O's (not to be mistaken with its old-line homonym Arnaud's) is a dependable first-meal fallback if ever there was one, a valuable utility infielder that we use as a convenient introduction to the city, its geography and culinary variety.

Of course, by the time we're on the road, the crew is usually salivating uncontrollably, primed with the promise of an R&O's specialty: a heaping plate of the infamous gravy fries.

Cheese fries may be more of a bar food standard, but gravy fries will take you on the meat-and-potatoes ride of your life. A dish that sounds like a line cook's afterthought turns out to be the pinnacle of diner-level appetizer culture, delivered on oversized stoneware platters and coated with a thick layer of beefy shrapnel.

The fries alone— standard bigger-than-shoestring russets tipped with squares of dark potato skin—aren't particularly notable; it's the gravy that makes them sing. Chocolate-colored, studded with morsels of tender beef and a little on the salty side, R&O's standard "brown gravy" turns fries into a distinctive and addictive starter. The rich, chunk-style liquid pools in the bottom of the oversized oval platter, and for true gravy aficionados, the sopping and savoring begins after the crisp potatoes are polished off.

Equal parts seafood house, Creole Italian joint and poboy emporium, R&O's is loud, smoky and, despite violating every healthy child guideline ever printed in *Parenting* magazine, alive with a family-friendly vibe. The dining room recalls a time before animatronic birthday rats roamed the earth, when restaurants had to serve at least two generations at every table. Sweet waitresses tend to the wee ones and provide parents with stout cocktails and pitchers of beer. Institutional chairs and plywood tabletops are all but indestructible; the indoor/outdoor carpet has seen more spills than any kid could dish out before high-school graduation. Even the twitchiest parents relax, comfortable that their kids couldn't possibly compete with the room's clamor and high noise level.

The big room is usually packed with locals digging into huge portions of downmarket local classics—immense poboys, towering mounds of fried seafood, softball-sized artichokes stuffed with garlicky breadcrumbs.

It's possible, of course, to stop after gravy fries and beer, but it would be criminal not to dig further into the menu. Poboys served on lengths of crunchy Italian-style bread all benefit from a quick run under the broiler. In addition to providing that distinctive shatter-crisp crust, the broil caramelizes and firms up any gravy-based poboy: roast beef for the brown team; meatball, Italian sausage and soft-shell crab parmigiana for the red. Diners without a meat tooth can dig into light fried seafood that comes pretty damned close to sushi bar tempura.

We've never had a houseguest leave R&O's hungry, so the drive back to the city is usually punctuated with groans of overstuffed satisfaction.

Verti Marte

1201 Royal St. (at Governor Nicholls)
504-525-4767

zone: French Quarter
reservations: none

meals: round the clock
specialty: poboys and assorted drunkfood
fancy factor: lowbrow
price range: $4–9

caveats: don't wake the neighbors
bonus points: never closes, there when
you need it

Any kitchen can stay open 24 hours, but it takes a special one to become a bona fide temple of drunkfood.

Located in the quiet section of the Vieux Carré, the Verti Marte is a somewhat claustrophobic, approachably seedy takeaway establishment that never gave up its grocery-store roots. The busy kitchen hits its stride in the post-post-midnight hours and churns out an impressive range of cheap and satisfying fare—greasy, cheesy, saucy or crunchy; served on French bread or in transparent plastic containers; sweet, savory or salty. Whatever your post-crawl craving, the Verti Marte can usually satisfy it.

The Verti's wide list of options caters to various states of impairment—point-and-serve dishes liked cheesy au gratin potatoes or smothered cabbage speak to the visual crowd, while customized poboys favor those who can string their preferred list of ingredients into a coherent order.

One of my favorite poboys is an inspired Verti Marte classic: fried oysters with crispy bacon and cheddar, dressed.

The tender, subtly salty shellfish merges with crunchy cured pigflesh, a layer of iceberg and tomato; the whole megillah smoothed out with a layer of tangy cheese and a generous dollop of mayo. It's one of those combinations that could only be created by off-duty cooks midway through a post-shift bender.

For all its local fame, the Verti Marte has got to be a mixed blessing for its neighbors.

On the upside, there's the advantage of an outstanding 24-hour neighborhood grocery at walking-distance disposal. The benefit of a hardworking neighborhood kitchen that never shuts down; a deep poboy list, a cooler filled with prepared vegetable dishes and a full breakfast menu served anytime. Free delivery in the French Quarter and the nearby Faubourg Marigny.

On the downside, there's the constant stream of night owls who seek out this renowned drunkfood destination. Wobbly crews of eighth-round bar hoppers seeking a little early morning sustenance. Marathon pub crawlers who manage to turn any horizontal surface into a nocturnal picnic area.

Now, I'm not saying that you'd do this stuff *yourself*, mind you, but for the sake of neighborhood harmony, take your macaroni and cheese away from the Marte before you start oohing and aaaahing over its ballast-providing magic. Poboy lovers are a bit luckier, since they can munch and moan in motion.

Whatever your pleasure, be respectful of the temple so it'll be there the next time you need to make a late-night pilgrimage. Otherwise, you might just have to settle for slice pizza or Neon Zone slider-burgers, and nobody really wants that, do they?

creole ITALIAN

*W*hen a wave of Sicilian immigrants arrived in the late 1800s, they brought their food and traditions with them. The new arrivals settled in the French Quarter, and within forty years turned the waning Creole neighborhood into an ethnic stronghold commonly referred to as "Little Sicily" or "Little Palermo."

Today, you can taste the influence of this Italian population in New Orleans' neighborhood cuisine . Meatball poboys drenched with a garlicky "red gravy" (marinara sauce) are a staple throughout the city, as are gargantuan muffuletta sandwiches topped with tangy olive salad. Artichokes stuffed with seasoned breadcrumbs appear on many local menus. Decades before the New American movement had chefs hyphenating every possible combination of ethnic cuisines, the term "Creole-Italian" was already part of New Orleans' culinary lexicon.

These restaurants are a testament to the persistence of this Italian influence and how strongly the Sicilians contributed to the evolution of New Orleans cuisine.

Central Grocery
923 Decatur St. (at St. Philip)
504-523-1620

zone: French Quarter
reservations: none

meals: lunch daily
specialty: muffuletta
fancy factor: lowbrow
price range: $6–10

caveats: closes 5:30 PM
bonus points: good grab-n-go

With the neighboring Progress Grocery replaced by yet another high-markup Mardi Gras bead emporium, Central Grocery is the last of the Decatur Street muffuletta destinations; an endangered species that keeps on kicking despite overwhelming schlock incursion in the lower Vieux Carré.

As befits the last of a breed, Central Grocery seems unchanged with time—shelves full of bulk olive oil, boxes of imported pasta, kilo packages of marinated baby octopus, Parmigiano Reggiano by the wedge. In an era of updated specialty markets, this is still an old-style Italian grocery.

After looking around the well-stocked shelves (two-quart cans of clam juice, Louisiana hot sauces, Italian cookies) you order a muffuletta by the fraction (half, whole), add a quart jar of their famous olive salad, then eat while standing at the white Formica bar or, as many do, head

for Armstrong International for your outbound flight. A handwritten red cardboard sign answers the perennial question: Yes, indeed "Muffuletta sandwiches are cut and wrapped to travel already." The sandwich comes tightly wrapped in plastic and taped butcher paper.

Central Grocery's muffuletta is considered the classic—a circular loaf packed with layers of Genoa salami, thin-sliced ham, soft provolone and *mortadella*, a cousin of American baloney. Then a generous helping of oily olive salad fragrant with garlic and chunky with crunchy chopped vegetables. These days, the sandwich makers do a lot of construction in between rushes, stocking up on pre-wrapped sandwiches for the airport crowds. The practice has its up and down sides: on the bright side, a pre-made sandwich has plenty of time for the tasty oil to permeate the Italian loaf's dry crumb; on the not-so-bright, a tight wrapper compresses the fillings together, making it tough to appreciate the different flavors in each bite. You can fix this, of course, by separating the layers before your first bite, a ritual that never fails to get a few sideways glances from your fellow diners. The texture of the final sandwich, though, is worth it. To hell with 'em.

While you're at the counter, load up on a couple of 2-pound jars of olive salad. Not so much for making your own muffulettas (the bread is tough to replicate outside the city), but for glopping on hot pasta for quick weeknight meals. On your inaugural trip to New Orleans, you might haul one home. Seasoned veterans often allow extra room in their carry-on luggage for multiples.

Truth be told, many customers buy these pre-wrapped muffulettas with the best intentions—aromatic gifts for New Orleanians in exile or fans of traditional cold cuts—only to rip through the butcher paper halfway to the airport. If you're cabbing it into town from Armstrong, check the floorboards for telltale sesame seeds.

Eleven79

1179 Annunciation St. (at Erato)
504-299-1179

zone: Garden District
reservations: recommended

meals: lunch Thu–Fri, dinner Mon–Sat
specialty: Italian
fancy factor: high-middlebrow
price range: $23–33

caveats: hidden
bonus points: intimate

There was a time in New Orleans when the term "warehouse district" didn't mean upscale loft condominiums, spacious art galleries and hipster-heavy wine bars. It meant industrial service companies, deserted cobblestone alleys and . . . well . . . warehouses.

Eleven79, a decidedly upscale Italian eatery, sits in the quasi-industrial warehouse district that's officially part of the Lower Garden District. Secluded and unassuming, Eleven79 has the feel of a hidden mafia clubhouse; a bit of Sinatra's Hoboken in the shadow of the Mississippi River Bridge.

Inside, the crowd seems dominated by the downtown's executive class, who roam the dimly lit, clubby room and its bustling adjacent bar. At lunch, the emphasis is on leisurely business meals; legal pads stained with olive oil droplets and wineglass rings. At night, the smallish dining room plays host to trysts and celebrations; tight quarters make weeknight meals better for romance.

The straightforward Italian menu ignores the upscale *trattoria* trend with red-sauce pastas, veal variations up the wazoo and a few buttery seafood dishes for good measure. But impeccable sauces elevate these seemingly simple dishes to sublime levels: veal saltimbocca's Marsala-laced cream and garlicky butter sauce on barbecued shrimp can make the shellfish seem optional. An outstanding juicy rosemary chicken drizzled with savory demi-glace might well be the best upscale poultry dish in town. Prices can seem steep but dinner portions are definitely oversized— a half order of pasta makes a generous side for two diners.

Irene's Cuisine

539 St. Philip St. (at Chartres)
504-529-8811

zone: French Quarter
reservations: none

meals: dinner daily
specialty: Creole Italian
fancy factor: high-middlebrow
price range: $16–20

caveats: hidden, no reservations
bonus points: piano lounge

Tommy's Cuisine

746 Tchoupitoulas St. (at Notre Dame)
504-581-1103

zone: CBD/Warehouse
reservations: accepted

meals: dinner daily
specialty: Creole Italian
fancy factor: high-middlebrow
price range: $16–20

caveats: low light
bonus points: takes reservations

If you don't know the backstory, it's easy to mistake these two Creole-Italian restaurants for halves of a familial micro-chain: a successful French Quarter Creole-Italian and its newer spinoff in the up-and-coming Warehouse District. After all, the atmospheres seem complimentary in a traditional east coast kind of way, the offerings seem to have plenty of overlap, the casual, familiar vibes mesh perfectly. Everything seems to fit together.

That is, of course, if you don't know about the split that separated the fortunes of restaurateurs Irene DiPietro and Tommy Andrade, the couple behind Irene's Cuisine in the French Quarter.

Even though Irene's is smack-dab in the middle of the Quarter, it remains a classic local's haunt. The room at Irene's is a throwback that suggests a pre-touristy time in the Vieux Carré. With chaotically decorated walls and tall ceilings, the narrow dining spaces are intimate without feeling the least bit cramped. Pictures of regulars, Italian-American icons and a mystery nun line the walls. Mandolin tunes alternate with the smooth tones of Vic Damone on the soundtrack in a room made for evenings of romantic relaxation.

Irene's maintains a solid reputation for classic Creole-Italian cuisine. Shellfish dominate the starter list with oysters Irene—baked oyster on the half shell with savory pancetta/romano topping—taking well-deserved top billing. A short-ish list of entrées mixes Continental metaphors with excellent results. An ethereal soft-shell crab floats in a light-bodied crawfish/parmesan cream, while the trademark rosemary chicken packs a subtly sweet punch of roasted garlic. End with another hybrid knockout—a foster-sauced bread pudding with sautéed bananas and ice cream—or a letter-perfect tiramisu.

The couple ran the restaurant for years, until a marital rift forced Mr. Andrade to opened up his eponymous restaurant on a now-booming stretch of Tchoupitoulas, taking much of the menu, the vibe and the details with him; an Uptown déjà vu for regulars of the original and a textbook case of cross-town culinary cloning.

Comparing the two menus, some dishes differ in name only, if at all. The flavorful oysters Tommy, not so coincidentally, are topped with pancetta and romano. A light fried soft-shell crab with a light crawfish-tomato cream (another clone) also shines in new digs. Heady and sweet, a port demi-glace highlights outstanding seared lamb chops—small enough to qualify as a dainty entrée or finger food for hands-on carnivores.

Breakups are always tough, but in this particular case the dining public benefits quite directly from the couple's commercial separation. The best we can do, as friends and customers, is order up oysters and garlicky chicken and let the healing begin.

Artichokes

These woody vegetables still play a large part in Creole-Italian cuisine, even though they're no longer widely grown in Louisiana. Sicilian immigrants used the hearty vegetable in numerous dishes that have become part of the neighborhood Creole canon. In the summer or fall, the heart is cooked into creamy soups featuring shrimp or oysters. A few neighborhood restaurants (Liuzza's, Franky and Johnny's and R&O's Pizza Place) serve massive artichokes packed with garlicky bread crumbs.

At one time in the city's history, artichokes were so popular that huge farms were planted with the thistle-like plants. The land that comprises much of the modern-day Warehouse District was once an artichoke plantation.

Presently, however, artichokes are trucked in from California farms. There are a few farmers growing the plant in Tangipahoa Parish, but it's tough for local farmers to compete with the larger out-of-state farms. "Our artichoke farms are gone now," says Richard McCarthy, director of the Crescent City Farmers' Market, "but they've left an important footprint on our local menus."

Mosca's
4137 Hwy. 90 W.
Avondale, LA
504-436-8950

zone: Outtatown
reservations: recommended

meals: dinner Tues–Sat, closed Sun–Mon
specialty: family-style Creole Italian
fancy factor: low-middlebrow
price range: $25–35

caveats: a hell of a drive
bonus points: convivial atmosphere,
    legendary specialties

It's a forty-minute drive to get to Mosca's, but that's exactly what makes it an adventure. Literally over the river and through the woods, this nondescript roadhouse sits beside a deserted highway outside of Avondale in rural Jefferson Parish and since the 1940s, New Orleanians have made the swampside trek for home-style Italian cuisine and a dose of local legend.

According to the widely accepted lore, Mosca's (pronounced MOW-ska's) was the favorite restaurant of reputed mafia boss Carlos Marcello—and the retelling of classic mob stories is a kind of sport among regulars. Rumor has it that the Mosca's founder, Profino Mosca, cooked for Al Capone (an unconfirmed report that Mosca's son Johnny, the current owner, likes to keep alive) and relocated to become Marcello's personal chef. There are stories of bodies dumped in the swamps or sudden power outages causing the whole dining room to hit the floor in anticipation of gunfire. Each performance varies slightly and concludes with the qualifier "Swear to God." Factual or not, each telling adds to the joint's reputation and seedy charm.

On the weekends, the place packs with enthusiastic crowds from New Orleans and the Jefferson Parish suburbs—usually older couples willing to brave the narrow, shoulderless Huey P. Long bridge and traverse the marshy Avondale roads. (Again, it's part of the adventure.) Inside, the atmosphere is all roadhouse—happy regulars waiting their turn in the front room, swigging cocktails and red wine from thick glass tumblers, yelling over Louie Prima party tunes. Owner Johnny Mosca works the bar and tries to keep the crowds at bay as the tables turn.

The food is exactly what you'd expect from a reputed mafia joint—huge portions of simple Italian dishes, heavy on the garlic and served on huge family-style platters. The house specialties aren't particularly complex: chicken à la grande is a take on baked garlic rosemary chicken; house-made sausages with roasted potatoes soaked in olive oil; oysters baked in a pie plate with breadcrumbs and garlic; iceberg salads topped with a layer of marinated crabmeat. Just about every dish carries a distinctive sheen of olive oil and the heady scent of garlic.

One of the greatest dishes isn't even on the menu—a plate full of gimmes for regulars, friends of regulars or folks willing to wait a long time for a table. Tiny crab claws are pre-cracked and marinated in wine vinegar, Worcestershire and raw garlic. The perfect nugget of moist claw meat clings to the blunt end, insanely delicious and off-limits to the general public.

The Mosca's experience, with its long travel requirement and huge portions, favors larger groups and good timing. Larger groups can make reservations from Tuesday to Friday, though Saturday nights are strictly first-come first-served. Off-peak eating (Tuesday–Thursday) can leave you without the convivial vibe, the bellowing laughter from both rooms—which contributes to the clubhouse atmosphere.

When the kitchen's on, all is right with the world and the feast seems worth the journey. But on the nights when the signature dishes falter—oysters are shriveled and tough, chicken cooked to the texture of oily jerky—you can't help but feel a bit cheated. Those are the nights when you concentrate on the adventure—the trip back in time—and hope the echoes of Mr. Prima can sooth you on the long ride home.

Pascal's Manale
1838 Napoleon Ave. (at Dryades)
504-895-4877

zone: Uptown
reservations: accepted

meals: lunch Mon-Fri, dinner nightly
specialty: barbecue shrimp, Creole Italian

CLASSIC

Barbecue Shrimp

Saucy instead of smoky, this classic Creole-Italian seafood dish has been a New Orleans standard since the 1950s, when it first showed up on the menu of Pascal's Manale (page 148) on Napoleon Avenue. Whole shrimp—heads on and shells attached—are baked in a hot butter sauce spiced with copious amounts of black pepper, Worcestershire sauce, lemon juice and a little garlic. Usually served in a wide soup plate, the dish is a full-contact eating experience that's been a boon for local dry cleaners over the years. The shrimp have to be shelled by the diner, resulting in accidental butter sloshes and finger-licking cleanup. When all the shrimp are gone, you've got the pure goodness of buttery sauce just begging to be soaked up with a hand-torn morsel of crusty French bread.

According to most accounts, the original barbecue shrimp was an oven-based recipe that called for shallow pan baking—a process still followed at Pascal's. (Slow-smoke purists take note: the name allegedly comes from what the cooks *thought* barbecue would taste like. So relax.) This classic preparation became popular with home cooks, especially during the peak of shrimp season when the crustacean is plentiful and cheap in local markets.

But diners familiar with other restaurant versions of the dish might think of a different aesthetic when it comes to barbecue shrimp: heavier on the garlic, tinted dark brown with Worcestershire, and smelling ever so slightly of rosemary. The texture of the sauce is more consistent than the baked version, with the buttery sauce holding as a smooth emulsion.

This particular variation allegedly came from the kitchen of K-Paul's in its early days, when Prudhomme and his staff were looking to adapt the traditional recipe to the single-portion requirements of a busy restaurant line. The result was a quick pan sauce fortified with Worcestershire sauce, shrimp stock, a little beer and plenty of garlic—all cooked to order in a single sauté pan. This much darker version of the dish has since become the standard in most New Orleans restaurants.

Contemporary chefs have reinterpreted barbecued shrimp in various ways— replacing the butter with olive oil, substituting Asian chili and garlic sauces for the black pepper and—in what seems like heresy to traditionalists—using pre-shelled instead of the unpeeled shrimp for the sake of cleanliness. The latter seems to make its way to plenty of appetizer lists, but be forewarned: if you're not peeling your own, you miss the essence of this finger-lickin' New Orleans classic.

fancy factor: low-middlebrow
price range: $12–26

caveats: summer closed Sun
bonus points: parking lot, great oyster bar

If you grew up in metropolitan New Orleans, odds are the barbecued shrimp at Pascal's Manale looks and tastes most like the dish that your mama made in her home kitchen. Huge, heads-on shrimp languishing in a deep pool of drawn but-

Muffulettas

In a town known for its plentiful poboy joints, this mammoth Sicilian sandwich often gets overshadowed by its oblong, overstuffed cousin, but this doesn't lessen its status as one of New Orleans' outstanding culinary achievements. It's a lowbrow specialty to be sure, but inside every oversized, crunchy bite is edible evidence of New Orleans' proud Italian heritage.

The classic muffuletta starts with a round loaf of coarse-crumbed Italian bread about ten inches in diameter. This oversized flattened disk is cut in half heightwise, and the bottom "slice" is brushed with fruity olive oil. Next come layers of hearty, delicatessen-style meats and cheese—fragrant Genoa salami, layers of Swiss and provolone, smooth-textured mortadella and delicate shavings of ham.

But before final "press and cut" assembly, the top of the giant seeded bread is ladled with a generous helping of "olive salad"—the muffuletta's trademark condiment with a simple name and complex nature. Essentially antipasto in a jar, the basic formula calls for crushed olives (green and Kalamata), various pickled vegetables (celery, cauliflower chunks, crinkle-cut rounds of carrot, sliced sweet pepperoncini) and plenty of garlic, capers and slivers of red pimento. Each maker seems to introduce signature flavors with the addition of herbs and spices—most often oregano, parsley and more garlic—into an olive-oil base. The ingredients marinate and mix their flavors, resulting in a mélange of tastes that hits every part of the mouth and sets your nasal passages free. Tangy, salty and full of complex flavors, it's the olive salad that keeps the muffuletta from being a Frisbee-shaped poboy with a Mediterranean pedigree.

Most histories of the sandwich (none are definitive) trace their origins back to family-run Italian groceries of the French Quarter (along Decatur Street, specifically) around the turn of the twentieth century. The muffuletta has its roots in these markets, which served the burgeoning population of mostly Sicilian immigrants who flocked to New Orleans during the latter half of the 1800s. By 1910, the French Quarter's Italian community flourished, making up 80 percent of the Quarter's population, and though the neighborhood's current ethnic makeup is decidedly different, the muffuletta hasn't changed much since the turn of the last century.

Just saying the word "muffuletta" can get tricky because of a tomato/tomahto split among locals. Sure, it might *look* like "muff-uh-LET-ta," but diehard counter folk might correct you to the preferred local version: "muff-uh-LOTT-a."

ter fragrant with garlic and finely powdered black pepper. The simple unpeeled presentation means that utensils won't do you much good here—you'll need nimble fingers and a disposable bib if you want to avoid greasy droplets on your shirtfront.

In a rare concurrence of local food historians, this Creole-Italian restaurant is where the oddly named dish was first prepared. Sometime in the 1950s a diner named Vincent Sutro, yearning for a dish that he once tasted in Chicago, asked chef Jake Radosta to improvise a version. Next thing you know, it's a fifty-year tradition and Pascal's logo features a happy go lucky shrimp playing a concertina and sporting a Tyrolean yodeler's hat.

In business since 1913, Pascal's Manale has had a great run on an oak-shaded stretch of Napoleon Avenue. Originally named for owner Frank Manale, the restaurant was purchased by his nephew Pascal Radosta in the 1930s and added his name to the sign. Pascal's (or Manale's—people refer to it as either) shows its layers of history in its various dining rooms: one looks like a grandmother's parlor, another an early-60s shrine to the Saints.

The crowd seems to skew toward long-time regulars and tourists steered here by well-meaning concierges. On a busy night it's like simultaneously stepping into someone else's childhood memory and a random regional sales conference.

The best seats in the house are in the dark, moody front bar. Immediately inside the doorway, busy shuckers work away at one of the most atmospheric stand-up oyster bars in town. It always takes a while to get a dozen ready to go, but the shuckers are quick with the ban-

ter and the selection of autographed celebrity pictures goes on forever—Cyndi Lauper, Ernest Borgnine, Jack Dempsey, Bear Bryant, a young Abigail Van Buren, Merv Griffin and the guy who played Doogie Howser's dad. Where else can you find show-biz personalities of this caliber in one place?

The bar is also a good place to order up a version of the house's signature dish in poboy form. It's not quite the peel-and-eat experience you'd heard about, but it's more economical than the pricy entrée serving and you're closer to the oysters. And besides, you can munch away without the bib as TV funnyman Jack Carter smiles down upon you.

Rocky and Carlo's
613 W. St. Bernard Hwy.
Chalmette, LA
504-279-8323

zone: Outtatown

meals: breakfast, lunch and dinner daily
specialty: Italian bar food
fancy factor: lowbrow
price range: $8–15

caveats: loooong drive from the city
bonus points: portions MUCH larger than your head

When certain locals *really* want to get out of New Orleans, they point the car toward Rocky and Carlo's, a blue-collar Italian bar in industrial Chalmette, Louisiana. The 30-minute drive out to neighboring St. Bernard Parish (locally known as "Da Parish") shows a different side of southeast Louisiana. Highway 47 takes you past chemical refineries instead of suburbs, shrimp docks instead of strip malls.

Rocky and Carlo's sits across the road from steam-belching industrial smokestacks and serves a jumpsuit-clad crowd of on-break or off-duty shift workers; the front windows marked with the somewhat unexpected invitation LADIES INVITED. The huge room feels like an institutional church hall: open kitchen to the rear, long tables on terrazzo floor, poster of the Pope gesturing from the Masonite-paneled wall. A long bar, worn from years of use, hugs the left wall. If you need rosaries made of lucky Sicilian fava beans (shellacked and some painted with the face of Christ), they're on sale near the register.

As you'd kinda assume, the fare and portions here run simple and gargantuan, respectively. The kitchen's steam tables are laden with five or so specials of the day—red beans, chicken parmesan, stuffed bell peppers, fried chicken—with poboys and signature sides always available. In an area known for ample portions, Rocky and Carlo's reigns supreme: an $8 lunch can feed three average-capacity diners; a single order of crispy/sweet onion rings weighs well over a pound.

Fans of the joint routinely crow about Rocky and Carlo's roast beef poboys, red-sauced dishes and house specialty macaroni and cheese, but unfortunately the standouts tend to be a lot bigger than they are tasty. The roast beef poboy measures well over a foot long but requires plenty of salt and Crystal to make it flavorful. The chicken parmesan is cooked down in a watery red sauce, making for tender meat but a goopy fried coating. The best of the lot is the mac and cheese, served up in huge plates and drenched in your choice of red or brown gravy. Creamy and comforting, it's a childhood cafeteria favorite served with a beer on the side as a young John Paul II blesses you from across the room.

seafood HOUSES

New Orleans seafood houses often got their starts as casual two-trick ponies tied directly to the local fishing culture—serving fresh-boiled seafood during the peak seasons and fried variations year-round. Dependable, family friendly, and pretty much shockproof, these no-nonsense eateries play to big crowds with bigger appetites; easily accommodating raucous multifamily gatherings and beer swilling post-softball-game celebrations.

Even though some of the bigger names have moved into the city, the lakeside neighborhood of Bucktown—just across the Jefferson Parish line on the shores of Lake Pontchartrain—is the traditional home of these welcoming, unfussy seafood joints.

Bozo's Seafood

3117 21st St. (at Causeway Access Rd.)
Metairie, LA
504-831-8666

zone: Metairie
reservations: none

meals: lunch and dinner Tues-Sat, closed
 Sun–Mon
specialty: fried seafood, hamburgers
fancy factor: lowbrow
price range: $10–17

caveats: no reservations
bonus points: good oyster bar

If you find yourself wandering lost through Metairie's suburban backstreets, here's the way to find Bozo's: it looks like an aging dentist's office instead of a seafood house. There's no visible signage, no circus motif, no gigantic neon oyster that attracts drive-by traffic on the northbound Causeway overpass. Despite violating the realtor's ironclad rule of success ("location, location, location"), this oyster bar institution draws serious oyster-hungry crowds. Most dentists couldn't pack two parking lots during the Saturday lunch rush.

Opened in 1928, Bozo's migrated from its original location in Midcity sometime in the 1980s—leaving New Orleans for the promise of the suburbs. In its previous life, the joint served hungry crowds from the nearby Fairgrounds horse track; nowadays the Vodanovich family serves its famous shellfish to a mostly suburban clientele. Current chef Chris Vodanovich, who goes by the moniker "Chef Bozo," is the second generation to hold the title, the nickname and the keys to the kitchen.

CLASSIC

The Seafood Platter

Scanning the menu of an average New Orleans seafood house, it's hard to resist the siren call of the combination seafood platter. For the uninitiated, there's a compelling logic to the "little bit of everything" philosophy—shrimp, oysters, catfish, soft-shelled crab—with the only obstacle being a hefty price tag (about twenty bucks in most places).

But here's the thing: a traditional New Orleans seafood platter isn't a "little bit of everything" proposition. You get a LOT of everything. It's a mountain of deep fried goodness so packed with shrimp, fish filets and fries that it can't help but go vertical. The rounded nuggets—oysters and hush puppies—are strategically placed around the crunchy foundation, and the growing tower is often crowned with a fried soft-shell crab reaching for the sky.

It's pretty safe to say that these platters, even though listed as a single menu item, could feed two to four average eaters. To polish one off solo, you'd better be a Guinness-level endurance eater or championship sumo wrestler—or both.

As is the tradition in local Croatian-owned restaurants, oysters are the stars here—plump and cold on the half shell or fried in a toasty cornmeal crust—but the delectable fried catfish filets give the bivalves a solid run for their money. The kitchen is serious about its frying—each high-traffic product (shrimp, oyster, catfish, fries) gets its own station (fryer, skillet or stovetop pot) to eliminate murky mixed-oil flavors.

Any meal at Bozo's starts off with addictive loaves of French bread, thoroughly buttered and fresh-broiled to a shattering crunch. Like hot-from-the-oil tortilla chips at a Tex-Mex restaurant, this complimentary starter can quickly become an accidental obsession as you call for basket after basket of the airy/rich treat.

Bozo's has been in its new location almost twenty years—plenty of time for local families to build their traditions around the suburban incarnation without ever knowing the original. Saturday lunch is a perfect time to see traditions in action. Twelve-seat tables packed with three generations from bent grandfathers to toddlers in high chairs, older siblings barely able to keep their seats. And scattered around the room, middle-aged men taking their mamas out for a nice midday meal; each staring into opposite directions, silent except for the crunching of crispy toast.

Crabby Jack's

428 Jefferson Hwy. (Between Knox Road and Dakin St.)
504-833-2722

zone: Metairie
website: www.jacquesimoscafe.com
reservations: none

meals: lunch Mon–Sat, closed Sun
specialty: eclectic Louisiana seafood
fancy factor: lowbrow
price range: $5–12

caveats: lunch only, wait times during peak service; specials can run out, large groups problematic, kind of a schlep
bonus points: quick seating, huge portions, parking lot

With so many good seafood restaurants in New Orleans, why exactly would anyone drive out to an industrial section of Jefferson Parish for lunch?

The two-word answer would be "Crabby Jack's"; expand it to three and it becomes "Jacques-Imo's Junior." Looking at the menu, fans of Jack Leonardi will see a distinct family resemblance: Crabby Jack's does double duty as the off-site commissary (bare-bones kitchen and prep zone) for the Uptown favorite and a lunchtime destination in its own right.

It doesn't look like much from the road—a small plate-glass room on the front of the all-aluminum Louisiana Seafood Exchange—but inside, this workaday lunch counter delivers with outstanding fried seafood and daily specials showing the creativity that made Jacques-Imo's consistently wait-worthy.

Seating can be tight; a familiar line of waiting workers from nearby Oschner Hospital, area construction sites and downtown offices give it a somewhat clamorous vibe. The setup doesn't make many accommodations for privacy—a wall-length Formica bar and a long, unbroken island of tables occupy most of the available floor space, and often force communal dining. But once seated, conversation won't be the midday priority. You'll be lucky to have time to breathe.

Many of the dozen or so whiteboard specials will seem familiar to Jacques-Imo's fans—fried green tomato salad topped with a tangy shrimp remoulade, a generous hunk of blackened Gulf fish topped with spicy hollandaise, Austin Leslie's famous fried chicken—priced at more than reasonable lunchtime rates. The portions are still huge, but manageable compared to Jacques-Imo's generous overkill.

There are also "permanent specials" on the poboy list that locals crave and can get nowhere else. Sandwiches filled with gravy-drenched stewed duck or crispy fried rabbit are both set off with the pronounced burn of coarse-grained Creole mustard. In a nod to Jazzfest and Cajun smokehouse traditions, the list can sometimes contain a *cochon de lait* (suckling pig) poboy packed with chunks of tender smoked pork that some say is the best barbecue in town. Though these seem a bit pricy for "just a poboy," remind yourself that they're anything but simple.

Fried seafood fans won't be disappointed at the selection or quality of the standard plate and sandwich selections. Tender catfish filets hit the table still sizzling. Shrimp and calamari are cooked to the perfect stage of doneness. But then, what else would you expect from the front room of a seafood market?

If you're on your way home or are simply craving a few pounds of boiled crawfish to go with your meal, CJ's is also a "pack and go" seafood market with many of the featured fish—fresh from the Gulf—displayed proudly in a well-iced case.

Weekday lunch rushes make for a bit of a mob scene, so skew late to guarantee a sit-down dining experience. The only tradeoff here is that a late arrival cuts your chances at the daily specials—but even if the duck or rabbit poboys are all gone, there will be plenty of other tasty temptations to explore.

Deanie's Seafood

841 Iberville St. (at Dauphine)
504-581-1316

1713 Lake Ave. (at Metairie Hammond Hwy.)
Metairie, LA
504-831-4141

zone: French Quarter or Bucktown
website: www.deanies.com
reservations: none

meals: lunch and dinner daily
specialty: fried and boiled seafood
fancy factor: lowbrow, low-middlebrow
price range: $12–19

caveats: no reservations

When Deanie's opened up their new place on Iberville Street, they brought a little bit of Lake Pontchartrain tradition

with them. After all, if there were a million mid-market seafood houses in the French Quarter, why shouldn't a Bucktown crew have a crack at all those free-flowing tourist dollars?

The French Quarter Deanie's has a few more frills than its predecessor. Of course, that wouldn't take much, since the Bucktown Deanie's is currently housed in a utilitarian aluminum building a few blocks from the lakeshore. The new place has a classic New Orleans feel to it, with a prominent bar breaking up the single cavernous room.

The menu has the same selection as the original location with seasonal boiled seafood, raw oysters, a few salads and, of course, the legendary Bucktown-style fried seafood platter piled high with golden brown catfish filets, oysters,

shrimp and French fries, topped off with a soft-shell crab reaching for the sky. (Words to the wise: the "half platter" could easily feed three. The $40 "full platter" might require your waiter to maneuver a forklift to your table.)

In the interest of diversity, there are also a few other seafood standards on the list (crawfish étouffée, cheesy crabmeat au gratin, huge buttery barbecue shrimp). And of course, if you're really craving some greens, they offer a few salads, including a fried oyster spinach version for the half-heartedly health-conscious.

Boiled seafood (crabs, shrimp and crawfish) are all listed on the menu as "market price." Get a firm number before ordering and you'll avoid the possibility of after-meal sticker shock.

CLASSIC

Boiled Seafood

Just about every diet-conscious diner headed for New Orleans looks to boiled seafood as delicious penance for their other mealtime sins—most of which will be deep fried, slathered with mayonnaise, soaked in butter or a combination of all three. Three of

Louisiana's major seafood catches—crawfish in spring, crab in summer and shrimp in summer and fall—are awfully damned tasty boiled or steamed with aromatic spices and a healthy shot of fiery peppers, usually served in a "peel it yourself" environment.

But if you're going to be ordering from the boiled side of the menu, you should be familiar with two critical phrases: IN SEASON and MARKET PRICE. It's a simple economic concept—seafood is freshest and best when it's cheapest and vice versa. More than any other cooking technique, boiling seafood requires fresh, in-season ingredients. In the case of crawfish and crabs, this means live, healthy animals plucked from local waters, so get in the habit of asking about your dinner's home address. Once the critters have to be trucked in from other areas—summertime crawfish can come from ponds in California—the price goes up as the quality goes down. Be aware that just because they have it *on hand* doesn't mean it's *in season*—you might end up paying dearly for tiny, tasteless crustaceans.

Middendorf's

30160 US Hwy 51
Ponchatoula, LA
985-386-6666

zone: Outtatown
reservations: none

meals: lunch and dinner Tues–Sun
specialty: fried catfish
fancy factor: lowbrow
price range: $9–17

caveats: long drive

When Middendorf's kitchen is on its game, one mouthful of fried catfish justifies the long drive from the city.

A bite of the thin, yellowish filet yields to the teeth with a pliable crunch, then melts onto your tongue with a flavor of toasted cornmeal and salt. The fish flesh beneath the soft yet crispy crust maintains an ideal amount of moisture—not too dry, not too gooey—and a palate-tender consistency. Dipped in homemade tartar sauce or munched obsessively out of a Styrofoam "go box," it's perfect fried catfish, deserving of its multigenerational local following.

A destination seafood house since 1934, Middendorf's draws a consistent crowd despite the fact that it's a 30-mile round trip off Interstate 10—the main artery between New Orleans and the western reaches of south Louisiana. This simple seafood house is a deep-fried version of Mosca's—a far-flung restaurant that New Orleans locals proudly claim as one of their own, as if the tiny fishing town on the western edge of Lake Pontchartrain qualifies as metropolitan Bucktown.

Some people head out to Middendorf's for a full-blown sit-down meal—a dark-wood and Formica experience with waitresses who seem evenly split between perky, high-school-age local gals and their sixty-something mothers. Others just grab a hot box of catfish for a filling on-the-road snack. Either way, the place does so much business that the owners opened up a second location a few doors down to handle overflow during the busy summer season.

It's the restaurant's way of cutting catfish that makes the final product so distinctive. A standard-width catfish filet is carefully cut into slabs a scant $1/16$–$1/8$ inch thick, then lightly dusted with a seasoned corn-flour fish fry and thrown into hot oil. Fresh from the fryer, the filets almost look like aquatic potato chips—

folded over themselves in irregular ways and piled in a tall, luscious heap on a simple white platter or packed into a Styrofoam container.

The traditional deep-fried sides are mostly an afterthought: tiny, onion-flecked hush puppies have a hard, savory crunch; missable seafood house fries and coleslaw fill out the traditional three fried and one green configuration.

Hit Middendorf's during an off shift and the easily overcooked house specialty can be all crunch with jerky-tough fish underneath. The slightest frypit miscalculation can result in dry fish and a most disappointing journey back to the city. But if you get a batch that's bite after bite of melt-in-your-mouth perfection, you'll dream of the stuff and hope that your next trip out will mark another good day at Middendorf's.

Sid-Mar's of Bucktown
1824 Orpheum Ave. (at Metairie Hammond Hwy.)
Metairie, LA
504-831-9541

zone: Bucktown
website: www.sidmarsofbucktown.com
reservations: none

meals: lunch and dinner Tues–Sun
specialty: fried and boiled seafood
fancy factor: lowbrow
price range: $5.25–$21.95

caveats: closed all holidays
bonus points: outdoor dining/waiting
    area, lake views

Talk to any local about Bucktown seafood houses and you're likely to get a response that's based mostly on family tradition. As long as the portions are huge and reasonably priced, the phrase "it's where we always went" determines where they eat out at the lake.

Sid-Mar's has a leg up on a lot of the lakefront competition when it comes to ambience, since it's one of few with an actual waterfront atmosphere. Park in front of the building and you'll nose your car near the 17th Street Canal boat moorings. Meander back to the patio waiting area and you'll get a partial view of Lake Pontchartrain as you wait for a table.

As you'd expect, seafood reigns at Sid-Mar's, though they've got plenty of meaty poboy and sandwich options, just in case. Towering seafood platters practically block out the sun. The boiled selection shows that they're serious about their shellfish—crabs are offered individually or by the dozen in three different sizes. Choose your size and your portion, then get cracking.

The inside dining room is about as straightforward as it gets—beige on beige, an enclosed wraparound porch for additional seating. But if you're in the mood for a trip outside the city and an excuse to smell the brackish water of the lake while sipping a few beers, it might be the perfect place. And of course, if you grew up eating at the lake, you're probably already halfway there.

St. Roch Market
2381 St. Claude Ave. (at St. Roch)
504-943-5778

zone: Bywater
reservations: none

meals: lunch and dinner daily
specialty: seafood poboys

fancy factor: lowbrow
price range: $2–9

caveats: lowbrow seafood market
bonus points: cheeeeeap!

By just about any measure imaginable, St. Roch's Market is a dump.

Now that's not to say that this Bywater landmark isn't without merit—it's got rich history, gritty authenticity and good food—it's just, shall we say, not for everyone. In the words of Tom Waits, "For those who love adventure, perhaps . . ."

And if "adventure" includes solid fried seafood, all the better.

Long before at-home refrigeration was a plug-and-play affair, the market was an open-air vending space named for its downriver neighborhood. In 1937, it was deemed important enough to merit a full renovation from FDR's Works Progress Administration, and the modern-day St. Roch Market was born. Photos from the WPA era show modern, sanitary fish stalls and butcher's counters, concrete floors instead of dirt, cast-iron columns built to endure—the newly-renovated promise of a new age.

Today, pretty much the opposite is true. The building still houses a working seafood market and walled-in kitchen, but the operation lacks the spic-and-span approach of the old days. All around, you see subtle signs—floors half-mopped, video poker machines beeping away, signs warning "Don't open your drink until after you pay"—that this is a struggling business in a somewhat dicey neighborhood. Try as they might, vividly painted ocean/aquarium murals provide little contrast to the generally dank scene.

The kitchen is a walled-off cube with a plate glass window—for viewing today's steam-table options—and an ordering window staffed by businesslike, usually cranky Vietnamese cashiers. The specialty here seems to be whatever's big and cheap: fried seafood poboys are huge, overstuffed and a great bang for the buck; dark okra is stewed to a silky consistency, packed with shrimp and ham, and available for about a buck a pound. Asian specialties aren't all that special—a tepid fried rice seems to be the extent of the Asian influence.

But play the kitchen's strengths and a lunch at St. Roch's can give you insight into a city's history and the nature of urban decay. The iron columns are still standing, if a little grungier and less hopeful.

Again, if it's lunchtime and you love adventure, perhaps, this might just be what you're looking for.

The Pearl Restaurant & Oyster Bar
119 St. Charles Ave. (at Canal)
504-525-2901

zone: CBD/Warehouse

meals: lunch and dinner Tues–Sun
specialty: seafood
fancy factor: middlebrow
price range: $19–16

bonus points: on streetcar line

Pedestrians walking up St. Charles from Canal Street can't help but notice the Pearl. Even if you manage to miss the antique neon sign (OYSTER BAR RESTAURANT CREOLE SEAFOODS), you'll probably see the pink terrazzo sidewalk inlaid with enormous oyster shells—arranged stepping stone–style—that lead into this downtown eatery.

In earlier days, the Pearl's hallmarks were its eponymous oyster bar and an unexpected show—savory meats carved in the restaurant's front window. Whole hams, roasted turkeys and beef roasts made for a great gimmick, drawing in passersby for a plate or sandwich. Natives still recall the meaty bounty as their enduring image of the old Pearl. In business since the 1920s, it was a lunchtime standby for busy office workers or for oyster lovers on their way home from the office.

The Pearl's historic shell is pretty much intact and in good repair, but the modern-day dining experience—overpriced and underflavored—makes it just another tourist joint. If you've got good memories of the place during its heyday, just let 'em ride.

A new-century renovation changed the look of the place—adding an layer of stylized 60s aesthetic to the original Art Deco–influenced room. The renovation also removed the room-length oyster bar and the prominent carving station, recap-

turing floor space for additional seating and a banquette unit.

Roast beef, turkey and ham sandwiches are still on the menu—but the emphasis is now on post-Prudhomme Cajun and Creole mainstays. The winner of the lot is a hearty seafood gumbo, filled with small shrimp, chunks of sausage and halved gumbo crabs. A tomato sauce–topped jambalaya isn't quite as appealing; the lackluster seafood poboys didn't show any evidence of seasoning whatsoever.

All this would be forgivable if the menu prices were reasonable, but they're not. With every overpriced plate, you get

Saltine Syndrome

At the more old-school neighborhood joints, you might be surprised by an unexpected pre-dinner treat—a small wicker basket filled with cellophane-wrapped crackers instead of French bread. Sometimes the saltines are a prelude to bread, sometimes an invitation to order some garlic toast—the policy varies—but if your stomach grumbles while perusing the menu, do as the locals do: slather them with a little butter and munch away.

the feeling that you're paying a surcharge for a renovation budget that went terribly awry. Any place close to the Quarter can be cut some slack for location costs, but the Pearl's prices go beyond acceptable tourist premiums by just about any measure.

Fans of mystery novelist James Lee

Burke might overlook the prices because of the Pearl's literary legacy—the author has mentioned the place in half a dozen of his Dave Robicheaux novels. No need to to bring your dog-eared paperbacks along for evidence: the owners have framed copies of the passages—cut, matted and highlighted—as wall decorations.

TECHNIQUE

Rapture of the Deep (Fryer)

C'mon . . . admit it. Whether it's an order of crinkle-cut potatoes or the season's plumpest soft-shell crab, everything tastes better when it's deep fried. It's a shame that the fast-food mega-chains have sullied this fine and noble cooking method by making the term "fried" synonymous with the terms "greasy," "sodden" and "hazardous."

In New Orleans, cooks aren't so quick to dismiss deep-frying just because diet trends point toward broiling, baking and steaming as more healthful alternatives. Well before the fast-food chains invaded middle America, it was a cornerstone of our seafood-centric cuisine.

Local chefs talk of "respect for the fry pits" as a prerequisite for entering a kitchen and many establishments maintain generations-long reputations for sublime fried specialties—succulent mahogany-colored fried chicken topped with a couple of crinkle-cut pickle slices or fried oysters with a toasty cornmeal crust and a nearly liquid center. Austin Leslie, one of the legends of New Orleans cookery, proudly wears the title of "fry cook" instead of chef, though he'd qualify for both.

Throughout the city, respect for the pits can takes many different traditional forms. Some kitchens fry in stovetop pots instead of electric deep-fryers. Others keep food-specific fryers to prevent the cross-contamination of flavors (i.e. onion rings with fishy aromas). Some insist on frying in hot liquid lard for the distinctive flavor it imparts to the final product.

But most of all, the respect requires paying attention to the food as it's burbling away in the fryer. There's a world of difference between the human touch and a preprogrammed electronic timer. An experienced fry cook can, to paraphrase Austin Leslie, tell what's going on in a fryer without even looking at it, because he can *hear* how it's cooking.

So even if you've sworn off the fried stuff for years, try at least one fried shrimp poboy or order something off an upscale menu (where they cleverly camouflage the technique with the less controversial term "crispy"). You won't be disappointed.

notable BARROOMS

*N*ew Orleans serves up more than its share of bar food, but the kitchens of the "bar and grill" school usually do justice to this food-crazy town's reputation. You can get chili-cheese fries and breaded jalapeño poppers anywhere; belly up to a Crescent City bar and knock back a good poboy, hot muffuletta or steaming bowl of gumbo with your late-night beer.

Here are a few watering holes where the cook behind the scenes is as popular as a friendly bartender with a heavy whiskey-pouring hand.

Cooter Brown's Tavern and Oyster Bar

509 S. Carrollton (at St. Charles)
504-866-9104

zone: Uptown
website: www.cooterbrowns.com
reservations: none

meals: lunch and dinner daily
specialty: poboys and bar food
fancy factor: lowbrow
price range: $5–13

caveats: a billion TV screens, parking across the railroad tracks
bonus points a billion TV screens, wide beer selection

As a well-stocked beer bar in a cocktail town, this Riverbend staple gets a lot of play from its selection of imports and microbrews. Being close to the Uptown universities doesn't hurt either, as a good chunk of the crowd at this bar tends to have Loyola or Tulane affiliations.

Some folks are drawn in by the "round the world" selection of beers (40 draft and countless bottled), some by the cheap oysters on the half shell, and others by the zillion plasma-screen TVs broadcasting every sporting event in the Western hemisphere. Saturdays and Sundays, the spacious main room is packed with sports fans following six football games, three screens of televised poker and a horse race in between sips. Among these superhuman multitasking spectators, whiplash is not an uncommon affliction.

If you're able to resist the draw of action-packed high-def sports, you'll probably spy the impressive, if kinda creepy, "Obeertuary and Barsoleum." Thirty bottles of beer held by carved wooden caricatures: giant heads, tiny bodies. Hitchcock, Nixon, Judy Garland, Van Gogh. The more you drink, the weirder they get.

The kitchen pumps out deep-fried or griddle-seared bar food with the best of them, with a specialty menu that pays homage to former employees and regulars. A wide range of folks are immortalized on the poboy list: owners (pastrami and kraut on the onion roll), bartenders (pastrami and Swiss cheeseburger) and members of local music fixtures the Radiators (shrimp, oysters and cheese). But the classic has to be the "Coonass Special" poboy—spicy fried pies (ground meat or crawfish, your choice) with gravy and provolone. It's just what the doctor ordered when the big wooden heads start talkin' to you.

Liuzza's

3636 Bienville St. (at N. Telemachus)
504-482-9120

zone: Midcity
website: www.liuzzas.com
reservations: none

meals: lunch and dinner Mon–Sat
specialty: bar food and Creole-Italian
fancy factor: low-middlebrow
price range: $7–17

caveats: no reservations, mistaken identity
bonus points: bowling balls fulla beer

Even if Liuzza's didn't have an outstanding kitchen in the back, it would still qualify for blue-collar landmark status. From the 40s-era neon sign advertising the bar's alphanumeric phone number (HU2-9120) to icy oversized schooners of draft, this Midcity barroom has occupied a slot in the well-populated pantheon of neighborhood joints since the Truman years.

Just past the bar's elbow-rubbing camaraderie and jangling video poker machines, a powerhouse kitchen plies a brisk trade in Creole Italian pasta dishes,

seafood specialties, solid burger variations and just about ANY food that can be covered in tomato-based "red gravy."

Liuzza's main dining room is simple and seemingly always busy—pink paint and dark paneling with a crush of wood-grain Formica tables and few aisles to speak of. At peak mealtimes, the blur of activity is nothing short of overwhelming. Nimble servers float through narrow spaces between the crowded tables and manage to treat every customer like a regular. It's a delicate balance of grace, familiarity and subtle impatience that marks the best seasoned professionals. In the middle of a midday crush, they can still make you feel well cared for—even in ten-second chunks.

Fizzy drinks (beer, root beer, red soda for the kids) are served in the joint's trademark beer schooners—thick fishbowls of bulletproof glass that heft in at about two pounds apiece. (Imagine drinking a slightly slushy brew from a hollow crystal bowling ball.) Liuzza's is justly proud of these frosty wonders—the unmistakable spherical silhouette appears on signs, cards and in the imagination of every customer who's ever bellied up to the bar.

It's hard to resist the fried foods here as a nice cold brew almost pulls the palate toward the salty/crunchy end of the culinary spectrum. And the cooks here do it all—crispy eggplant rounds, dill pickle chips, artichoke hearts or onion rings cut whisper thin, then cooked to just-caramelized perfection.

Fried green tomatoes sport a crispy crust of seasoned bread crumbs and a lush topping of sautéed shrimp and a garlic-heavy remoulade sauce. The thin slices are cooked just enough to provide two layers of crunch—one from the toasty crumb layer and the other from the barely soft-ened tomato underneath. The house gumbo, double thickened with dark roux and okra, combines the Cajun staples (chicken and spicy andouille sausage) with the added sweet bonuses of shrimp AND oysters—a kitchen-sink approach that does justice to all the ingredients with-out sacrificing a flavorful balance of taste.

Liuzza's also lays claim to its own variation of the muffuletta with the "Frenchuletta," a hot version of the spicy sandwich served on a foot-long sec-tion of crusty French bread instead of the traditional round Italian loaf. Thin slices of ham and salami are griddle-cooked and topped with a layer of melt-ing Swiss cheese and a salty house olive salad. The toasted loaf is simultaneous-ly crisp and soft as it soaks up the caramelized meat juices and seasoned oil from the olive salad. The Frenchuletta isn't exactly a sandwich purist's choice, but it's a damned good experience for muffuletta lovers willing to eat outside the traditional circle.

The biggest danger here is, strangely enough, ending up in another Liuzza's by mistake. You'd think that a distinctive Italian name would be enough of a dis-tinguishing mark, but you'd be wrong.

Another Midcity Liuzza's—located near the Fairgrounds—fits the broad descrip-tion of "old bar with great food," and can cause confusion for visitors. If some-one suggests you meet for a beer at Liuz-za's, ask them to choose between "by the track" or "the one on Bienville."

Liuzza's by the Track

1518 N. Lopez St. (at Ponce de Leon)
504-943-8667

zone: Midcity
reservations: none

meals: lunch Mon–Sat, dinner Mon–Fri,
specialty: eclectic bar food
fancy factor: lowbrow
price range: $6–10

caveats: early kitchen closing, closed Sun,
  smokey room
bonus points: diverse, well-executed
  menu

If you're set to meet friends at a bar called Liuzza's, you need to ask a follow-up question. Otherwise, you might just end up drinking alone.

Both Liuzza's are located in Midcity; both are known for their good drinks and strong kitchens; both serve beers in oversized spherical schooners; both share a common spelling.

So the million dollar question is: *"By the track or the other one?"*

"The other one" is on Bienville. "By the track" is smack on the corner of North Lopez and Ponce de Leon, mere steps from the local horse track, the New Orleans Fairgrounds.

Liuzza's by the Track is celebrated as a Jazzfest headquarters during the festival's annual two-week run and a standout dive the other fifty weeks of the year. Coming from a tiny kitchen in back of a not-quite-renovated bar, there are some menu items that you'd expect—good poboys spring to mind, fried seafood and a decent roast beef are pretty much required. But owner Billy Gruber manages to put simple but amazingly flavorful twists on the usual poboy suspects. Wonderfully sloppy roast beef gets a savory jolt from a liberal dose of garlic and a sinus-clearing drizzle of creamy horseradish sauce. Oyster poboy gets the not-so-traditional drizzle of potent garlic butter—a breadbound variation of fried oysters "Bordelaise" like you'd find across town at Restaurant Mandich. Crave a Reuben? Out by the track they corn their own beef. How about a dose of barbecue shrimp? Their poboy variation is a hollowed-out section of soft French bread filled with tiny sautéed shrimp and a gooshy overdose of thick, garlicky gravy. If you're a fan of lemon pepper and want to perfect your elbow-licking technique, here's your chance.

Other surprises on the menu come in the soup and salad departments. Close proximity to video poker might lead you to expect iceberg wedges, but the crispy pannéed chicken or sautéed shrimp salads feature generous portions of mixed leafy microgreens. Dressings are all made in house, with a green onion vinaigrette scoring high points on the savory scale.

Soup lovers face a terrible/wonderful choice with a trio of signature soups. A sweet corn chowder with meaty crawfish tails sings in springtime while the thick Creole gumbo packs it all in (chicken sausage AND sautéed-to-order seafood in abundance). Bivalve fans should dip into a bowl of the oysters Rockefeller soup—Gruber's take on the traditional milk-based oyster stew taken to new heights with a little bit of spinach for texture and a hint of anise-flavored Herbsaint for aroma and flavor. (A portion size warning seems appropriate here: a cup is a bowl and a bowl is a vat.)

And while you'd assume that a bar kitchen would be open until well after midnight, the cooks start their cleaning routine on the early side (9 PM at press time). If you skew early, you're golden. If you miss the last kitchen call, at least you can have a stout cocktail to sooth your disappointment.

Napoleon House
500 Chartres St. (at St. Louis)
504-524-9752

zone: French Quarter
website: www.napoleonhouse.com
reservations: none

meals: lunch and dinner daily
specialty: muffulettas, classic New Orleans cocktails
fancy factor: middlebrow
price range: $5–8

caveats: no parking, early close Sunday
bonus points: amazing atmosphere, patio
dining, Pimm's Cups

If I've heard this story once, I've heard it a thousand times: a small group of tourists is tromping around the French Quarter, not really paying attention, when the skies open up for a summer rain shower. Looking around, somebody spies a run-down corner bar and the group ducks in to escape the storm. The bar is ancient and quiet, plaster walls peeking through layers of old paint, classical music on the stereo, waiters clad in bow ties and short-sleeved polyester shirts. The group sits down for a few minutes, orders a drink, maybe a muffuletta, and the next thing you know, they've spend the whole day sipping Pimm's Cups (see page 214) and watching the street traffic amble by.

"Do you know the place? It's called the . . . what is it? Yeah! The Napoleon House."

As one of the city's great "hidden in plain sight" institutions, this aging bar

A Pimm's Cup refreshes at the Napoleon House bar

has a knack for getting accidentally discovered by first-timers. Across the street from the sprawling Supreme Court building and a couple of blocks from Jackson Square, the unassuming structure contains more than its share of history, a supremely relaxing atmosphere and a dependable kitchen all under one 18th-century roof.

The building's name comes from an offer made to Napoleon in the 1820s— former mayor Nicolas Girod allegedly invited the then-exiled emperor to set up shop in New Orleans. The Chartres Street apartment, constructed in 1797, would be a perfect getaway for the Little General; an alternative to the rat race on Elba.

The two dining areas—a perfectly aged bar space and intimate interior courtyard—trigger a sense of French Colonial déjà vu, a feeling of what the city felt like before those damned Americans came to town in 1805. The weathered courtyard has a distinctly Caribbean feel with banana trees, flickering gaslights and shaded under-gallery seating for when the rains come. The streetside bar has arguably the best historic ambiance in town—earthy ochre walls covered with historic photos and artwork, wall-height doors flung open to the street, a romantic alcove containing a tête-à-tête two-top and 70s-era pay phone.

Though it's listed in just about every possible guidebook (including this one), the Napoleon House remains a local's favorite, for lunch or afternoon cocktails. The kitchen does a dependable job with the standard poboy offerings, and updates the rest of its menu with standard New American influences (goat cheese panini served on focaccia, artichoke and sun-dried tomato spread, raspberry vinaigrettes).

Veterans usually choose the house

Fried Pies

If you've got a weakness for fried pies, then, my friend, New Orleans is your kinda town. Savory or sweet, fresh out of the oil or cool enough to scarf by the dozen, these little beauties are a guilty pleasure that are damned near irresistible whether you pick 'em up at a convenience store or a Jazzfest concession stand.

Nachitoches Meat Pie—This bar kitchen staple hails from the north Louisiana city of Nachitoches (pronounced NACK-uh-dish. Really.) Stuffed with spicy ground meat, these crispy-crusted beauties bear a strong family resemblance to Latin *empanadas*.

Crawfish Pies—Imagine a Nachitoches pie stuffed with a thick crawfish étouffée—tails smothered with onions, bell peppers and celery. Same crispy crust and just as habit-forming as their meaty counterparts, but safe for the fish-eating crowd.

Hubig's Fried Pies—You don't usually find these at bars, but these sweet dessert pies are an impulse purchase just about everywhere else: poboy shops, gas stations and even hardware stores. Lovingly made down in the Faubourg Marigny, these sweet little turnovers are filled with a wide range of gooey flavors: tart lemon, cinnamon-spiked apple, peach, chocolate and coconut cream. They're all fantastic, but true connoisseurs seek out the seasonal flavors like sweet potato, blackberry and blueberry, all of which are made when the Louisiana crops are at their peak. Their simple white wax-paper envelopes printed with a picture of the best-named cartoon mascot ever: Savory Simon the Hubig's Pieman. Vegans should sit this one out—there's a bit of animal product in both the crust and frying oil. Sorry.

---

sandwich specialty, a muffuletta (see page 150) heated just long enough for the seeded Italian bread to crisp up and the cheese to become gooey. Though toasting this particular sandwich is seen as borderline heresy to some purists—read as "Central Grocery loyalists"—the overall flavors are nonetheless excellent.

For a sit-down muffuletta meal, you're not likely to find a more comfortable spot in the Quarter, whether you've been coming for years or you're just trying to get out of the rain.

Parasol's Restaurant and Bar
2533 Constance St. (at 2nd)
504-897-5413

zone: Garden District
website: www.parasols.com
reservations: none

meals: lunch and dinner daily
specialty: poboys and bar food
fancy factor: lowbrow
price range: $5–9

caveats: smoky as hell
bonus points: St. Patrick's Day chaos

Aaaaaah, the dependable neighborhood dive. A gathering place for friends, a beer-soaked social club and a deafening echo chamber for sports fans whenever there's a game on the tube. Since the early 1950s, Parasol's has been an important fixture in the Irish Channel, a formerly Celtic section of town just riverside of the Garden District.

That's half a century as the natural successor to the dockside saloons that dotted the neighborhood when it actually qualified as an Irish stronghold—a period roughly spanning from the 1850s to the suburban exodus of the 1970s. Dingy, cramped and much beloved, Parasol's leads a normally quiet existence, roaring to life, logically enough, every St. Patrick's weekend, when the bar throws its annual Irish-themed block party. The annual event is an all-out brawl of a party complete with excessive amounts of murky green beer, countless Kelly green Jell-O shots and the inevitable sickly green aftermath.

Food lovers usually know Parasol's from its famous roast beef poboy, which on its good nights can be heaven on a flimsy paper plate. The house-cooked roast beef is braised until spoon-cutting tender and soaked in flavorful, garlic-infused brown gravy. In keeping with tradition, the mayo used to dress the sandwich mixes with the gravy in rich, sultry ways, making for a glorious mess of a meal. Of course, that's on a good night. Unfortunately for roast beef fans who aren't quite Irish Channel loyalists, the sandwiches miss about as often as they hit (gummy, floury gravy, flavorless beef). Luckily, there are other poboy variations available as well as bar snacks like sear-

ing hot buffalo wings and other deep-fried goodies.

Port of Call
838 Esplanade Ave. (at Dauphine)
504-523-0120

zone: French Quarter
website: www.portofcallneworleans.com
reservations: none

meals: lunch and dinner daily
specialty: burgers, no fries
fancy factor: low-middlebrow
price range: $8–24

caveats: lines out the wazoo, no French fries
bonus points: open late-night

Maybe it's just me—and by all accounts it is—but this one is a stumper. If you drive past this bustling corner bar just about any time of day or night, you'll see groups of prospective diners milling around Esplanade Avenue. Most are sipping sweet, fruity cocktails from white plastic cups to pass the time, patiently waiting for tables that can take hours to turn. And at any given time, well over half of the milling crowd seems to be from out of town. (Really. After a while, you can just tell.)

The big draw of this kitschy Polynesian-themed bar isn't an obscure Pacific specialty (poi, mahi mahi, SPAM sushi) but common food that makes the appeal that much more confusing: a hamburger. Sure, it's a *good* hamburger—a perfectly circular puck of beef just under two inches thick, heavy for its size, the exact diameter of a seeded grocery-store hamburger bun. Cooked medium rare, it's

Local Beers

There was a time, a magical time, when the German immigrants set up shop in our fair city and brought with them the gift of beer. The Crescent City had more than its share of breweries and the town was awash in suds. We could choose from Jax, Falstaff, Regal, George Auer, Armbruster, Fasnacht's.

But sadly, those days have passed. New Orleans has become more of a cocktail town, and those looking for huge selections of draft beer go sadly wonting. There are a few bars that stock 50+ different beers on tap, but those joints are few and far between. In terms of local beer, there are a couple of holdouts available in local saloons:

Abita Brewing. Odds are, if a bar stocks any local beer on draft, it'll be the malty amber ale from this North Shore microbrewery. Located in Abita Springs, they consistently produce a solid brown ale (snazzily named Turbo Dog), a hoppy pilsner (Abita Golden), raspberry-flavored wheat beer (Purple Haze) and the now-required low-cal version (Light, of course). At different times of year, Abita's seasonal offerings include a Christmas ale, Mardi Gras bock, and various other brews that vary by season. Available in draft and bottled form.

Dixie Brewing. When you've got an image, you go with it. Regular Dixie, a medium-bodied beer that's a notch above the standard industrial brews, gets a lot of play among the tourist crowd. The genius move of naming their sweet brown lager "Blackened Voodoo" guarantees a steady following among those looking to hit two of the city's biggest clichés in a single order. Available in bottles only.

lick-your-arms juicy and the perfect shade of deep pink in the center. It's the kind of burger your dad would make on the backyard barbecue if he really knew as much about grilling as he pretended to. On the side, a foil-wrapped baked potato packed with a fistful of shredded cheddar; the kitchen apparently a fry-free zone. Steaks and pizzas round out the list, but it's the burgers that lure the crowds.

The bar plays its "Mutiny on the Bounty" shtick without the slightest bit of irony. Schooner prints and other nautical paraphernalia (wooden ship's wheel, lifesaver float) cover the walls; a grid of woven rope provides a net-like drop ceiling over the whole place. Sug-

ary signature cocktails have names like Windjammer or Neptune's Monsoon—along with appropriately fictional origin tales.

Now a good burger is a wonderful thing, but again, it's the *standing in line* part that puzzles me. Faced with a more or less universal food or a city's specialty sandwich, wouldn't you prowl around for a poboy?

If you've got an unshakable burger jones, smaller groups tend to have the advantage, so break your party into pairs and jockey for a seat at the bar if there's one available. You'll likely be rubbing elbows with other patrons, but the burgers are just as good and at least twice as quick.

DOWN-HOME soul

The "Southern soul food" school doesn't dominate the Crescent City's food scene as it does in most of the Deep South, but New Orleans has more than its fare share of soul food in its everyday repertoire. Many of the standard dishes will be instantly recognizable to fans of southern home-style cuisine—crispy fried catfish, long-stewed collard greens, crunchy fried chicken and sweet potato pie to wash it all down. Others have a distinctively Creole twist—ubiquitous Monday red beans and numerous seafood dishes on Friday to name only two—that let you know you're dining in New Orleans.

Barrow's Shady Inn
2714 Mistletoe St. (at Belfast)
504-482-9427

zone: Uptown

meals: lunch Thurs–Sat, dinner Tues–Sat
specialty: fried catfish
fancy factor: lowbrow
price range: $8–14

caveats: tough to find, limited menu
bonus points: huge portions

The bill of fare at Barrow's Shady Inn embodies the essence of southern-fried simplicity—if you're a fan of fried catfish, you're in the right place.
Tender filets have a thin mantle of pale yellow cornmeal that crackles with every bite. The meat is moist, nearly creamy and falls apart on the tongue. It's miraculously greaseless, served in huge portions and best washed down with a snifter of potent, tartsweet lemonade. Creamy, mustard-heavy potato salad on the side, a few slices of white bread (plain or toasted) to add a little starch.

Now, if you're not a catfish fan, you're out of luck. Prefer fried chicken or some French fries? Nope. An order of hush puppies on the side? Nope. Barrow's menu is streamlined to a single note— catfish filets and potato salad. Period.

It seems that even the most humble country fish shacks usually offer at least a few different variations on the fried critter theme—even if it's just for kicks. Whole fried fish? Nuggets for the kids? A grilled option for fish-friendly dieters? Not likely. Barrow's stands firm: if you've made the trek, you'll eat the fillets. And for catfish fans, this is a very good thing indeed.

Since 1943, this remote eatery in the Hollygrove neighborhood has nurtured a sterling local reputation as "The Catfish Specialist"—so say generations of loyal fish fans, so reads the burned-wood sign hanging on the mirrored wall. The single dining room seems like more of a neighborhood lounge—a Naugahyde bar that got a supper-club facelift sometime in the 1970s, complete with wall-to-wall mirrors and a burbling aquarium behind the bar. Photo portraits of kitchen workers cleaning gigantic catfish ring the room.

At Barrow's, fried catfish is a given: your only choice is serving size, which are best considered as communal portions. A small plate, which runs for about twelve bucks at press time, will easily feed two moderately hungry diners; a dollar more will get you more than enough to make two heavy eaters roll out the door in search of a nice siesta. The largest plate would probably crack the restaurant's foundation or block out the sun.

There is, however, an insider's tip for those who love the crunch: a request for "extra crispy" means that the fish will stay in the oil a few minutes longer than usual, resulting in a firmer texture, a toastier crust and a good deal more ambient crunch.

For years, Barrow's has been a standard Friday pilgrimage spot for observant Catholics—after all, what else can they order?—and to this day, the kitchen maintains a nonstandard weekend-centric schedule (dinner Tuesday–Saturday, lunch Thursday–Saturday). If you're often seized by the need for the whiskered fish, take note.

Café Reconcile
1631 Oretha Castle Haley Blvd.
(at Euterpe)
504-568-1157

zone: Midcity
website: www.cafereconcile.com
reservations: none

meals: breakfast Mon–Fri, lunch Mon–Fri
specialty: down-home Creole
fancy factor: middlebrow
price range: $4–7

caveats: weekday early meals only, not walking neighborhood, watch the noon rush
bonus points: great prices, for a great cause

CLASSIC

Fried Chicken

Crisp on the outside, tender on the inside and splashed with a little hot sauce, a properly fried chicken has primal appeal that's made it a southern classic, and an integral part of America's culinary identity.

New Orleans has its share of bona-fide chicken masters, some of whom stick to the old ways when cooking their birds. Modern deep-fryers have simplified the big-batch production, but the outstanding practitioners of the craft believe that proper frying takes personal attention.

Local experts include Austin Leslie (the cook in charge of the fry pits at Jacques-Imo's Café [see page 64] and Ms. Willie Mae Seaton [see page 177]). They'll both serve up the best fried chicken of your life, but it won't be quick. Perfection might require a bit of patience on the diner's part, but it's always well worth the wait.

Midway through the lunch rush at Central City's Café Reconcile, the young restaurant staff is neck-deep in frenzied activity. On one side of the cavernous space, a five-person crew works the café's shining kitchen line—the hum of a 25-foot vent hood punctuated by sizzles, chops and whooshes as food meets fire. Finished dishes—steaming bowls of red beans, plates loaded with fried catfish, platters of roasted chicken—hit the stainless serving shelf, only to be whisked a few steps to tables packed with name-tagged office workers and city employees. Teenage waitstaff and bus workers move steadily through the rush—with the occasional misstep here and there—but the action never lets up for a second. And in a couple of months, if everything goes well, they'll be gone.

"Except for a few of the staff, they're all nesting here," says Reconcile's chef Don Boyd. "The program usually takes from six to eight weeks, and we try to get them placed around town. We got guys at Acme Oyster House, Arnaud's, The Hilton, Palace Café . . ." His voice trails off as he scans the one-room restaurant to make sure the whole show runs smoothly. "A lot of times, I can get them better jobs than I can supply."

Dressed in an embroidered chef coat and requisite houndstooth pants, Boyd works with Café Reconcile as chef, manager and teacher. During most lunch shifts, he's a roving presence, troubleshooting kitchen problems, or talking up the causes associated with the café and its symbiotic partner, the St. Regis Hospitality School.

The two programs—restaurant school and school's restaurant—are bound together in both structure and mission. Café Reconcile is the public face of a nonprofit job-training program for the city's at-risk youth. The hospitality school is the educational component, providing valuable training and employment connections for its students. The two share community sponsors, a physical home (a renovated furniture warehouse on Oretha Castle Haley Boulevard) and a common goal (providing practical restaurant experience for inner city youths).

From a diner's view, Café Reconcile has a reputation that any neighborhood restaurant would envy. The busy kitchen specializes in reasonably priced Creole and southern-style lunch fare (po-boys, collard greens, pot roast) that's worth a cross-town pilgrimage. Rotating specials—creamy white beans with shrimp, meatloaf and hand-mashed potatoes in spicy tomato-rich Creole sauce—attract devotees of the blue plate. It's good food for a great cause, and a bargain to boot. The Thursday special—white beans and shrimp—are more than worth the drive. Presentation couldn't get any simpler—a shallow stoneware soup plate filled to the rim with beige-tinged beans slow-cooked and blended to a thick, smooth consistency. The individual beans are barely discernable in the creamy potage flecked with thyme and green onion. You might go a few spoonfuls tasting only the essence of seafood mixed with hearty beans, then hit a few chunks of tender shrimp tail, sautéed with garlic and the same color as the soupy beans. Camouflaged in the bowl, these tasty morsels are hidden in plain sight, just waiting for the spoon to find them. Served with a chunk of jalapeño cornbread, it's a hearty meal that the "no red meat" crowd can embrace with a clear conscience.

Reconcile's huge portions make it tough to save room for dessert, but ease up a bit on the entrée and you'll be rewarded. The house desserts (a dryish strawberry shortcake, rich chocolate brownie and Bananas Foster bread pudding) come topped with an irresistibly sweetened, almost puddinglike whipped cream.

Dunbar's Creole Cooking

4927 Freret St. (at Robert)
504-899-0734

zone: Uptown
website: www.dunbarscreolecooking.com
reservations: not needed

meals: breakfast, lunch, dinner Mon–Sat, closed Sun
specialty: home-style Creole and soul food
fancy factor: lowbrow
prices: entrées $5–10

caveats: closed Sun, no bar
bonus points: daily specials, all-you-can-eat challenge, almost familial service

After my second plate, the waitress came over for a routine table-check.

"Get you another?"

She had already brought me two full plates of Dunbar's house specialty—red beans and fried chicken—and was obviously only asking as a formality. All around the packed dining room, big eaters worked their way through third and fourth servings, but during this particular Monday, I just had to stop.

"You know that it's all you can eat, right?" Her concerned voice trailed off as she motioned to the kitchen. "I can bring you another . . ."

And therein lies Dunbar's lunchtime challenge—the toughest thing is knowing when to stop.

Though seemingly interchangeable with hundreds of other white-frame neighborhood eateries around New Orleans, Dunbar's sets itself apart with an infamous all-you-can-handle lunch offer—red beans and fried chicken for about five bucks. Other rotating specials (smothered chicken, meatloaf and potatoes, gumbo) provide a bit of midday variety, but most of the customers belly up for Dunbar's trademark multiplate challenge. It's printed on the menu in bold letters: RED BEANS & CHICKEN ALWAYS AVAILABLE.

In keeping with local laundry-day tradition, the red beans are spicy and substantial, with tender chunks of onion and pepper floating in the mix. Served "center plate" on a pile of rice, the beans strike a good balance between firm and creamy without a hint of long-cooked mushiness. Even without the chicken, this dish (served with its sides of green salad and cornbread) would be a great standard lunch option.

But as luck would have it, there's also a near-endless supply of dark-meat fried chicken included in the bargain (white meat available for a reasonable surcharge). Judging from the color of the chicken, Dunbar's cooks don't like to be rushed when it comes to frying, since the crisp skin always occupies the darker end of the color spectrum. This long cooking makes for deeper, more developed flavor in the chicken's protective crust without drying out the bird's moist meat. Once you start crunching it's pretty tough to stop, and provided you finish before 4:00 (the all-you-can-eat cutoff time) the cheerful waitstaff will keep your plate perpetually full.

If you're not in the mood for poultry, but still want a heap of beans for lunch, Dunbar's offers a smoked sausage substitution—a full link split down the middle and deep fried until the ends curl up like clown shoes. Not an option for the fat-phobic, but sausage fans should give it a try for its great flavor and amazingly delicate texture. The link slices clean with the slightest fork pressure and melts on the tongue.

There are other items on the multimeal menu ranging from breakfast platters and poboys to seafood and steak options for dinner. Desserts (if there's room) change daily with a lineup of chunky homemade cakes and other sweets. The individual-sized sweet potato pie makes up in pure richness what it lacks in size; yet another case of big tastes coming in small packages.

If you're going to go for sweets, start your day at Dunbar's with a strict two-plate limit, or bank on an afternoon nap. The charming waitress might worry a bit ("You *sure* that's enough, baby?"), and some days she may just talk you into one too many helpings, and sometimes "too much" can be just perfect. Those are the days to lunch at Dunbar's.

Praline Connection
542 Frenchmen St. (at Chartres)
504-943-3934

zone: Faubourg Marigny
website: www.pralineconnection.com
reservations: none

CLASSIC

Grits and Grillades . . . and Grits

A gut-warming standard of the Creole brunch, this gravy-rich dish consists of beef or veal steaks pounded thin, browned and braised in a gravy of roux, onions, tomatoes, and peppers.

Grillades bear a distinct family resemblance to a classic dish of the Deep South—round steak smothered in dark gravy. Flattening the steak reduces cooking time and makes the meat tender enough to cut with a spoon.

If you're unclear on the concept of grits, consider it the American version of the now-trendy *polenta*—a thick, slow-simmered porridge made from ground corn. (In the case of grits, the corn is actually hominy, a treated kernel that's had its germ and hull removed.) Though grits don't as commonly appear on New Orleans breakfast tables as they do in other parts of the Deep South, many contemporary chefs interpret traditional dishes that feature the versatile grain, including shrimp and grits, a classic of the coastal Carolinas.

hours: lunch and dinner daily
specialty: home-style Creole and soul
   food
fancy factor: lowbrow
Prices: Entrées $5–10

The catchy name of this Marigny soul food joint may sound oddly familiar—especially if you fly into Armstrong Airport's Concourse B or wander the streets near Morial Convention Center, prime spots where their second and third locations operate. The original location on Frenchmen Street is a dependable little soul food café that specializes in a vast array of "greens and beans"—a mix-and-match setup of red or white beans, crower peas, mustard greens, collards or cabbage—served every day. Top these off with a meaty "one from column B" setup (including but not limited to stewed chicken, meatloaf, turkey necks, smothered pork chop, smoked sausage) and you've got a hefty meal for under ten bucks.

The kitchen works best with dishes that are either slow stewed or deep fried. The fried chicken is crisp and moist, as is the fried catfish. Their jambalaya is a good take on the no-tomato country style, with one puzzling addition: formerly frozen mixed vegetables, presumably thrown in for color. (In a lifetime of eating jambalaya, I haven't seen it before or since.) Adventure eaters drawn to the barbecue oysters and alligator sausage are in for two separate (but equally disappointing) surprises: the oysters are poached in a sweet Kraft-style barbecue sauce instead of sautéed in garlicky butter sauce and the sausage cooks down to a ridiculously small portion after its dip in the deep-fryer. The amaretto-praline sauce served with the bread pudding is pretty potent, like a sticky shooter for the grade-school set. The sweet potato pie goes the other direction—just a bit on the savory side.

The Connection's service is always familiar, snappy and dressed in the restaurant's trademark uniform of crisp white shirts and stylish fedoras.

Tee-Eva's
4430 Magazine St. (at Jena)
504-899-8350

zone: Uptown
website: www.tee-eva.net
reservations: none

meals: lunch and dinner daily
specialty: Creole seafood
fancy factor: lowbrow
price range: $3–6

caveats: selection limited
bonus points: year-round snowballs

Some days, the hot lunch at Tee-Eva's just doesn't happen.

"I usually do a baked chicken or a barbecue chicken or something," she says with a grin. "But today . . ." She shrugs

Des Allemands Catfish

The noble whiskered wonder doesn't get the same kind of play in New Orleans that it does in drier areas of the Deep South—but then, there's tough competition for "marquee fish" status this close to the Gulf.

In nearby Mississippi, aquaculture turned the Delta into a veritable fish factory, churning out tons of grain-fed catfish that can safely escape the "bottom feeder" stigma that's plagued the species for decades. These days, marketing campaigns have presented the Fish Formerly Known as Mudcat into a palate-friendly, not-gamey-at-all version of the *other* other white meat.

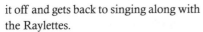

New Orleans cooks, always the contrarians, tend to dote on catfish caught in the waters near Des Allemands, Louisiana, on the Lafourche/St. Charles Parish line. Because these "wild catfish" eat what they please, they're known for having a more pronounced fishy flavor than their farm-raised counterparts. An overheard comment on the subject: "I want my catfish to taste like catfish instead of nothing."

it off and gets back to singing along with the Raylettes.

It's not that the cupboards are bare at Tee-Eva Perry's little sweetshop and restaurant on upper Magazine—there always seems to be seafood gumbo thickened with filé, tomato-based jambalaya on the menu, but most days they're in the fridge. If you've got a few minutes she'll heat them up for you, and tell you stories while you wait. Like the Mardi Gras day that she danced her way into labor before delivering her first child at Charity. Or the times she hung out with Ray Charles in the 60s at the legendary Dew Drop Inn. Or the grocery trip that turned into a roadhouse weekend in Pass Christien, Mississippi. Or tales of her favorite cousin-in-law, the infamous

Ernie K. Doe, the city's Emperor of the Universe.

She tells the stories with a sparkle in her eye and a laugh that lights up the neighborhood. Meanwhile, tiny savory crawfish pies heat in the microwave or the snowball machine roars to life for a sweet summer cooler.

It's pretty hard to miss Ms. Eva's little cinderblock shop—it's painted bright yellow with a cartoon-style mural of her smiling visage gracing the Napoleon Avenue side—and during the Carnival season, it's usually buzzing with neighborhood folks grabbing a crunchy praline or sweet potato pie before they catch the Uptown parades.

Rumor has it that on the days when hot lunches *do* happen, they're good and cheap. If you're craving a big plate of red beans or baked macaroni and cheese, you should probably call ahead, but even if you're just wandering the neighborhood, you'll do well to stop by for a visit, something sweet and, if you're lucky, a story, a song and a smile.

Willie Mae's Restaurant

2401 St. Ann St. (at Tonti)
504-822-9503

zone: Tremé
reservations: none

meals: lunch daily
specialty: seafood, fried chicken
fancy factor: lowbrow
price range: $3–6

caveats: be on good behavior
bonus points: fried chicken

Based on my own good luck in the extended family department, I live my life by a simple, nearly foolproof rule: Whenever possible, eat at Grandma's.

Whether it's for Sunday dinner or Passover Seder, there's something magical about an invitation to Grandma's table. It's often a window into family traditions and life before the microwave. Any cross-generational meal takes on a somewhat formal air, and even if the grandmother in question never pokes her head out of the kitchen, there's a sense of theatre, a sense of the sacred and a bit of showing off. At various grandmothers' tables, I've tasted foods that provide true comfort—whether I was digging in to a dish of meltingly tender *tripa Fiorentina* in Italy, the best chicken fried steak in all of Texas or my own grandmother's roast, rice and gravy.

Ms. Willie Mae Seaton is the literal grandmother in the kitchen at her simple Faubourg Tremé restaurant, which is basically a front parlor that's open for the lunch trade. Willie Mae's is a quiet place to get away from workaday office business; a favorite for local lawyers and politicos who need a break from power-lunch mode. The room inspires a special kind of informal respect that's just about the opposite of a neighborhood bar—you'll find yourself feeling completely at ease, yet keeping your voice down and sitting up a little bit straighter than usual.

Single-page paper menus are a new thing at Willie Mae's; tradition is to ask her son, Charlie "Slim" Seaton, what's cooking on the stove. Most days, it's a home-style variation on the big pot theme—creamy butter beans on Monday and Wednesday, smothered cabbage Tuesday, red beans anytime—with a choice of meats on the side (smothered veal, breaded pork chop, fried trout on Friday).

But it's pretty hard to get away from Willie Mae's fried chicken, hand battered, cooked to order, and bone-munching good. Like all good fried bird, it involves a bit of a wait (no heat lamps here), but when your mahogany-crusted pieces appear, they're often still crackling from the fryer and sizzling against a pool of silky bean gravy. Though it's not the coveted pan-fried variety, Ms. Seaton's chicken is good enough that customers often request another portion of the crunchy-skinned specialty for a savory dessert course.

During my first couple of lunch trips, my esteemed lunch companion, a Willie Mae's customer since boyhood, would disappear into the kitchen to pay his respects just before departure. In true grandma fashion, Ms. Willie Mae doesn't go into the dining room much, preferring instead to keep her eye on the stove.

Usually, it's traditional to pass good wishes through Slim, but if you happen to be on your way through the kitchen for a restroom stop, she'll allow a momentary distraction. For a second, you'll forget this is a restaurant: you'll thank her for the wonderful meal and feel your best manners bubbling to the surface, even if you haven't used them in years. And she'll take your hand, graciously thank you back and make sure you've had enough to eat—then turn her attention back to the stove.

After all, she's got other people to feed, and she's the only grandma on duty.

ASSORTED standouts

Every system of categories needs a catch-all—and how many of us really want to spell miscellaneous? Desperation hot dogs, drive-up fried chicken and a couple of options from New Orleans' most influential latter-day ethnic population. Enjoy . . .

Kim Son
349 Whitney Ave., Gretna, LA
504-366-2489

zone: West Bank
reservations: none

meals: lunch and dinner Mon–Sat, closed Sun
specialty: Vietnamese
fancy factor: low-middlebrow
price range: $6–16

caveats: over on the West Bank

Sometimes change comes slowly to the American palate. It's hard to think that even ten years ago, most diners couldn't name one of the dishes from the Pacific Rim pantheon. There were only a few recognizable Asian traditions, and the most popular was by far Chinese.

In the years since, our collective taste-buds have expanded. In New Orleans, the small Vietnamese eateries in the suburbs have done steady business, first masquerading as more accessible Chinese-American restaurants, then slowly gaining an audience for their native specialties. And as time passed, more locals took the Crescent City Connection across the Mississippi River to the hidden Asian enclaves in the West Bank towns of Gretna and Harvey.

Recalling a time before Vietnamese cuisine became trendy, Kim Son still bills its specialties as "Chinese and Vietnamese" on its signs and menus—the better to attract diners in search of the familiar Asian flavors. And indeed, you can get a good selection of Chinese dishes at Kim Son, but its real standout items come from the Vietnamese sections of the menu.

There are steaming bowls of *pho*—a complex beef noodle soup topped with crispy mung bean sprouts, cilantro and a squeeze of lime juice—and huge helpings of rice vermicelli *(bun)* topped with crispy vegetables and delicate slices of grilled pork or beef.

The Vietnamese seafood traditions are also high points of Kim Son's menu. Experimental diners clamor for sweet scallops baked in a salty crust or the plump crab steamed in beer and served in a traditional earthenware "hot pot."

Vegetarians, so often disappointed in omnivorous New Orleans, are in luck with Kim Son's plentiful meatless options. One of the best is a variation on the "hot pot" theme featuring melt-in-your-mouth strips of tender eggplant mixed with slightly crunchy white onion in a garlic-spiked savory brown sauce. Cubes of firm-textured tofu soak up the tasty sauce and would make any anti-soy activist reconsider the often maligned cakes of bean curd.

The menu goes on for days, and it's pretty easy to be distracted and/or lost in page after page of options. But even if you're set on slurping a huge bowl of noodles, do yourself a favor and order a bowl of the hot-and-sour soup as a starter.

Vietnamese hot-and-sour soup—unlike its starch-thickened Chinese-American counterpart—is an amazing mingling of light, powerful flavors and aromas. Take a big whiff of the steaming stock and you'll catch cilantro, hot pepper, lemon, and fragrant *nuac mam* (fish sauce) wafting through your nostrils. Dip your spoon and you'll scoop a mouthful of pinkish broth, filled with crunchy bean sprouts, whisper-thin slices of scallion, plump shrimp and the occasional sweet chunk of pineapple or tomato. If you love spice, it's all there—from the sweet kick of garlic to the subtle afterburn of Vietnamese chile paste.

Lucky Dogs Carts
no fixed address
no phone

zone: French Quarter
reservations: none

meals: catch as catch can
specialty: desperation dogs
fancy factor: lowbrow
price range: $3–7

caveats: as tasty as you'd expect
bonus points: you usually don't expect much

As much as we'd *like* them to be, Lucky Dogs are NOT a variation of the proud immigrant hot dog cart tradition native to cities like New York, Chicago and (strangely enough) Birmingham. Usually purchased between stops on Bourbon Street, the Lucky Dog might be the only street-food purchase that qualifies as an obvious blood alcohol test.

In other words, if you're buyin' one of these to eat, you definitely shouldn't be driving.

The familiar and kitschy "bun and weenie" carts prowl the Quarter and the other tourist-heavy districts at all hours, but become more of a temptation for

unsuspecting drinkers in the wee small hours of the morning. Roughly the size of a horizontal home refrigerator, the metal carts are essentially steam tables on wheels packed with water-logged hot dogs and all the required accessories (buns, onions, chili, squirtable condiments). And on the palate, they're exactly as tasty as you'd think they'd be. Take that however you'd like.

Like a lot of Bourbon Street specialties, the appeal of the Lucky Dog breaks down to equal parts well-lubricated impulse and empty-gut desperation. If you find yourself swilling fluorescent frozen cocktails out of a plastic alien's head for nine consecutive hours, there might just be a Lucky Dog in your future. If you've got five bucks in your pocket and a powerful need for some food, ANY food, NOW, you're their target demographic. In other words, they're a lot more convenient than they are good.

Unlike the beignets at Cafe du Monde—a French Quarter staple that locals seek out when they're in the neighborhood—these long-boiled sausages probably haven't passed a native's lips since Ignatius J. Reilly ate himself out of a job in *The Confederacy of Dunces*. Locals know that the Lucky Dog moment is best fought off with a stroll around the block, where an all night diner or decent after-hours kitchen might be ample reward for a little patience.

But the Lucky Dog has its own cult, its own band of fans who swear by the wurst's magical restorative powers. They have fond, hazy memories of buying a foot-long from Ignatius himself and having the life-saving epiphany triggered by a daybreak weenie binge.

Here's hoping that these people—bless 'em—have the good sense to call a cab.

Pho Tau Bay
216 N. Carrollton Ave. (at Canal)
504-485-7687

zone: Midcity
reservations: none

meals: lunch and dinner Mon–Sat, closed Sun
specialty: Vietnamese
fancy factor: low-middlebrow
price range: $5–9

bonus points: on the Canal streetcar line

The owners of this local Vietnamese chain hit paydirt when they opened up their fourth restaurant in the New Orleans metro area. After the success of two suburban locations (one in Metairie, one on the West Bank) and a takeout operation near the LSU Medical Center downtown, the Cao family found a choice spot for their latest casual café-style eatery—on a convenient Midcity avenue, steps away from the revived Canal Street/Carrollton streetcar line and right next door to a fabled Italian ice-cream parlor, Angelo Brocato's (see page 192).

True to its name, the newest Pho Tau Bay specializes in casual soup and noodle dishes of Vietnam, including the heady beef noodle soup called *pho*. Native to Hanoi, *pho* starts out a thin, slow-simmered beef broth spiced with cinnamon and fragrant star anise. Rice noodles are commonly added to the mix, as are a number of meaty optional toppings, including thinly sliced beef brisket, flank steak, or (for the offal-compliant crowd) beef tendon and tripe. Steaming bowls of the soup are served with a side plate piled high with fresh

The Vietnamese in New Orleans

The Vietnamese community in New Orleans is one of the better-established latter-day immigrant groups. After the fall of Saigon in 1975, volunteer organizations of the local Catholic diocese launched an effort to resettle refugees in New Orleans East, where the area's largest Vietnamese population is concentrated. The burgeoning Vietnamese restaurant scene, however, is mostly across the Mississippi River Bridge in the towns of New Orleans' West Bank suburbs (Algiers, Gretna and Harvey), home to a separate but active Vietnamese Buddhist community. In recent years, simple, no-frills restaurants specializing in all manner of Vietnamese cuisine have sprung up and flourished.

basil, mung bean sprouts and chopped chili peppers so the diner can customize their own bowl of pho. It's the perfect wintertime treat on the biannual "really cold night" in New Orleans.

The rest of the menu covers the Vietnamese standards including various incarnations of *bun* (vermicelli noodles topped with a range of savory toppings), plump spring rolls and an assortment of ridiculously cheap *banh mi* sandwiches. And of course there's always the gold standard of super-sweet coffee beverages—*cafe sua da*—that's essentially equal parts slow-dripped chicory coffee and sweetened condensed milk.

Any of the restaurant's specialties end up being a welcome option for vegetarians and butter-soaked travelers looking for a one-meal respite from the city's riches. But its new location always presents its own temptation. After a light but satisfying meal, what's to stop you from heading next door to see what gelato flavors old Angelo is peddling?

Virtue in New Orleans, it seems, never comes easy.

Popeye's Fried Chicken and Biscuits
various locations

zone: various
website: www.popeyes.com

meals: lunch and dinner daily
specialty: fried chicken and fast-food Cajun
fancy factor: lowbrow
price range: $2–9

caveats: beware the afterburn
bonus points: great for Mardi Gras takeout

After many, many stories of celebrated culinary traditions, we will now praise a corporate fast-food chain.

Now to be fair, Popeye's isn't just *any* fast-food chicken chain—it's a genuine local institution. Founder Al Copeland opened his first location downtown in the 1970s and now boasts forty-eight locations in the metro area. Always a pillar of the local community, Copeland mounts an annual display of Christmas lights that's clearly visible from the International Space Station. His local color credentials are also stellar: he's sued novelist Anne Rice for defamation of character and battled a fellow millionaire businessman to a steakhouse fistfight.

But that's not the reason why locals love Popeye's. It's another case of tasty default cuisine that tastes more or less like New Orleans. Crunchy, cayenne-spiced fried chicken that's got the hot sauce built into every bite. Red beans that don't skimp on porky flavors and meaty rice dressing with just the right amount of black pepper kick. Hand-dipped onion rings instead of frozen. Biscuits so drenched in margarine that it's hard to tell of they were baked or fried. It may not be lunch at Galatoire's, but it sure beats the hell out of the Golden Arches.

There's also the convenience factor, especially during Carnival season, when house parties and impromptu parade gatherings require only two stops: the convenience store and the nearest Popeye's. It's a no-brainer menu that could only be easier if the chain installed beer taps for to-go orders. But then, if that happened, Copeland might easily rule the city.

It's also nice to know that the chain's "Louisiana-inspired cuisine" isn't completely off the mark when it comes to flavor. The standard menu includes a few passable fried seafood selections (shrimp and catfish) along with shrimp étouffée and smothered chicken—all of it a reasonable fast-food interpretation of the real thing, in a guilty pleasure kind of way. So when a customer in Minneapolis, Mannheim or Paramaribo, Suriname, get a craving for New Orleans food, they're at least eating the same quick-stop specialties that the locals scarf down as the parades roll by.

morning FOOD

CAFÉS AND BREAKFAST JOINTS

Even if vacationers start their days a bit later than back home, there's still need for some kind of morning meal, even if it's just a nice cup of café au lait and an order of crispy beignets.

Many travelers take an appropriately Continental approach to breakfast, since it's not uncommon to wake up still a bit full from the night before.

Sometimes the lure of the morning foods or a nice cocktail at brunch is just enough rouse you from a comfortable bed. Or if you're heading home on the far side of midnight, the magic words "breakfast served anytime" might end your evening on the perfect note.

Bluebird Café
3625 Prytania St. (at Antonine)
Cross Street: St. Ann St.
504-895-7166

zone: Garden District
website: www.bluebirdcaferi.com
reservations: none

meals: breakfast, lunch and dinner daily
specialty: diner and short order specialties
fancy factor: lowbrow
price range: $4–10

caveats: weekend lines out the door
bonus points: breakfast anytime

Just about every city has a beloved breakfast joint, a place where folks seek out a steaming plate of late-morning eggs as they test the limits of the "free coffee refills" category with a Sunday *New York*

Times. Such a place usually draws a line of late risers who are content to queue up and dream about pancakes.

Located near the Touro Infirmary complex, the Bluebird fills this role for the Garden District. Unlike the neighborhood newcomers that offer a bit more eclectic menu, this comfortably unadorned diner sticks to the basics—breakfast standards

(omelets, huevos rancheros), a few short-order grill specials (burgers, sandwiches and salads) and salads for the ladies who lunch.

Cafe du Monde
800 Decatur St. (at St. Ann)
504-525-4544

zone: French Quarter
website: www.cafedumonde.com
reservations: none

meals: open 24 hours daily
specialty: beignets and café au lait
fancy factor: lowbrow

caveats: tables coated with sugar
bonus points: open 24 hours

As the anchor of the historic French Market, Cafe du Monde is one of New Orleans' most visible landmarks. Tourists taking in the other sights around Decatur Street—Saint Louis Cathedral, the riverside walking parks, the Jax Brewery shopping complex—are drawn to the spacious open seating area like moths to a flame, regardless of weather, season or time of day. If you're walking around the Quarter, a coffee and beignets break is just part of the package, and Cafe du Monde is there to fill all your caffeine and fried dough cravings—24 hours a day, 363.5 days a year.

Billing itself as "The Original French Market Coffee Stand," Cafe du Monde has operated in the market since 1862, originally catering to two separate crowds—farmers and vendors during the night shift and shoppers during the day. The business went through several changes with various market renovations—most notably the Depression-era WPA program and 1974 French Quarter renovation—and now occupies a huge space in the old meat market. The company has since opened up other locations in the suburbs and various shopping malls, but for most folks, the French Market ambience defines the Cafe du Monde experience.

For most of its history, the café's sign proudly advertised "Coffee & Doughnuts"—the doughy fritters weren't officially called beignets until the 1950s, when veteran waiters raised in Cajun south Louisiana started using the term. Even in Cafe du Monde's high-trafffic setting, the deep-fried treats usually arrive in close to prime condition—crisp and golden brown on the outside, tender and puffy on the inside. As with any fried food, freshness is key—as the doughnuts cool, they lose their crunchy surface and the pillowy interiors turn tough.

Cafe Du Monde's coffee is in many ways the New Orleans standard—a thick, black brew cut with an equal amount of hot milk. The addition of roasted chicory serves a dual purpose by adding a distinctive nutty flavor and drastically reducing caffeine content. Generations of locals grew up on the taste of "CDM"—the café's grocery-store version of its coffee/chicory mix. Adventurous and/or lactose-intolerant sippers can order their coffee without milk.

The huge open-air arcade is always bustling, with bow-tied waiters shuttling trays of beignets and coffee underneath whirring ceiling fans. The streamlined operation—cash only, limited options, whambamthankyoumaam—is made for quick turnaround, which can often lead to a rushed vibe and tables coated with a shift's worth of sugary glaze. Street musicians, who know a semi-captive audience when they see one, perform on the café's sidewalk: heat-sensitive patrons usually retire to the café's smaller air-conditioned room.

Any visit to the Cafe du Monde usually concludes with a vigorous round of gentle self-flagellation as sated diners try to brush stubborn deposits of powdered sugar from their shirt fronts.

The café is another of the trusty local establishments that never shuts down for the night—open 24 hours for club hoppers instead of the produce vendors these days. Except, of course, for the 36 hours spanning the two-day Christmas holiday (6 PM Christmas Eve until 6 AM December 26) and if a killer hurricane has the city in its sights.

CC's Coffee House
various locations

zone: various
website: www.ccscoffee.com
reservations: none

meals: morning–night daily
specialty: coffee and pastries
fancy factor: lowbrow

Well before Starbuck's became the nation's high-dollar caffeine pusher, Louisianans sipped thick, flavorful cups of Community-brand coffee and wept when forced to travel outside the state (also known as "Clear Coffee Country"). City dwellers depended on chicory-cut "New Orleans Blend," while the rest of the state brewed up stout pots of dark roast, often in a manual French-drip pot. When the coffee-shop mania swept the country, Community responded with its own version of the "sit and sip" coffeehouse. The chain currently boasts about a dozen locations in the New Orleans metro area, half of them scattered through the neighborhoods of the city itself.

The high-profile shop on Upper Magazine beckons a steady crowd with a line of shaded sidewalk tables and plenty of indoor seating. The main room is airy and spacious, with plenty of natural light close to the counter. The perky caffeine technicians pump out a wide range of coffee drinks (hot, iced, blended, frozen and sweet) and a matching selection of smoothies and teas. Truth be told, the quality of the standard coffee isn't quite as high as Community's supermarket brands, so if you're a stickler for flavor, opt for an espresso variation. Pastry selection is pretty meager, but somehow covers offering something to most fad dieters (low-carb, low-fat, sugar-free, dolphin-safe).

A complimentary wireless Internet connection caters to the university crowd. During peak curricular times, the room resembles an off-campus study hall for the Tulane and Loyola crowds as well as neighborhood freelancers.

Fair Grinds

3133 Ponce de Leon
504-948-3222

zone: Midcity
website: www.fairgrinds.com
reservations: none

meals: morning-night daily
specialty: coffee and pastries
fancy factor: lowbrow

"Round the corner" proximity to the Midcity horse track gave this neighborhood coffeehouse its pun-compliant title and weathered (but well-preserved) equestrian murals on its beadboard walls.

Formerly home to a racetrack bar and gambling parlor, the Fair Grinds now serves as a de facto community center for the rapidly gentrifying Faubourg St. John. Many community groups—from youth chess leagues to morning tai chi groups—convene in the spacious upstairs room, which hosts acoustic music and open-mike performances in the evenings.

For such a small place, it has plenty of amenities—shaded patio seating, free wireless connection and water bowls for the canine customers. The Grind's art collection goes beyond the usual wall-based artist's shows to a more functional "permanent collection"—each of the café's wooden chairs has been decorated by a different local artist. (Read about their influences and other works on the convenient hanging tags.)

The menu offers plenty of pastries (muffins, cakes, pies) but is light on more substantial offerings. The Fair Grinds' coffees are organic and harvested from small, cooperative farms that earn the "Fair Trade Certified" designation.

Huey's 24/7 Diner

200 Magazine St. (at Common)
504-598-4839

zone: CBD/Warehouse
website: www.hueys247diner.com
reservations: none

meals: 24 hours daily
specialty: diner food
fancy factor: lowbrow
price range: $7–17

bonus points: 24 hours, full bar,
  breakfast anytime

Even in a city with a plethora of late-night eating options, nothing beats a 24-hour diner's no-brainer simplicity. Before or after a night on the town, there's solace in a balance-restoring plate of eggs any style, pork chop on the side, maybe a biscuit if someone baked a batch at midnight.

Located on the ground floor of the CBD's Pelham Hotel, Huey's is situated in a near-bulletproof setting—half a

block off bustling Canal Street, surrounded by the new high-rise hotels, and not very far from the Harrah's casino complex. Even the most dedicated gamblers tire of beeping slot machines and stale cigar smoke, and when they do, Huey's is a round-the-clock clubhouse for vacationing night owls.

The menu is heavy on tried-and-true breakfast standards and burger variations, most of which are perfectly fine, especially in the pre-dawn hours. The kitchen also tries its hand at familiar dishes from the casual restaurant canon (fried-chicken Cobb salad, beef medallion and scampi "surf and turf," roasted chicken breast with rosemary, pasta in seafood cream sauce). The more ambitious dishes don't do quite as well as the simpler ones, which should suit most diners just fine.

Any time of day, Huey's has a welcoming ambience that's a bit more upscale than your average breakfast joint. High-backed leatherette booths give the joint a bit of clubby sophistication—other architectural cues (patterned stainless steel walls, stools at the kitchen bar for solo diners, Art Deco clock) reinforce the traditional diner vibe.

But the genius of the place is in a particularly shrewd business plan—it's a 24-hour diner that also houses a full liquor bar. Think of it as a dream come true for hard-drinking conference types: after twelve or so hours of bar hopping, half the group wants to catch some food before turning in, the other half just wants one last round.

"Hey . . . didn't that diner have *drink* specials?"

The bar and the blue plates seem tailored to the party crowd. The meatloaf, for example, has a tangy brown gravy ladled on mashed potatoes AND toasted

brioche (perfect for capping a high-octane evening). As for the bar, Bloody-Marys and margaritas are cut price from 6 AM on the weekends.

Morning Call Coffee Stand
3325 Severn Ave. (at 16th)
Metairie, LA
504-885-4068

zone: Metairie
reservations: none

meals: 24 hours
specialty: beignets and café au lait
fancy factor: lowbrow

caveats: tough to find
bonus points: open 24 hours

At Morning Call, they make their café au lait the old-fashioned way—blended by gravity and mixed to order. It takes two long-spouted metal pots—one filled with dark chicory coffee, the other with heated milk—to fill a cup; each tipped gently, then raised a foot or so in the air. The twin streams of hot liquid never leave the cup, and the final product—a perfect, dark beige cup of steaming, slightly bubbly coffee—is whisked away to the waiting customer.

In any modern coffee shop, this pour—essentially a double-fisted version of the Turkish mint tea maneuver—would be considered legitimate tableside theatre, every cup capped with a triumphant flourish ("Tah daaaaaah!") at the end. But in this semi-historic coffee establishment, the traditional pour is taken for granted and performed at the café's back counter. For you, it's dramatic old-world tradition; for her, it's one of three hundred cups she'll dish out during her shift. If you don't keep your eyes peeled, you'll miss the whole damned thing.

Buried deep in the concrete hinterlands of suburban Metairie, Morning Call is a strip-mall coffee stand with solid French Market credentials. Sitting in the shadow of a 1960s-era shopping mall, the nondescript corner space houses a bit of French Quarter history.

From 1870 until 1974, Morning Call was a popular coffee stand in the Quarter and Cafe du Monde's main competition for fried dough supremacy. Situated at the split of Decatur and North Peter's Streets—the current location of the gold Joan of Arc statue—Morning Call had a devoted local following for its strong coffee and crisp, puffy beignets. It also had carhop service and lots of customer parking, which was eliminated by the French Market renovation in 1974. A casualty of tourist-friendly urban development, Morning Call beat a path to the suburbs.

The "new location," now thirty years old, still keeps a bit of the old days alive—the worn marble bar with its wooden archway made the trip from the Quarter. The arch's line of light bulbs stay lit and the doors stay open 24 hours a day, another holdover from Morning Call's days in the city. And given its secluded mallside locale, the crowd consists overwhelmingly of locals from Metairie and nearby Kenner.

As for the other half of the menu, blessedly small-batch beignets arrive steaming, crisp and unadorned. The customer is in

▦ CLASSIC ▦

Café au Lait and Chicory Coffee

Long before Americans embraced upscale *caffè latte*—an Italian import by way of Seattle—New Orleans started its mornings with rich, potent *café au lait*. A mixture of strong, chicory-fortified coffee and hot milk, café au lait is mostly an urban phenomenon—served in restaurants and homes throughout New Orleans and the outlying areas. In most of the old-line restaurants, after-dinner coffee is strong, flavorful, and black as night.

Roasted chicory—the root of Belgian endive and a close botanical relative of the radish—is what distinguishes the citified "New Orleans Blend" from the dark-roasted coffee preferred in the rest of south Louisiana. Originally used as a coffee extender or substitute during scarce times, the root became an accustomed taste and part of New Orleans' morning and post-meal routines.

The blend has a deep smoky fragrance and a pleasantly bitter flavor when brewed. And though a cup of black chicory coffee looks strong and mudlike, it's lower in caffeine than its unblended Cajun counterpart. And combined with equal parts of hot milk, it's one of the trademark tastes of a morning (or midnight) in the Crescent City.

Once you get out of the metropolitan area, though, you'll find the coffee in Acadiana served black as night, without milk or the telltale aroma of chicory.

charge of the oversized powdered sugar shaker, which invariably leads to Three Stooges–style physical comedy.

Quick flicks of the wrist rarely dispense enough of the sweet powder onto the doughnut's sizzling surface, especially on humid days. Dainty shakes are quickly replaced by more powerful blows to the shaker's base—which inevitably lead to a sweet explosion of sugar.

It's all part of the show, performed at Morning Call a few hundred times a shift. Laugh it off and, facing your audience of tablemates, take a bow. "Tah daaaaaah!"

PJ's Coffee & Tea Cafe
various locations

zone: various
website: www.pjscoffee.com
reservations: none

meals: morning–night daily
specialty: beignets and café au lait
fancy factor: lowbrow

As the city's largest local coffee-shop chain, PJ's has solid New Orleans connections—twelve of its stores, its corpo-

rate headquarters and roasting facilities are all in the city proper. They've got a knack for setting up shop in high-traffic areas (Armstrong Airport, D-Day Museum, the Tulane campus, strip malls) and pumping out tasty brew.

The coffee-shop experience can be hit or miss, depending on your location. The newer "concept stores" show good attention to atmosphere and detail, while the adapted spaces (notably the Uptown location on Magazine) tend to feel rundown and not terribly welcoming. If you're just looking for "joe to go," it's not a problem, but if you're looking for a more leisurely café experience, it's best to look elsewhere.

Rue de la Course
various locations

zone: various
reservations: none

meals: morning–night daily
specialty: coffee and pastries
fancy factor: lowbrow

The owners of this local cafe mini-chain have a knack for turning the city's landmark architectural forms into comfortable (if consistently smoky) coffee shops. The original location in the Lower Garden District is a reclaimed Creole cottage on Race Street (or in French, *Rue de la Course*) and flourished by serving the then-transitional neighborhood's caffeine-swilling needs. Success in the LGD led to citywide expansion—from locations in the Quarter and the CBD to the outer reaches of Uptown's Riverbend neighborhood.

The chain's flagship location—a renovated general store on the Garden Dis-

trict stretch of Magazine Street—closed its doors recently, only to reopen in a suitable space across the street. The new room, not quite as spacious as the old digs, lacks the pressed-tin ambience of the old place, but provides a home for the neighborhood's chain-smoking Bukowski disciples and frantic grad students. Like all the other Rues, an official indoor smoking section makes for hazy conditions, especially in the evening hours. If you're sensitive to tobacco, jockey for one of the plastic sidewalk tables underneath the streetside balcony.

Closer to the Uptown universities, the Rue crew took over a classic 20s-era financial institution (a branch of the old New Orleans Bank) to fantastic effect. Inside the stately sandstone structure—the same basic formula (spacious tables, ladderback chairs, green-shaded accountant's lamps) makes the space feel like an old gangster movie set. Smokers are relegated to the room's elevated vault platform near the 25-foot ceilings. Thanks to elementary physics— hot smoke rises—the lower section stays smoke-free for most of the day.

CLASSIC

French Fritters: Beignets and Calas

Though *beignets* (BEN-yays) are usually classified as a breakfast specialty, these deep-fried squares of puffy yeast-leavened pastry end up being the official snack food of French Market tourists. Served three at a time and dusted in fine powdered sugar, beignets are usually washed down with a cup of creamy café au lait. The prime purveyor of these doughnut-like sweets, Cafe du Monde (see page 184), has expanded to various suburban locations and shopping mall food courts, spreading the traditional treat beyond the Quarter.

The *cala* (kah-LAAH) is a close cousin of the beignet, but made with cooked rice bound together with sugar and egg. A dose of yeast or baking powder provides lift during the frying process—the finished product resembling a ball of light rice pudding with a crunchy "hush puppy" crust and a dusting of powdered sugar. Formerly a popular street food, calas are now on New Orleans' culinary endangered species list. Most often calas are prepared by home cooks (most notably African-American Catholics) as a breakfast food on special feast days—Mardi Gras morning and first communion parties. If you're not particularly faithful or connected, you can order calas at Elizabeth's in the Bywater (page 59).

The food selection is basic coffee-shop fare—sandwiches and tasty pastries to go with your mug o' joe. In a nod to the hotter months, iced coffees and teas also take up their share of the list. A seemingly innocuous chai milkshake is a nearly hidden knockout—a full pint of thick, creamy goodness with fragrant vanilla and a heady kick of cloves and cinnamon.

Slim Goodie's Diner
3322 Magazine St. (at Toledano)
504-891-3447

zone: Garden District
reservations: none

meals: breakfast, lunch and dinner daily
specialty: diner food
fancy factor: lowbrow
price range: $4–12

caveats: street parking scarce
bonus points: breakfast anytime

In a town where night life often bleeds into morning, the phrase "breakfast served anytime" can be utterly reassuring. Just knowing that you can score any manner of early-day specialties—eggs, pancakes, something starchy—well after the traditional lunch hour allows members of night-owl nation to oversleep with confidence.

Tall neon letters on this Magazine storefront announce its current occupant—DINER—as do the seating options (red leatherette booths, chrome stools at a low-slung counter) and utilitarian open kitchen. At most times of day or night, the place serves a hipster/student crowd along with workers on break from nearby Garden District boutiques.

Slim Goodies is a safe haven not only for the nighttime breakfast crowd, but for the meatless crowd as well. The list of short-order specialties runs the gamut from sugary (sweet potato pancakes) to savory (pork chops with grilled onions and gravy) and back again (fresh fruit smoothies). The deep burger and plate lunch menu has a surprising number of vegetarian-friendly options: soy burgers, smoked tempeh sandwiches, a meat-free jambalaya type concoction. "Eggs any style" can take a turn toward Central America (black beans and plantains) or the Midwest (a St. Louis Slammer—eggs, bacon and hash browns smothered in chili and cheese).

An unexpected standout at Slim's is a buttery crawfish étouffée—available on its own, as an omelet filling or ladled over pillowy biscuits or crispy potato pancakes. Smooth and silky, rich with just the right amount of radiant red pepper afterburn, it's literally just like the étouffée that Mama used to make (if yours used the Don's Seafood House cookbook for reference). Tender tailmeat makes it a great (and regionally appropriate) chili substitute for omnivores and shellfish-compliant vegetarians. An outstanding off-menu option is to get the étouffée ladled over a bed of crunchy, thin-cut French fries. It's not a heart healthy dish by any stretch, but a combination that might keep you up at night, or at least get you moving before noon.

Notable Brunches
- Brennan's
- Commander's Palace
- Dante's Kitchen
- Delmonico
- Lulu's in the Garden
- Mr. B's Bistro
- Ralph's on the Park
- Palace Cafe
- René Bistrot
- Ye Olde College Inn

THE sweet STUFF

PRALINE SHOPS AND SNOWBALL STANDS

Though there are plenty of savory treasures in New Orleans' edible pantheon, there are just as many sugary delights to bring out the kid in just about anybody. In the summertime, smooth snowballs help us cut the often unbearable heat and humidity. Rich pecan-filled pralines make the perfect late afternoon pick-me-up or after-dinner treat. Ice-cream shops are a draw just about anytime. And if you're lucky enough to catch Uptown's mule-drawn taffy cart, you'll get a sticky-sweet taste of old New Orleans, hand-pulled and sold by the paper-wrapped stick.

Angelo Brocato Ice Cream

214 N. Carrollton Ave. (at Iberville)
504-486-0078

zone: Midcity
website: www.angelobrocatoicecream.com
reservations: none

meals: morning–night daily
specialty: gelato, Italian pastries
fancy factor: nobrow
price range: $1–3

bonus points: candy-store atmosphere, on streetcar line

Inside this unassuming Midcity storefront, sweet temptations lurk at every turn. Toward the front window, a refrigerated case contains pre-made portions of tricolor spumoni, spicy *torroncino* and wedges of creamy baked Alaska. Along the back wall, an array of colorful Sicilian cookies taunt you from behind a thick layer of plate glass. And in between, a selection of rich gelati and sweet sorbets waiting to be hand-scooped into cone or cup.

In business for three generations and 100 years, Angelo Brocato's has the feel of an old-school soda shop with wire-backed chairs and nectar-pink walls. The aging neon sign outside (A. Brocato Spumoni and Cassatta Ice Cream) beckons a mostly local crowd for sugary fixes year 'round— ice cream in the summer, house-baked cannoli and coffee during the cooler months.

Pralines

Pralines are the most elementary of sweets—mix various sugars with butter, sometimes cream and cook over a low fire until smooth and browned. Add pecans for flavor and crunch (halves are best, bonus points for toasted) and dollop onto a marble cooling slab or a wax paper–lined countertop. The final product is one of the city's trademark snack foods and the perfect capper to a poboy-and-beer lunch break. Easy to make and pretty damned durable, this sugary nut-studded candy magically appears to satisfy the city's insatiable sweet teeth.

Historical accounts of the city describe other candies that carry the name *praline*—most notably white coconut candies often tinted pink with cochineal, a red dye made of crushed insects. The same sources describe " the old Creole women of New Orleans . . . the *Pralinieres*" as selling the pecan/sugar type around the city.

You'll see these simple confections in the most surprising places—souvenir shops, cashier stations, newsstands, even red wagons pulled by enterprising local youngsters. Down on Canal Street, a street-corner concessionaire carries on the *praliniere* tradition with a tray full of homemade goodness. In the city's restaurants, just about every dessert gives a nod to the local standby—usually with a nut-studded caramel sauce, cheesecake or ice cream.

In its familiar patty form, a praline can be one of three distinct textural types:

Crunchy—Usually thin and brittle, with a coarse crystal and a bit of a snap on the teeth.

Creamy—A smoother candy that melts on the tongue.

Chewy—More like a gooey caramel than the other two types. Don't forget to floss.

No matter which type you favor, make sure to *eat them while they're fresh*. Over time, even the best praline can dry out to a tooth-grinding puck of desiccated brown sugar and stale nut meats. If you're picking some up for the folks back home, ask your purveyor for "travel freshness" estimates.

Originally located on Ursulines in the French Quarter, Brocato's moved to Mid-city in the late 1970s, a strategic relocation that puts it within easy striking distance of Uptown regulars and suburban loyalists. (The original location currently houses Croissant D'Or, but ceramic remnants of its former tenant remain in the two tiled entryways of the old parlor. In front of

one, A BROCATO, and in front of the other, UNESCORTED LADIES ENTRANCE.

Brocato's current digs—a former Long's Bakery building now on the revived Canal streetcar line—retain a certain bit of the old-world charm. Circular marble tabletops are worn, chipped and smoothed by constant use. Labeled apothecary jars contain familiar candies and lesser-known traditional sweets.

House-made ice cream tends to dominate in-store traffic, because after all, who can resist a heaping scoop of rich chocolate/hazelnut *bacci* on a sweltering summer day? Or what about a cup of creamy coconut or praline gelato perfectly marbled with caramel and roasted pecans? On the lighter side, how about a shot of cooling lemon ice—a palate-cleansing shock of citrus that's only a *hint* grittier than sorbet? Mix or match.

Standard flavors are painted straight onto the menu board, with blank spaces conveniently left for seasonal favorites. Local crops of Louisiana strawberries, blueberries and peaches are transformed into batches of outstanding fruit ice that might last a week at peak season. Obscure Sicilian gelato flavors also make periodic appearances, including an intoxicating *gelsomino* (jasmine) flavor that's a floral variation on sweet vanilla.

As you wait in line, one of the pre-made ice-cream confections might catch your eye. Slices of spumoni sit next to cups of Bisquit Tortoni (frozen cream with cake and almonds) and fancy *sciallotti* (a molded dessert that mixes four different ice creams with three ices in a fancy pre-molded portion). Texturally, these confections are a bit harder than their hand-scooped counterparts and are perfect at-home dessert options. If you're buying one for immediate consumption, give it a little time to thaw.

Which is not to shortchange Brocato's baked goods. Notable options include cheesecakes, tira misu, light almond meringues, cookies such as clove-scented *scadalina* (dead man's bones), anise-frosted biscotti or fig-filled *cucidata*. And for the sentimental Sicilian in your life, Brocato's can ship many of these durable dipping cookies nationwide. (See the Louisiana Pantry section of the Appendix.)

Aunt Sally's Praline Shop
810 Decatur St. (at St. Ann)
504-524-3373

zone: French Quarter
website: www.auntsallys.com
reservations: none

specialty: pralines
fancy factor: nobrow
price range: $1–3

bonus points: convenient location

This candy and souvenir emporium seems to have locked down one of the best slots in the whole French Market— the storefront next to Cafe du Monde. And as is the custom with local candy makers, an employee is usually standing out on the sidewalk offering tiny praline bits as bait for passing tourists on their way to buy cheap sunglasses or African tribal masks. Odds are, if a passerby is in the mood for a crunchy-style praline, they'll pop in to Aunt Sally's for a quick look around.

Commercial vendors seem to favor creamy pralines over the crunchy variety— the kind with a little bit of snap but not so much grit on the teeth. Aunt Sally's bucks the trend by offering three different flavors of the thin, crunchy kind—original, chocolate and triple chocolate.

The last option consistently lures unsuspecting chocoholics into the shop, even as they're still buzzing from a recent beignet and coffee binge. Rich, creamy and delicate, these little pucks pack a concentrated fudgy punch; a crunchy candy version of your favorite chocolate cake frosting, just perfect for a walk through the market.

Creole Creamery

4924 Prytania St. (at Upperline)
504-894-8680

zone: Uptown
reservations: none

specialty: ice cream
fancy factor: nobrow
price range: $1–3

bonus points: sidewalk seating

The sleek, pale green glass façade of this Prytania Street ice-cream parlor will look familiar to any lifelong New Orleanian and pleasantly retro to newcomers. Foot-tall neon letters proudly advertise for the building's former tenant—the original McKenzie's Bakery, part of the much-beloved and recently bankrupted chain of neighborhood sweetshops. For years, the 40s-era bakery served Uptown's breakfast needs and sugary cravings with trademark pastries such as delicate frosted petit fours, chocolate-frosted shortcake "turtles" and dense but delicious buttermilk drop donuts.

CLASSIC

The Nectar Soda

Sweet, creamy and unusually wholesome, the nectar ice-cream soda looks like it was lifted from the pages of an *Archie* comic book.

In the heyday of the neighborhood drugstore, soda fountains were prime date spots for underage locals—and the nectar soda reigned supreme. The local version of New York's egg cream, the nectar soda starts off with a couple of shots of potent ruby-pink syrup flavored with almond and vanilla. Before the advent of "push and serve" soda technology, soda jerks mixed the syrup with short bursts of carbonated water from a soda fountain and dropped a scoop of vanilla ice cream into the thick cap of Barbie-pink foam.

For older New Orleans natives, childhood nectar stories are usually set in any of the now-defunct neighborhood drugstores, many of which had soda fountains on the premises. The family-run establishments—Schweighardt's, Bradley's, Berner's to name a few—figure heavily in local soda-fountain stories, as do chains like Walgreen's on Canal or the much-beloved K&B Drug Store. By the 1980s, K&B had shut down most of their soda fountains and the local soda-based tradition all but vanished.

For years, nectar fiends could get their fix, but only during the summer months. The flavor remained a seasonal favorite at the city's many snowball stands—thus keeping the cream-soda flavor on the palates of post-jerk generations.

Luckily for diehard fans, a recent wave of nectar nostalgia means the pink refresher is once again available in liquid form. A few local ice-cream parlors have revived the tradition of the hand-mixed nectar soda in all its sweet, baroque glory; a company on the North Shore is marketing a bottled version.

chocoholics a dedicated drool zone.

Sorbets follow the seasonal cues, but also seem to be influenced by the Uptown bar scene: mint julep and sangria are obvious riffs; the idea for blueberry mojito was probably hatched at nearby St. Joe's Bar, where the fruit and mint concoction is a signature cocktail.

Then there are outrageous flavors that seem to be off-limits for customers taller than about three feet. Judging from drip-stained Elmo shirts, bright pink bubble-gum ice cream studded with gummi bears and an unearthly "blue skies" flavor seem to be a hit with the under-9 set.

Sundaes, shakes and ice-cream sodas round out the lineup—including traditional nectar sodas and sugar-free sundaes for the no-carb contingent.

The seasonal flavor list includes some flavors that pay respect to the building's previous tenant—Sweet Cream Danish and TurtleMisu are already in rotation, and "Buttermilk Drop" is in the works. As homage, it's the next best thing. In the sweltering summertime, it might be even better.

A Creole Creamery nectar soda

Much to the chagrin of neighborhood pastry fans, the building lay fallow for a few years following the chain's untimely collapse. But around Mardi Gras of 2004, the building reopened to the sweet-snacking public as the Creole Creamery, an ice-cream establishment picked straight out of an *Archie* comic book.

Black-and-white checkerboard floors and pale pink walls make for an eerily wholesome ambience; well-placed benches on the sidewalk make for a bustling environment just about any summer night.

With 36 super-cooled tubs available at any given time—an easy one-uppance to Srs. Baskin and Robbin—the ice-cream scientists aren't happy to stick with the usual flavors. The standard options (vanilla, chocolate, mint chocolate chip, cookies and cream) share space with locally-themed flavors (café au lait, Creole custard, Creole cream cheese, and Rocky Rue). In a move of logistical genius, all eight chocolate-based variations are in a single section, giving

Hansen's Sno-Bliz
4801 Tchoupitoulas St. (at Bordeaux)
504-891-9788

zone: Uptown
reservations: none

specialty: snowballs
fancy factor: nobrow
price range: $1–5

caveats: closed March–October
bonus points: homemade syrups

Though some might consider snowballs to be an interchangeable summer-

time impulse item, regular customers of Hansen's Sno-Bliz pretty consistently beg to differ.

Chalk it up to a flavor preference, a sense of history or family loyalty—the snowballs churned out by this utilitarian cinderblock cube on industrial Tchoupitoulas Street inspires profound loyalty in its regular customers. Diehard fans of this Uptown landmark are quick to dismiss other stands as mere pretenders to the throne and routinely extol the virtues and pedigree of Hansen's over any other.

Oftentimes, the argument for supremacy is anchored in pure historical terms—the first is the best. They point to the legendary Sno-Bliz machine invented by Mr. Ernest Hansen in the 1930s as a breakthrough in shaved-ice technology. Other times, it's based on the texture of the ice, the quality of the syrups or obvious sense of neighborhood tradition. Snowball stands are a dime a dozen, the argument goes, but there is only one Hansen's.

And to a certain extent, they're right—Hansen's snowy texture can be spot-on in the consistency department, but the other legendary stands keep their blades equally sharp.

Hansen's flavor selection seems a bit slim by local standards—23 at a recent count, including all cream variations—but it's more than compensated for by an extraordinary amount of after-market accessories—everything from ice-cream stuffing to traditional sundae toppings. After 67 years of business, they've had plenty of time to run the permutations, add to the menu, and create new classics.

Their standard flavors, though, are favored by those who don't like too much sugar in their syrup, and who call Hansen's product "more of a grown-up snowball." Their standard Sno-Bliz flavor—a variation on the lemon ice theme—can make your whole head pucker up, and is sometimes mixed with grape or spearmint to take the edge off. The cream flavors—cream of blueberry and cream of peach, especially—work a subtle magic, all the way to the bottom of the cup.

The big draw for Hansen's is almost certainly family tradition. Folks who have lived here most of their lives have spend a goodly amount of their formative summers waiting in the line that often snakes in circles around the concrete block center space. They've had countless conversations with Mr. Ernest and Ms. Mary—who hold court from behind the glass counter and near the front picture window, respectively. Longtime regulars have watched their son Gerard grow up and become a local judge, and his daughter Ashley grow from a tiny girl to the third generation of Hansen to run the business.

Louisiana Snowballs

Even though this sweet frozen confection exists in other regional forms (Mexican *raspas,* ballpark snow cones, Hawaiian shave ice), a Louisiana snowball holds a sacred place in the state's summertime snack pantheon. A marriage of finely shaved ice and flavored sugar syrup, snowballs provide soothing relief from brutal summer heat with a universally appealing jolt of liquid sucrose and unnaturally bright food coloring.

The defining characteristic of a Louisiana snowball is its smooth, almost creamy texture. The other members of the "snow cone" family start off with pre-crushed chunks of ice, usually scooped from a waiting ice chest; authentic snowballs have to be shaved to order.

Every local snowball stand worth its syrup contains an important piece of industrial machinery—a high-torque electric shaving contraption capable of reducing 20-pound blocks of solid ice to endless cupfuls of ski-quality snow. The well-regarded stands are renowned for keeping their cutting blades sharp and their product's texture as smooth as a Squaw Valley snowdrift.

Once these delicate crystals are plowed into cups, the snow jockeys—nearly always a group of high-school-aged girls—pour on the flavor of your choice. Generations of Louisiana kids grew up staining teeth and tongue with the bold tricolor classics— spearmint green, cherry red or bubble-gum blue—but the flavor chemists at syrup companies manage to churn out new flavors for every hot season. Tutti-frutti pink, clear almond and chartreuse lemon-lime will be familiar to first-timers, while less obvious flavors like wedding cake, praline, Dragon's Blood, and Silver Fox cater to the more adventurous eaters. Flavor mixing—from half-and-half to full-on rainbow is another way of branching out across the flavor spectrum.

Most stands offer a selection of more delicate cream-based flavors that combine the sugary flavor with evaporated milk, which results in subtler flavors and pleasing pastel colors. While this category is dominated by fruit flavors—cream of blackberry, cream of blueberry, cream of cherry—a few wild cards slip into the dairy group as well (cream of nectar, cream of chocolate and the seemingly redundant "cream of ice cream.")

In an attempt to keep up with ice-cream-parlor competition, many stands offer a variety of toppings, drizzles and other add-ons for variety's sake. If a straight-up snowball just isn't sweet enough, it can be topped with gummi bears, crushed cherries or condensed milk. For a more sundae-like experience, opt for a snowball "stuffed" with a scoop of ice cream or a flourish of whipped cream.

On the other end of the sugary spectrum, many stands now offer sugar-free versions of their classic flavors. Not *quite* the same as a full-bore summertime sugar rush, but just as cooling.

Hansen's regulars have the biggest advantage when it comes to timing. The average snowball customer, driven by impulse and summer heat, might drop by on a steamy Wednesday afternoon, or perhaps make the trek for an after-dinner cooler—and in both cases, their quest would be thwarted by Hansen's ironclad hours (Thursday to Sunday, 1:00 to 7:00 PM). The loyalists know the rhythms and plan their cravings accordingly.

Loretta's Authentic Pralines
1100 N. Peters St. Suite 17 (in the French Market)
504-529-6170

zone: French Quarter
reservations: none

specialty: pralines
fancy factor: nobrow
price range: $1–5

bonus points: convenient location

Sugar fiends know that there's nothing quite as tempting or disappointing as a cash register praline. Wrapped in clear plastic wrap and charmingly irregular in shape, these simple, often homemade candies seem to be primitive slabs of firm caramel, but end up being gritty pucks of brown sugar with a few desiccated pecans thrown in for good measure.

A handwritten sign at Loretta's gives customers a quick lesson in the confectionary reality: "Our pralines are made with no preservatives and will crystallize in 3 weeks." In other words, freshness counts.

Of course, it's not the only lesson that's available at this French Market sweet shop. The well-windowed produc-

tion area, visible from the shop and the market's center walkway, looks like a folklife diorama of living local history. Several times a day, customers are attracted by the sights of an older woman scooping huge spoonfuls of liquefied sugar from an oversized copper pot. With a quick flick of the wrist, she makes a lopsided but consistent oval of batter-like syrup on the wide cooling table, then dips her spoon back in the pot. Consistent and measured, she repeats the process until the table is covered with shiny patties of sugary goodness.

In Loretta's tiny showroom, cooled pralines from previous batches are laid out like bakery cookies, deep brown in color with a subtle sheen reflecting bright fluorescent light. Each tray is marked with a different flavor label (original, rum, coconut, chocolate, peanut butter), each tray's contents differing just a bit in color and surface texture.

From the first bite, you understand the difference that freshness makes: the surface barely resists the teeth with just a whisper of a crunch; the center has its own thick, creamy quality, the consistency of super-sweet peanut butter. Pecans are tasty but largely beside the point; it's the candy that makes a handmade praline special.

Halfway through the patty, you're riding a rich, sugary high and are instantly spoiled: once you've eaten a fresh praline, it's tough to crunch your way through the cash register variety.

It's a little epiphany that seems completely appropriate given the shop's penchant for handwritten prayers and Bible verses. Looking through the praline maker's window, you catch a scriptural reminder scrawled onto masking tape: "Therefore I say unto you, What things so ever ye desire, when ye pray, believe

Doberge Cake

You probably won't find this on a restaurant's dessert list, but this towering multi-layered cake is a traditional birthday food for many New Orleans natives.

A specialty of local bakeries, the Doberge (pronounced DOW-bawzh) cake is constructed of 6–10 layers of standard butter cake, each coated with a thin layer of pudding (usually chocolate or lemon). The cake is frosted, decorated and frequently wolfed down before the honoree finishes blowing out the last candle.

that ye receive them, and ye shall have them.—Mark 11:24." And a foot or so away, an engraved plastic sign balances the Good News with a bit of hard-nosed business reality: ALL SALES FINAL.

Sophie's Ice Cream
1912 Magazine St. (at St. Mary)
504-561-0291

zone: Garden District
reservations: none

specialty: ice cream
fancy factor: nobrow
price range: $1–3

caveats: closed Mon
bonus points: courtyard tables, mini-scoops for easy sampling, open late

Don't let the nostalgic décor fool you. Even though this Lower Garden District upstart takes its aesthetic cues from the old *Happy Days* set, the stuff they're scooping is high-quality Italian-style gelato.

When the owners renovated this former auto parts store, they could have gone modern Euro-style and been convincing, but instead chose to go for the American drive-in motif. Chrome stools run the length of the boomerang-Formica countertop; wire-frame chairs cluster around tables closer to the front windows. Out back, a narrow courtyard matches the building's shocking pink exterior and holds a few tables for cooler nights.

The gelato flavors run the gamut from American standards to the Italian classics (intense pistachio, a potent chocolate/ hazelnut *bacci,* coconut that hits you right between the eyes) and local variations (tangy Creole cream cheese, caramelized sweet potato, Louisiana blueberry). The texture is rich, pliable and insanely creamy—just what you need on a tropical summer night.

If you plan on lingering awhile, you can get your cool treat scooped into old-style footed glassware. Or if you're in the mood for a foot-tall frosty pink delight, you can order an old-fashioned nectar soda—a nearly extinct native New Orleans refresher.

The whole process takes place on Sophie's 40s-era soda fountain; a three-ton, all-metal affair rescued from a Bywa-

Roman Chewing Candy

Mule carts aren't exactly a rarity in New Orleans. The steady clop-clop-clop of hooves on pavement is still an integral part of any French Quarter soundtrack. But very few of the tourist carriages contain an operational candy kitchen, and most of the drivers spend their time spinning tales instead of pulling taffy.

Since 1915, this mule-drawn sweetshop has been the family business for the Cortese family (from founder Sam to his grandson, current taffy man Ron Kotteman). In between batches, the distinctive white cart slowly makes its way down St. Charles Avenue most days, patiently parked outside the Uptown schools as they're letting out for the day.

Kotteman's only product is a thin, foot-long stick of handmade taffy in one of three flavors (vanilla, chocolate and strawberry) made from an old Sicilian recipe. When Ron's grandfather first drove the cart, the candy was just a sideline—produce and firewood were the real moneymakers—but eventually Sam switched over to full-time taffy sales and launched another durable New Orleans tradition. The candy is just like the older folks remember— tasty, sugary, a little tacky to the touch and strong enough to yank your molars straight out of your jaw. Back in the day, a stick sold for about five cents. Today, a wax-paper-wrapped dose of homemade nostalgia will set you back a mere seventy-five cents.

The Chewing Candy cart can be tough to find most of the year, but during Jazzfest Kotteman sets up shop at the Fairgrounds, making it easier to sample a sweet taste of Old New Orleans.

ter rummage sale. The soda jerk on duty pumps a few generous squirts of ruby-hued syrup into a slender fluted soda glass and moves in under the fountain's chrome and plastic nozzle. Ever so gradually he pulls the handle as the fountain gurgles loudly and spews a powerful stream of carbonated water into the syrup. With a series of quick upward strokes, the jerk uses a plastic spoon to mix the syrup and water in a contained explosion of tiny pink bubbles. The mixture lightens progressively as he adds more seltzer—burst by burst, inch by inch—and after a minute of wrist-action agitation the glass glows a vivid pale red topped with an inch-thick layer of matching froth. A scoop of vanilla tops off the colorful treat.

Sophie's vanilla has the perfect taste and texture for topping a nectar soda. After a few minutes, the melting cream blends in with the pink soda, and a hint of lemon in the ice-cream base keeps the flavors from being too sickly sweet.

If you've sampled all the flavors and still can't narrow it down, opt for a collection of "mini-scoops"—walnut-sized portions that come in groups of six or more for about the price of a single portion. Served in a footed glass sundae dish, they can make you nostalgic for old New Orleans or, if you close your eyes, the gelaterias of Rome.

Southern Candymakers
334 Decatur St. (at Bienville)
504-523-5544

zone: French Quarter
website: www.southerncandymakers.com
reservations: none

specialty: pralines, candies
fancy factor: nobrow
price range: $1–3

It's almost a shame that this French Quarter candy shop keeps its doors closed most days. If they didn't, the whole upriver half of the neighborhood—easily from Jackson Square to Canal Street—would smell a whole lot sweeter.

As it is, you walk into the unassuming Decatur Street shop and immediately start breathing air super-saturated with sugar, heady with vanilla and laden with invisible fudge fumes.

Most of the other neighborhood praline shops are just that—one-trick ponies that peddle a few different praline flavors from a well-situated storefront and fill the rest of the shop with cookbooks, boxes of beignet mix and historical postcards.

Southern Candymakers distinguishes itself with its wide selection of homespun bonbons. Their glass cases are packed with homemade candies you haven't seen since Grandma swore off the sweet stuff—chocolate-dipped toffee; pecan-topped mounds of white divinity; fudge by the pound; sticky, rich *tortues*—their take on the caramel/pecan turtle theme; sugar-glazed pecans.

Their creamy-style pralines have an amazing deep-roasted, almost butterscotchy flavor and toothsome texture with an addictive, slightly salty aftertaste—just enough to keep you going back for another bite. The pecans—plump, intact halves instead of precrushed bits—are a pleasant surprise, but sadly rare in this praline-heavy town.

William's Plum Street Snowballs

1300 Burdette St. (at Plum)
504-866-7996

zone: Uptown
reservations: none

specialty: snowballs
fancy factor: nobrow
price range: $1–5

caveats: closed Oct 15–Mar 15, leaky
  square containers
bonus points: endless flavor list,
  homemade condensed mlk, open seven
  days in season

Inside the cramped ordering area of William's Plum Street Snowballs, you can't help but feel like you've uncovered Willie Wonka's wet bar.

"Inside" is really little more than an enclosed pick-up window, with rickety screen doors at either end and a chest-height counter running the length of the room. Above the counter, a huge, bright yellow sign lists upward of a hundred different snowball flavors, ranging from vanilla to fuzzy navel and beyond. Underneath the sign, narrow shelves display a four-row rainbow of brightly colored bottles filled with flavored syrups.

There are always the classics: ruby-pink nectar, syrupy brown root beer, chartreuse lemon-lime, off-clear almond and rich chocolate mixed with evaporated milk. Some arise out of dietary demands—no-sugar and color-free varieties for the low-carb and clean-tongue crowds. Many of the flavors are deep, perfect colors that we associate with grade-school art class—Kelly green spearmint, deep blue bubble gum, strawberry the tint of pasty red finger paint. Poured onto a cup of snow-tender shaved ice, these concentrated flavors taste like summer to generations of New Orleanians.

William's Plum Street Snowballs has been an Uptown phenomenon since the 1940s, and to this day, it exudes a kind of Norman Rockwell wholesomeness. From mid-March until October, narrow picnic benches fill with families digging into super-cooling summer treats, risking the dreaded brainfreeze, and tinting their muzzles and tongues in all the colors of the rainbow.

One hot afternoon, struck with option anxiety and borderline heatstroke, I asked the owner for an offhand recommendation. "Orchid cream vanilla with condensed milk," she said, without missing a fraction of a beat. "It's what I always get. We make our own condensed milk, you know."

She presented a lavender-domed cup drizzled with a thick layer of sugary beige syrup. The pale purple syrup had its own deep vanilla flavor, but the homemade condensed milk—noticeably different from the Eagle-brand variety—added its own super-sugary dimension. For a simple "syrup on ice" confection, it had at least three levels of creaminess—the syrup's evaporated milk, the viscous condensed milk, and the velvety texture of the snow underneath.

By the time I hit the screen door leading out, I was nursing a weapons-grade sugar rush and a third-degree brainfreeze.

That's one down, ninety-nine to go.

MARKET groceries

NEIGHBORHOOD AND OPEN-AIR MARKETS

Not all of New Orleans' food culture flows from the city's restaurant kitchens. The Crescent City's open-air markets, neighborhood groceries and specialty stores also play a crucial role in the city's food traditions. From the historic French Market to the nomadic farmer's stands, here are a few of the places where the locals go to "make their groceries."

Crescent City Farmer's Market
various locations

zone: various
website: www.crescentcityfarmersmarket.com

specialty: locally grown produce and homemade specialties
fancy factor: nobrow

caveats: the markets move around
bonus points: the best local products

There's no better place to find the best regional produce, seafood and home-grown specialties than the Crescent City Farmer's Market. Portable tables groan under the weight of juicy Creole tomatoes during the summertime and sweet Louisiana satsumas (mandarin oranges) as Christmas nears. Shrimpers measure out tangled handfuls of jumbo white shrimp for boiling; fishermen advertise "Wild Des Allemandes Catfish" year-round. Ponchatoula strawberries, water-melons from Washington Parish, sweet potatoes, okra, mirliton or eggplant: if a crop grows within a hundred-mile radius of the city, you'll be able to buy it from the folks that picked it from the fields or plucked it from the water.

In its present form, the farmer's market resembles a roving gypsy camp more than a stationary marketplace. On Tuesday the tent city opens for business in a Riverbend parking lot across from the levee, Saturday brings the vendors to the Warehouse District, Thursday after-noons in Midcity near City Park, and Wednesday mornings the farmers return to the old French Market on Decatur Street.

Sweet Citrus and Summer Melons: Louisiana Fruits

Watch the farmer's markets and dessert lists for the distinctive seasonal flavors of these Louisiana fruits.

satsumas—This sweet, easy-peeling version of a Mandarin orange reaches its peak around Christmas. Along with much of the Louisiana citrus crop—oranges, grapefruit, Meyer lemons—satsumas enjoy their peak season from late November through January.

Ponchatoula strawberries—This specialty crop from the North Shore's Tangipahoa Parish has a double season with tasty berries in January, then again in March–April.

Louisiana blueberries—Bushes bearing these tasty berries peak just as summertime reaches full swing (late May–early July).

dewberries—These tangy wild blackberries start ripening on the vines in late April, with cultivated varieties ready for picking through the heat of July.

Ruston peaches—A specialty crop from north Louisiana, these juicy summer stone fruits appear from June to August.

watermelon—Melons from the Mississippi borderlands, Washington Parish watermelons are at their best right around Independence Day (early July).

Finding the markets might take a little research, but once you're there, the delights of the season are there for the taking. And while you're there, you can pick up locally raised organic meats, traditional hand-pounded filé powder, fresh-baked pastries.

The farmer's market is currently run by the Economics Institute of Loyola University, and the road show format fits well with the institute's overall dual goals: to serve a broad range of the city's population and to connect rural food producers with urban consumers.

Over the course of ten years, the market has grown from one market to four—effectively bringing the farmers to a cross-section of New Orleans citizenry instead of an exclusively affluent foodie community. Executive director Richard McCarthy is always trying to get closer to the poorer sections of town that have fewer food shopping options.

"Each market reflects its neighborhood," he says. "Our French Quarter market is more heavily tattooed than our Tuesday version, where the Uptown ladies come in straight off the tennis court."

As of February 2005, the market locations are as follows:

Monday morning
Uptown
Parking lot of 200 Broadway at River Road

Wednesday morning
French Quarter
In the French Market at French Market Place and Governor Nicholls

Thursday afternoon
Midcity Market
3700 Orleans Avenue

Saturday morning—Warehouse District
700 Magazine Street at Girod

For a list of current locations, check the market's website at www.crescentcity farmersmarket.com

French Market
1008 N. Peters St. (at St. Ann)
504-522-2621

zone: French Quarter
website: www.frenchmarket.org

fancy factor: nobrow

caveats: mostly souvenirs and such
bonus points: historical touchstone

There was a time when the Vieux Carré's French Market was a bustling, vibrant part of workaday New Orleans culture—a place where you could find food of every description, live animals, the freshest seafoods, and the only legal meats in town. Today, unless you're shopping on Wednesday mornings, the bumper crops are cheap sunglasses, reasonably priced tourist kitsch, patchouli oil, sandalwood incense and tiny shellacked alligator heads.

Before supermarkets became the primary purveyors of American foodstuffs, the French Market, like many other neighborhood markets around town, was filled with vegetable stands, butcher stalls and poultry pens—signs of guaranteed freshness, if not cleanliness. The market got a series of facelifts during its history, with the two most recent being the Depression-era work done by the Works Progress Administration and the reinvention of the market as a tourist plaza in the mid-1970s.

This sprawling arcade complex that now covers the swath of Decatur from Jackson Square to the old U.S. Mint retains a little bit of its historic feel—the downriver sections are sheltered from the elements but still have an open-air feel—but much of the old market has become little more than a strip mall full of postcard shops, craft vendors, praline factories and T-shirt boutiques. In addition, the complex contains a few restaurants and the New Orleans Jazz Historical Park, run by the National Park Service. There are still a few vegetable vendors, but by and large the market now serves the city's booming tourist industry.

In recent years, there has been a small revival in the market, with farmers returning to the Quarter to sell their products fresh from the fields. On Wednesday mornings, the Crescent City Farmer's Market (page 204) brings its migratory operation to the parking lot outside the crafts market, providing the French Quarter and Faubourg Marigny residents with a seasonal alternative to supermarkets when they want to "make their groceries."

Martin's Wine Cellar
3827 Baronne St. (at Peniston)
504-899-7411

zone: Uptown
website: www.martinwine.com
reservations: none

meals: lunch daily
specialty: sandwiches and lunch specials
fancy factor: middlebrow
price range: $5–12

caveats: no dinner
bonus points: great selection, great by-the-glass wine selection

It happens to the best of us—even in the land of butter and deep-fried goodness, a powerful, all-consuming craving for raw green vegetables sets in, and you just gotta have a salad.

I see this all the time with houseguests who manage to break the long-weekend barrier. They *want* to keep up a brisk pace of culinary indulgence, but need a one-meal break from a steady diet of high-carb, high-fat local classics. They need an infusion of fresh leafy greens—and that's when I send them over to a certain Uptown liquor store.

To call Martin's Wine Cellar a liquor store is only partly accurate: this beige cinderblock structure on Baronne houses the city's best wine market, an outstanding specialty grocery and, tucked way in the back, an outstanding contemporary delicatessen.

From the front of the store, you'd almost never know the airy, well-lit café is hidden beyond the bottle racks and shelves of every imaginable spirit. If you're there to eat, head for the glass-front display cases and by the time you can make out individual items, the ceilings have jumped four feet, revealing a semi-secret clubhouse for prim Uptown ladies and lawyers on lunch break.

The term "deli" doesn't exactly do this creative kitchen justice. Sure, the chalkboard sandwich list runs for days and includes a damned fine gravy-soaked roast beef poboy, but the rotating list of eclectic specials shows amazing depth and quality—duck enchiladas, tuna Niçoise, Moroccan lentil soup and, in a nod to tradition, creamy red beans on Monday and grillades and grits for Sunday brunch.

The salads contain almost comically large servings of perfectly dressed field greens, crisp romaine or tender spinach, depending on your pleasure. Martin's everyday salads have an impressive range (pulled roast chicken with raisins, pecans and blue cheese, several pasta variations, Caesars with and without grilled chicken), but the daily specials can rival anything put out by a fine-dining establishment (grilled lamb loin with teardrop tomatoes and chutney vinaigrette, grilled duck breast) at a fraction of the price. It's not uncommon to see three dainty "ladies of a certain age" working their way through a single oversized salad divvied up family-style onto tiny plates. If you don't have an afternoon of office work waiting, this is the place to sample great wines at bargain by-the-glass prices. Customers have come up with a host of creative strategies to blur the line between the market's take-out and sit-down aesthetics. Do-it-yourself wine and cheese samplings "spontaneously" break out on weekend afternoons. Wine lovers peruse the specials board and then the wine section, essentially turning the whole shop into their lunchtime wine cel-

lar—without the standard 250 percent restaurant markup.

It's tough to pass by Martin's prepared food section without adding a bit to your basket—wine-marinated herring, red velvet cake, or both; likewise for the far-ranging artisanal cheese and charcuterie selection. It's especially tough not to roam the wine aisles if you've had a few glasses with lunch. In fact, it's almost guaranteed that any midday meal will turn into a shopping trip—and with any luck, you'll feel virtuous enough to explore the city's bounty by dinnertime.

Vietnamese Market, New Orleans East

informal: around 4600 Alcee Fortier Blvd. (at Peltier)
no phone

zone: Outtatown

specialty: home-grown Asian produce
fancy factor: nobrow

caveats: early morning
bonus points: not in Kansas anymore

If you're willing to rise at Saturday dawn and drive a half-hour to New Orleans East, you can end up on the other side of the globe.

The Saturday-morning market off Chef Menteur Highway might as well be somewhere in suburban Saigon; a slice of southeast Asia on the swampy side of the Intercoastal Canal.

Located in and around a weathered motor court–turned–apartment simplex, this outdoor market has a thrown-together feel and a funky homegrown vibe to it. There are a few wobbly card tables, but mostly the wares—from whole barracuda to tied bunches of yard-long beans—are spread out on improvised ground coverings (plastic dish drainers, bright blue tarps, flattened-out cardboard boxes). Not so great for fresh seafood, but perfectly acceptable for the seasonal variety of vegetables that are grown on small farms or tilled yards flanking the bayous and canals nearby.

The vendors are mostly older women—some tending tables in housedresses or American garb, others wearing dazzling purple silk shirts as they crouch next to the ground, chewing betel nuts as they sit on their haunches, broad bamboo hats protecting them from the emerging sunlight.

Without a doubt, this is the city's most active immigrant marketplace—unless you speak Vietnamese, you'll end up relying largely on sign language. Signs, when they're used, advertise the name of products—dimpled bitter melons, shimmering gold gourds, fresh-dug nuggets of ginger—in Vietnamese script. There are little shops around the main action that sell piping hot fried sesame dumplings, strong Vietnamese coffees and various other specialties.

Dedicated early birds will see the best action, but you have to race the sun to do it. Usually by 8 AM, the market's already winding down for the day.

Zara's Lil' Giant
4838 Prytania St. (at Upperline)
504-895-0581

zone: Uptown
reservations: none

specialty: groceries and poboys
fancy factor: nobrow

In the age of "big box" grocery chains, it's hard not to have a soft spot for the few surviving neighborhood grocery stores. They remind us that at some point in the not-too-distant past, stocking an urban kitchen wasn't a one-stop experience. Each line item had a different address and a separate specialist—butcher, baker, vegetable seller.

Zara's Lil' Giant, an outwardly tiny Uptown grocery, manages to live up to its ambitious name and fulfill the original promise of the all-in-one "supermarket."

The building itself—a simple cinderblock cube with a single strip of about a dozen convenient parking spaces—only dates from the 1980s, but its business approach is decidedly old school. In a space the same size as a standard-issue convenience store, Zara's covers all the bases of a fancy boutique grocery—fresh seafood delivered daily, a fantastic poboy counter, a *real* butcher on duty and a prepared foods section featuring house-made portions of macaroni and cheese, lasagne, home-cooked vegetables for neighbors too busy to cook. Packed to the rafters with merchandise, the Lil' Giant never feels cramped or overwhelming.

And while a solid neighborhood supermarket might not be particularly notable, it's the range of products that never ceases to amaze. In the store's tiny footprint, Zara's packs an amazingly varied inventory that's been honed by years of individual customer requests.

This being the land of the red-bean Monday, you'd expect to see fresh local green onions and two kinds of parsley in the 20-foot produce line. But turn on your heels, scan the nearby condiment racks, and you'll find upward of twenty different hot sauces. Place an order at the deli counter (fifty different poboy options) and you can browse the pre-roasted chickens or wrapped muffulettas while you wait for your number to be called. The dairy case carries standard-issue milk along with heavy cream, three varieties of soy, and Creole cream cheese made by nearby Mauthe's dairy.

Whatever you're looking for, someone else has already put in a request to the manager. Oxtails? Frozen edamame? Brocato's lemon ice? Kosher, rock, sea and anodized salt? Vanilla-scented chestnut paste from southwest France? It's all there.

It actually wouldn't take much for Zara's to redo its outward image and remake itself as a boutique market—most of the raw materials are already on the shelves. But Zara's charm is its contrast with the mega-marts and self-consciously upscale grocery stores: whether it's a stewing hen or a sushi-grade tuna, they've got just what you need because they've been listening to you for years.

And if you're looking for the heads-on Gulf shrimp, check the ice chest by the wine rack. They came in fresh this morning . . .

chapter 4
BARS AND CLUBS

This might come as a surprise to some people, but New Orleans has developed a bit of a reputation as a drinking town.

Maybe it's the fact that the bars here never close or that a few notable cocktails (the Sazerac, the Ramos Gin Fizz, the Pimms Cup) were either invented here or have strong historic ties to the city. Maybe it's the rough-and-tumble saloon tradition that survived both Prohibition and the white wine spritzer. Maybe it's because we still have a population of dedicated old-guy bartenders who specialize in whiskey drinks and have never even SEEN a tiny paper umbrella. Or the fact that in some sections of town, you can buy beer out of a doorway or order a drive-through daiquiri from your rental car.

Whatever the reason, most locals would probably be shocked, SHOCKED to discover that there's drinking going on in New Orleans.

This chapter covers the salient points of the city's drinking tradition along with a sampler tour of a few of New Orleans' outstanding bars and nightclubs. (And by a few, we mean two dozen or so.) After all, you might need a little help finding the *good* bars, but if you can't find a drink in this town, you're just not paying attention.

"Go-Cup" Culture

The long-standing New Orleans "walk and drink" tradition never fails to amaze visitors from less permissive liquor cultures—which, to be honest, is just about everywhere else in America.

Walking out of a bar carrying a half-finished cocktail, while a fairly simple act, somehow brings out the frat pledge in the most straightlaced tourist. Sometimes even teetotalers buy a goofy frozen drink just for the thrill of NOT getting a pubic drunkenness ticket.

For residents, there's a different dynamic at work: once you get accustomed to alcohol *al fresco*, you're more likely to get a public drunkenness citation while on vacation. From secondhand accounts, police in other cities tend to frown on the seemingly commonsense explanation ("What? I'm from New Orleans. It's legal there").

Inside Orleans Parish, mixing a stout cocktail with a brisk stroll won't get you a ticket, but carrying a glass container might. Most bars will cheerfully provide nonbreakable plastic cups for their wandering clientele, available on request. If your buddies decide to move on halfway through a round, your bartender or the nearest bouncer will provide you with a smash-free container for the road. Just ask for a "go cup."

Understandably, go-cup culture blossoms during springtime Carnival season. In the interest of public safety and toast-the-float tradition, most Mardi Gras krewes fling colorful go cups to the enthusiastic parade crowds. Locals stock up and use them for street-friendly cocktail cups—disposable, no-maintenance and, best of all, perfectly legal.

french quarter

Monteleone Carousel Bar
800 N. Rampart St.
504-523-3341

vibe: Salvador Dali designs a tourist hotel bar
peak times: Thu–Mon, 8:30 PM–close
music: live
games: none

Elaborate merry-go-round bar spins at near-glacial pace—just fast enough to discombobulate heavier drinkers. Tables beneath a "starry-night" paint job for the motion-sensitive.

Donna's Bar & Grill
800 N. Rampart St.
504-596-6914

vibe: big bumpin' tubas
peak times: Thu–Mon, 8:30 PM–close
music: live

Brass band headquarters on the Rampart Street border of the Quarter and Tremé.

Funky Butt
714 N. Rampart St.
504-558-0872

vibe: jazz club
peak times: show nights
music: live
games: none

Deco-styled jazz club in the shadow of Congo Square (modern-day Armstrong Park).

House of Blues
225 Decatur St.
504-529-2583

vibe: funky by design
peak times: show nights
music: live
games: none

The local outpost of Dan Ackroyd's corporate roadhouse chain. Draws plenty of national-level acts in the main room and their smaller venue—The Parish.

The Pimm's Cup

A somewhat unexpected British import, the Pimm's Cup is an icy highball made from a spicy English liqueur mixed with ginger ale or lemon-lime soda and traditionally garnished with a cucumber slice. It's a cocktail that's slightly sweet, vaguely spicy and just fizzy enough to make your tongue tingle.

In England, the Pimm's Cup is a standard at summer's outdoor sporting events—marathon cricket matches and Wimbledon's extended tennis-fest to name only two—but in the U.S., this refreshing drink has become a happy-hour standard in New Orleans, a not-so-British American city. Sipped in a dark barroom (Napoleon House serves the gold standard) or savored on a breezy balcony, the Pimm's Cup is a perfect late-summer drink for the Crescent City, where subtropical summers take their toll on traveler and local alike.

The active ingredient of this classic cocktail is a complex gin-based English liqueur, Pimm's Number 1. Sipped on its own (as it rarely is), the sticky liqueur is thick with sugar and "secret spices" including juniper and aromatic bitters. At the peak of Pimm's popularity, there were six numbered variations of the liqueur, each with a different alcoholic base (from Number 2's whiskey to the vodka-infused Number 6). With time, the brown-liquor versions fell out of production, leaving the vodka and gin variations to carry on Mr. Pimm's tradition.

Recipes for a "proper Pimm's Cup" vary wildly on the drink's fizzy mixer. Some of the more traditional formulas call for a tangy ginger ale to compliment the liqueur's spicy notes, while other bartenders use sweet-and-sour mix topped off with a frothy shot of lemon-lime soda (7UP or Sprite being the most common). Some variations call for lemonade, others for fresh-squeezed juice and club soda. Whatever the specifics, the soda component adds a balanced sweet/sour flavor to the spicy Pimm's.

In the garnish department, there's a lot less variation—the one nonnegotiable component being a chunk, spear or disk of raw cucumber. This distinctive vegetable addition is there for more than visual appeal. The clean, almost astringent flavor of the cucumber plays off the sweet, sour and spicy sensations of the liquor and soda, giving the taste buds a welcome change of pace. Optional additions include a squeeze of lemon (always nice) and a sprig of fresh mint (less common, but welcome nonetheless).

Lafitte's Blacksmith Shop
941 Bourbon St.
504-522-9377

vibe: perfectly dank
peak times: evenings, weekends
music: jukebox, live piano
games: none

Away from the bustle of Bourbon, this Creole cottage still does business as God intended—pumping out spirits to the French Quarter crowd. The bartenders have heard every damn pirate joke in the world, so save your breath.

Molly's in the Market
1107 Decatur St.
504-525-5169

vibe: local's watering hole
peak times: evenings, weekends
music: jukebox
games: none

Aging, welcoming, open to the street. This old journalists' hangout wears recent history on its sleeve.

Pat O'Brien's
624 Bourbon St. (at St. Peter)
504-525-4823

vibe: old -chool tourist bar
peak times: any damn time
music: live
games: none

First stop for most first-timers. Big bar, sing-along piano lounge, froofy rum drinks in curvy, foot-tall glasses. Fiery courtyard fountain is good for the "thousand yard stare" crowd.

bywater

Saturn Bar
3067 St. Claude Ave.
504-949-7532

vibe: rapidly decaying funk
peak times: late-night
music: jukebox
games: junk-stacked pool table

Buzz Bombers: Hurricanes and Frozen Daiquiris

These are the potions that make Bourbon Street what it is today. They're high in the stuff that kids like (sugar and food coloring) and the active ingredients that adults crave (alcohol). Dump these ingredients in a refrigerated slush machine, pull the plunger and next thing you know, you're sipping a puréed popsicle that kicks like a mule.

The Hurricane is the grandfather of the bunch—a strong rum-based cocktail popularized by Pat O'Brien's in the French Quarter. Served in a foot-tall curvy glass, this bright red cocktail set the standard for excessive tourist cocktails in the Vieux Carré.

There are other sweet "tourist drinks" these days, and most of them are served frozen. Just about any cocktail you can name has a frozen counterpart swirling in the neon-bathed bars of Bourbon Street. Frozen White Russians, Long Island Iced Teas, flavored Piña Coladas and (yes) Hurricanes swirl alongside bizarre beverages named for just about anything.

A good rule of thumb is the more imaginative a drink's name (Shipwreck, Cherry Smasher, the Hulk, Blue Voodoo, Ghostbuster) the less it actually resembles an actual cocktail. Daiquiri bars tend to go through a lot of the more extreme liquors (151-proof rum, pure grain alcohol) in the never-ending quest to give the people what they want.

Another good guideline: If you have to sample the Double Shot Electric Lemonade in a fluorescent alien glass, you'd better have just one. The combination of high sugar and high alcohol makes for vicious mornings-after. Consider yourself warned.

Hipsters (local and imported) dote on this St. Claude über-dive for its funky atmosphere, old-school neon and never-ending collection of yard-sale clutter and dissected AC compressors. But if there's a line between funky and unsavory, it might well be an ever-present aroma of free-range cat piss. Your call.

Vaughn's
800 Lesseps St.
504-947-5562

vibe: hoppin' Bywater barroom
peak times: late-night show nights
music: live
games: off-night ping-pong

Don't reach for the corner door (it's been blocked for years). Instead, get buzzed in at the side entrance of this rough-hewn Bywater classic. Kermit Ruffin's more-or-less standing gig on Thursdays is a New Orleans classic, complete with red beans and rice in between sets. (Because even a late dinner was hours ago . . .) On show nights, the dance floor's packed; otherwise, there's always barfly ping-pong available.

cbd/warehouse district

Circle Bar
1032 St. Charles Ave. (at Lee Circle)
504-588-2616

vibe: your neighbor's basement (in a good way)
peak times: evenings, weekends
music: jukebox, live acts
games: none

Patched-together dive bar and music venue in the shadow of the Robert E. Lee monument. Strong drinks, neighborhood atmosphere and a full-ceiling homage to the dear-departed K&B Drugstore (the big clock).

Howling Wolf
1544 Tchoupitoulas St.
504-522-9653

vibe: loud room, basic bar
peak times: show nights
music: live

Cavernous live music venue with plenty of dancing space. Specializes in rock and road shows.

Loa Lounge
221 Camp St. (at Gravier)
504-553-9550

vibe: sleek and urbane
peak times: evenings, weekends
music: barkeep's choice
games: none

Sophisticated hotel bar in the International House—white on white, beautiful windows. A hit with the local martini crowd.

Loft 523
523 Gravier (at Camp)
504-550-6523

vibe: secluded, urbane
peak times: evenings, weekends
music: barkeep's choice
games: none

Dark, romantic, minimal. Backstreet modernist bar in hidden boutique hotel setting.

Sazerac Bar
123 Baronne St. (at Canal)
504-529-7111

vibe: sophisticated, historic
peak times: evenings, weekends
music: barkeep's choice
games: none

Dark wood and a sense of history in the Fairmont's grand old hotel bar. The room's eponymous cocktail is a little on the sweet (and overpriced) side.

garden district

Bull Dog
1017 Pleasant St.
504-891-1516

vibe: beer bar for the sports junky
peak times: Wed–Thurs nights, game day
music: barkeep's choice
games: video trivia

An unabashed beer bar in a cocktail-centric town. Fifty taps and twice that many bottled selections; hard liquor if you need it. Their over-the-top chili-cheese fries rank as a world-class high-grease beer ballast. Crowds skew to the college crowds on Wednesday and Thursday nights; weekend afternoons belong to the sports crowds.

Balcony Bar
3201 Magazine St.
504-891-1225

vibe: high-traffic student bar, great balcony
peak times: evenings, weekends
music: jukebox
games: pool

If this aging Victorian bar was a horse, it would be "rode hard and put up wet"; but the Magazine Street institution pulls in crowds for cheap drinks and a pleasantly urban al fresco experience.

Delachaise
3442 St. Charles Ave. (at Delachaise)
504-895-0858

vibe: casual swank
peak times: late-night
music: barkeep's choice
games: none

An upscale after-hours wine bar/tapas kitchen with an impressive selection of brandies, spirits and vintages from the four corners of the wine world. A narrow room and long bar packs with the

The Mint Julep

Though New Orleans is definitely a whiskey town, the mint julep isn't one of our native cocktails. Maybe it's the stately plantation-like manses on St. Charles, but something about New Orleans puts some into the julep mood, despite the fact that the drink most likely originated in Kentucky.

It's a relatively simple recipe—fresh mint leaves muddled with simple syrup for sweetness and plenty of bourbon for kick. In most bars, it's served in a rocks glass, but true connoisseurs demand that their juleps be poured over freshly crushed ice in a silver cup. In Lexington, bars might spring for the silver, but in New Orleans, silver cups and julep connoisseurs aren't so common.

usual Uptown suspects (students, young professionals, *Sex in the City* wannabes) who don't want to stray too far from home. Check the chalkboards for finds from lesser-known wine regions.

RC Bridge Lounge

1201 Magazine St.
504-299-1888

vibe: trendy minimalist wine bar
peak times: evenings, weekends
music: barkeep's choice
games: none

This trendy neighborhood joint does a brisk wine trade as it catches Uptown commuters on their way home from the CBD. Evening traffic usually spills out onto the sidewalk tables, making for a café-style party vibe. Dogs welcome.

The Saint

961 St. Mary St.
504-532-0050

vibe: punks pourin' drinks
peak times: late-night

music: jukebox
games: pinball, foosball

The tattooed hipster crowd invades a punkified 1960s rec room.

faubourg marigny

DBA

618 Frenchmen St.
504-942-3731

vibe: cavelike and cozy
peak times: evenings, weekends
music: live
games: none

One of New Orleans' perfect all-purpose bars. Young but not trendy crowd, music in the side room, comfortable dark wood soothes the spirit day or night. Great chalkboard selection of high-end spirits and draft beer lineup (with clearly posted prices).

Mimi's in the Marigny
2601 Royal St.
504-942-0690

vibe: split-level, loungy on top
peak times: evenings, weekends
music: jukebox

Great mix of spacious street-level bar and cozy upstairs room, furnished in 60s yard-sale aesthetic. Good tapas kitchen serves both levels.

The R Bar
1431 Royal St.
504-948-7499

vibe: relaxed, eclectic, just surreal enough
peak times: late-night, Carnival
music: jukebox
games: pool

Also known by its more regal moniker The Royal Bar is an easygoing neighborhood establishment that serves the tattooed hipster contingent and walking-distance barflies alike. Solo drinkers should jockey for the barber chair at the end of the bar (which, ironically, gets a more traditional use during Sunday night's "$10 haircut and shot" specials. On Mardi Gras day, the R is ground zero for the Marigny's "Krewe of St. Anne" parade, where you can get a glimpse of the city's best "do it yourself" costume culture. If you can make it up by 8 AM, the party's already in full force, and you wouldn't want to miss a second.

Snug Harbor
626 Frenchmen St.
504-949-0696

vibe: all about the music
peak times: show nights
music: live

Premier jazz venu and home of the local Marsalis dynasty. Never fails to pull a crowd.

midcity

Mid City Lanes Rock N Bowl
4133 S. Carrollton Ave.
504-482-3133

vibe: bowling alley with dance floor
peak times: show nights
music: live
games: bowling

≡ CLASSIC ≡

Ramos Gin Fizz
This creamy, gin-based cocktail is best sipped as a brunch or breakfast tipple, and is most common at restaurant bars that specialize in morning meals. It's got a thick texture (from heavy cream and egg whites) that's great for settling the stomach; a hint of orange-flower water adds a distinctive, mysterious aroma.

The Ramos Gin Fizz (always use the full name) has its roots in New Orleans, where it was first mixed up by bartender Henry Ramos sometime in the 1880s.

INGREDIENT

Peychaud's Bitters

If you've got a weakness for the classics—cocktails like the Old-Fashioned or the trendy Manhattan—you're probably familiar with the spicy-rich taste of aromatic bitters, a potent semi-medicinal distillation of various plant parts (barks, roots, etc). Clove-heavy Angustora bitters are the universal barkeep's standard, but in New Orleans, local tradition requires that a bar stock a second variety—Peychaud's—or face open ridicule as a two-bit daiquiri joint.

Developed by apothecary Antoine Peychaud in the early nineteenth century, this reddish fluid looks a lot like a tall bottle of Mercurochrome or wild cherry snowball syrup. Nipped straight from the bottle—not the suggested serving method—it tastes like double-strength cough syrup from hell. But shaken dash by dash into a cocktail glass, it's a critical flavoring element to a proper Sazerac and the reason why a properly made version has a slight pinkish cast in muted barroom light.

Peychaud's can be picked up at just about any liquor-purveying establishment in the city, but outside of metropolitan New Orleans, it's usually a special-order item. Just for the hell of it, pick up a bottle for a cocktail-themed souvenir.

Bowling, beer and bands (pick your order) in an aging but active upstairs alley. Required night stop for the Jazzfest crowd. Zydeco bands most Thursdays.

Pal's

949 N. Rendon (at St. Philip)
504-488-7257

vibe: cozy neighborhood bar
peak times: evenings, weekends
music: jukebox
games: air hockey, pinball

Locals-only neighborhood bar with a vague Vargas theme. Liquor in the front, air hockey in the back.

faubourg tremé

Mother-in-Law Lounge

1500 N. Claiborne Ave.
504-947-1078

vibe: surreal shrine to the Emperor
peak times: evenings, weekends
music: Ernie's ghost

The house that Ernie K-Doe built. Play the R&B hit that built the career of the self-styled "Emperor of the Universe," have a viewing of his life-sized mannequin and raise a toast with his personal catch phrase "Burn K-Doe Burn!"

uptown

Columns
3811 St. Charles Ave. (at Peniston)

vibe: historic, epic veranda
peak times: evenings, weekend brunch
music: barkeep's choice
games: none

The Columns (backdrop for the controversial cathouse film *Pretty Baby)* is all about the ambience. Inside or out, this aging mansion-turned-hotel on St. Charles corners the market on plantation-style ambience. The towering eponymous columns and broad veranda provide an enviable (and somewhat genteel) perspective on the Uptown oaks and broad avenue. Inside, the dark bar and attached parlor room provide various romantic or nostalgic seating options (church pews in hidden alcove, circular settee, Victorian sitting room). Weekend nights can find the rooms packed with frat kids, pledge-class refugees and wedding parties. Adjust your plans accordingly.

F&M Patio Bar
4841 Tchoupitoulas St.
504-895-6784

vibe: pleasantly grungy fallback
peak times: late-night
music: jukebox

Rough and tumble corner bar on an industrial stretch of Tchoupitoulas. Renowned for their gut-bomb chili cheese fries and round-the-clock service.

Kingpin
1307 Lyons St. (at Prytania)
504-891-2373

vibe: comfortable hipster with law school contingent
peak times: evenings, weekends
music: jukebox, occasionally live
games: shuffleboard

Uptown upstart near the popular Prytania Street restaurant cluster and streetcar line. Occasional music in the back room, bar shuffleboard always available.

Le Bon Temps Roule
4801 Magazine St. (at Bordeaux)
504-895-8117

vibe: neighborhood music hall
peak times: weekends, weekday show nights
music: jukebox, live
games: pool

Stiff drinks, solid "burger and poboy" kitchen and free music most weeknights in the back room. Popular with students.

Maple Leaf Bar
8316 Oak St.
504-866-9359

vibe: close quarters with a funky backbeat
peak times: show nights
music: live

House of local funk that usually packs with the late-night party people. Rebirth Brass Band's weekly gig (Tuesday nights) here always draws crowds.

Miss Mae's
4336 Magazine (at Napoleon)
504-895-9401

vibe: grungy and just a bit sketchy
peak times: round the clock, Carnival
music: Uptown
games: pool

Central location, cheap beer, full-contact barflys. For those who love adventure.

Snake & Jake's
7612 Oak St. (at Hillary)
504-861-2802

vibe: funky, dark, on till the morning
peak times: late-night
music: barkeep's choice
games: none

More a pieced-together shed than an actual bar, this ramshackle Uptown standard is low on light and rich in ambience. The ceilings top out at about 7 feet, and the glow of Christmas lights and various 70s-era Schlitz signs. If it wasn't such an organic piece of its largely residential neighborhood, it would be pure kitsch, but the mixed crowd (construction workers, musicians, students) lets you know that its heart is in the right place. During the wintertime, gas heat provides all the comfort of the womb—with a better soundtrack. Good selection of bottled beer and solid, if limited, draft offerings.

St. Joe's
5535 Magazine St. (at Joseph)
504-899-3744

vibe: dark wood, Catholic-school overtones
peak times: evenings, weekends
music: jukebox
games: pool

Mixed crowd (students and younger professional types) in this semi-gothic barroom. For the sake of balance, the colorful rear patio makes for good open-air lounging when the front bar gets too smoky.

Tipitina's
501 Napoleon Ave. (at Tchoupitoulas)
504-895-8477

vibe: timeless musical warehouse
peak times: show nights
music: live

Needs no introduction. The shrine to piano legend Professor Longhair still pulls in an amazing array of road acts and music fans from here and abroad.

chapter 5
BAYOU BACKROADS

A Cajun-Country Side Trip

New Orleans has such a well-developed tourist scene that most travelers are content to stay in the city, getting around mostly by cabs, on foot, and on public transit. For culinary explorers, it's tough to tear away from the meal-to-meal opportunities of the city, but sometimes, the countryside beckons and calls even the most dedicated foodfolks out onto the open road.

Many tourists scratch the itch with a quick jaunt out of town for a swamp tour or day at the plantations upriver from the city.

But the food-obsessed usually want to head a bit further off the beaten path—in most cases to the land where Cajun food was born. Armed with a rental car and a detailed road map, a south Louisiana day trip is a great chance to explore the land that feeds the city and to see the region's amazing, if somewhat waterlogged, topography.

The mid-1980s oil bust caused a major shift in the regional economy—from petrochemicals to cultural tourism—which is a boon for hungry travelers. Prior to the changeover, many of south Louisiana's foodways were primarily home-based instead of available in restaurants. If you didn't have a way into Mama's kitchen, your options were somewhat limited. But the tourist shift spurred a boom in restaurants—from simple roadside diners to meat markets advertising their wares (SPECIALTY MEATS!) on highway billboards.

The city of Lafayette, a mid-sized oilfield city two and a half hours west of New Orleans, makes a great base of operations whether you've got a spare night in your schedule or want to do a long "out and back day." Lafayette is the de facto capital of Acadiana, a name given to the French expanse of the state that lies between New Orleans and the Texas border. Equidistant from bayou country, the coastal prairie and coastal marshlands, Lafayette is a great reference point for novice travelers seeking a non-urban Louisiana experience. It's also a pilgrimage point for lovers of Cajun and zydeco music and heaven for home-grown accordion fetishists.

This chapter provides a thumbnail sketch of Acadiana with a few food-based recommendations to get you started. Needless to say, there are plenty of other options—some of them hidden, some all too obvious—but this short read should give you the lay of the land with a few good meals along the way.

THE BIG PICTURE

With its distinctive French culture and equally unique set of food and musical traditions, south Louisiana has accurately been described as "a tiny coastal country that shares a common border with the United States."

The highway planners that brought the Eisenhower Interstate Highway System to south Louisiana also defined an important cultural boundary—a four-lane paved borderline between French-flavored Cajun Louisiana and the more Protestant northern section of the state. Of course, the simple "south of I-10" guideline for defining Cajun Country excludes huge chunks of the Francophone prairie and the sweet potato capital of Opelousas, the natives of which prefer Highway 190 as the primary border between Cajun Country and the United States. This, of course, leaves out the town of Ville Platte, and on and on.

Still, the border-to-border stretch of Interstate 10 provides a good guideline for first-time travelers in rural Louisiana. From New Orleans in the east, it runs up the Mississippi through plantation country, crosses the river at the state capital of Baton Rouge and cuts west across bayou country and the rice fields of southwest Louisiana as it makes for the Texas border. South of the highway are expanses of sugar cane, rural fishing villages, brackish marshlands and sheltered coves and bays of the Gulf. The cattle country of the prairie, also the birthplace of hard-rocking zydeco music, stretches out to the north before giving way to the rolling hills of central Louisiana and with it, the American South.

The Zones

South Louisiana, often identified with the nickname Cajun Country, is a diverse region that encompasses a broad range of coastal land forms—slow-moving bayous and meandering rivers, freshwater swampland, the flat salt marshes and flat coastal plains.

Historically, these geographic differences determined local food traditions, since the tendency to "eat from your backyard" varied from area to area. Before modern trucking and refrigeration opened up trade among communities, coastal residents depended on the Gulf for much of their sustenance, bayou dwellers cooked freshwater seafood specialties and prairie people depended on the bounty of the barnyard. And of course, with an amazing diversity of wild game, just about everybody hunted and/or trapped for the family table—a practice that continues today.

Cultural Zones

■ **New Orleans**
The City

■ **Acadiana**
Cajun Country

□ **North Louisiana**
The Deep South

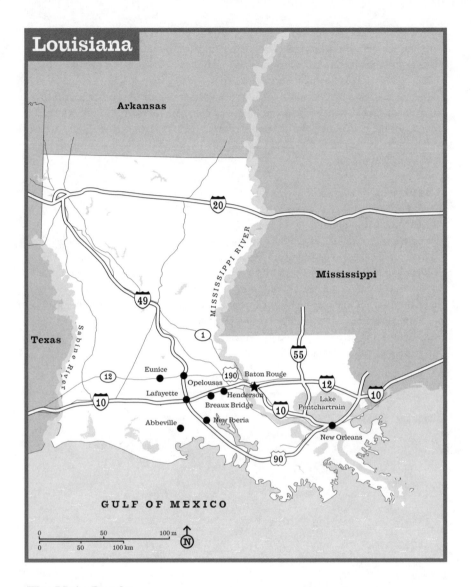

The Main Roads

If you're headed west from New Orleans for a short trip through Cajun Country, the two main east-west arteries are US Highway 90 and Interstate 10.

Highway 90 is the west bank road that runs parallel to the coast and through the flat fields of sugarcane country. Though it's not a modern expressway, the highway is four lanes most of the way and connects the cities of Houma, Morgan City, Franklin, New Iberia and Lafayette. A trip down the "oil patch road" is a glimpse into the state's rural/industrial complex as broad fields of bamboo-like sugarcane give way to pipe yards and machine shops that service the few remaining offshore oil rigs. Truckstop casinos, an increasingly common sight in the countryside, dot the roadside along with welding shops and farm supply stores. Between cities, it's not unusual to see crop dusters turning tight circles over the highway, squaring themselves for a spraying run over the roadside cane fields. In wintertime, plumes of smoke rise over the cane fields as farmers burn off the cane stubble following the harvest.

Interstate 10 is more of a modern expressway with limited access and, some contend, less to see than its slower counterpart. In contrast to Highway 90, I-10 runs along the eat side of the Mississippi, crossing over the river seventy miles northwest of New Orleans at Baton Rouge, Louisiana's state capital. Twenty miles later, the highway crosses the broad Atchafalaya Basin Swamp on an 18-mile stretch of elevated roadway that crosses over a strikingly beautiful section of the fertile freshwater wetland. Even if you generally prefer the smaller "blue highways" to the modern highways, the Atchafalaya portion of this trip is well worth braving the interstate truck traffic.

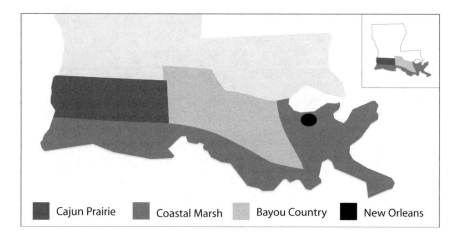

Cajun Prairie   Coastal Marsh   Bayou Country   New Orleans

CAJUN FOOD CULTURE

Get a group of Cajuns together and within two minutes the conversation will turn to food. Either they'll compare notes on how local crawfish have been small this season or the location of a "knock you down good" crab au gratin served only at a particular general store by the coast. Stories spin, personal recipes change hands, and by the end of the conversation, they part ways to go home for dinner.

That's the kind of dedication that keeps Cajun food culture going strong, with no signs of wavering. There's ALWAYS cooking (and eating) to be done . . .

While New Orleans natives have a well-honed sense of restaurant culture, Cajun food is traditionally more focused on the home table.

With strong connections to both family and the land, Cajun culture expresses these ties most strongly at the family table. The lands of south Louisiana provided an ample bounty of raw materials, which the Acadians-turned-Cajuns adapted into their trademark cuisine. The frontier survival experience mixed with the thoroughly Gallic "eat everything" tradition to create a style of cookery unique to the Louisiana landscape.

From Coastal Canada to the Crawfish Country: Cajun History in a Nutshell

Cajun culture (and by extension, its edible culture) is deeply rooted in the frontier experience and the most unlikely of places, the Canadian Maritime Provinces.

In 1604 the first French colonists settled Acadie—the North Atlantic peninsula currently known by its English name of Nova Scotia. The Acadian settlers, mostly fishermen and subsistence farmers, lived off the land in relative isolation, oblivious to the realities of New World colonial politics. Their homeland of Acadie, strategically positioned between English and French territorial holdings, changed political hands several times in the seventeenth and early eighteenth centuries without changing everyday life in the region.

Cut off from French culture and oblivious to English political intentions, the settlers developed a steadfastly independent cultural identity. They definitely weren't British subjects, but neither did they completely relate to French culture—after 150 years of surviving in the wilderness, they were Acadians.

But in 1755, British forces drove Acadians from their homes for refusing loyalty to the English crown. Known as the Grand Derangement, this dissolution of Acadian communities ended with a boatbound diaspora that was to last for over ten years. Farms were burned, families separated, and tattered groups of displaced Acadians dispatched for what few ports would accept them. Many died aboard ship awaiting a chance to resettle. Some would seek refuge in French holdings, while others returned temporarily to France—all awaited news of family and the possibility of a new home.

After ten years of exile, the first Acadians arrived in Louisiana—ironically as guests of the ruling Spanish Colonial government, who offered them farms in the lesser-populated territories west of New Orleans. The initial land grants were along the bayous and other waterways, but the Acadians (now referred to as "Cajuns") spread throughout the region, content to be left to their own devices.

In their new home of Acadiana, the Cajuns adapted the same fishing and survival skills that served them well in Acadie, and flourished in another era of relative isolation until well into the twentieth century.

That's not to say, of course, that there weren't significant influences from other cultures. German immigrants, for example, brought sausage-making traditions. Free people of color and Caribbean transplants settled in south Louisiana and founded "south Louisiana Creole" communities that gave birth to both a distinct dialect of French and in zydeco music. Smaller immigrant populations settled among the Acadians, and eventually blended into the communities—with names like the German Himmel becoming the Cajun Himel, the Spanish Rodrigues morphing into Rodrigue. The Germans brought with them, among other things, a rich sausage-making tradition that adapted well to the south Louisiana landscape.

CLASSIC

Rice and Gravy

Just about every dish from the Cajun repertoire is served on a bed of steaming, long-grain white rice. Like the Irish penchant for potatoes, our collective rice lust stems largely from the fact that they grow the stuff "right down the road"—in the flood-prone fields of Acadiana's prairieland. (Well . . . that and it tastes good.)

One of the hidden classics of Cajun cuisine is "rice and gravy," served as a staple side dish in just about every plate-lunch joint in the area. A thick brown gravy—usually beef or pork-based—is ladled over rice for a comforting dish that beats the hell out of mashed potatoes any day.

The settlers adapted their cooking styles to the freshest, most plentiful ingredients around. Bayou Cajuns knew how to prepare freshwater fish pulled from the murky brown streams while coastal communities work the Gulf's salty waters and marshlands. Farther upland, the prairie Cajuns made their gumbos from their most abundant resources—barnyard staples like chicken and pork. Household gardens provided fresh vegetables and spices well suited to the native climate (sweet potatoes, peppers, tomatoes). Styles varied from town to town, but the common spicing and cooking techniques united these variations into a coherent cuisine.

Even today, the descendants of the original Cajuns take pride in their collective and individual food traditions. Everybody cooks and everybody loves to sit around for hours and talk about great meals past, present and future. Approaches to a simple gumbo vary from person to person and can be as individual as a fingerprint. Fishermen and hunters take pride in catching AND cooking their prey. Both men and women prepare their own special dishes—an unusual case of edible culture transcending gender lines. Most households have a complete outdoor cooking setup—industrial butane burners and large pots to match—for impromptu crawfish boils or fish-frying parties.

The fame of the region is built on fresh seafood, with different towns renowned for local specialties. (For example, a Cajun in Lafayette will gladly drive 20 minutes to the oyster houses of Abbeville if she's craving the salty shellfish, and another 20 to the shrimp docks in Delcambre for the freshest catch of the day.)

But driving through Acadiana, you get the feeling that your stomach and taste buds are well provided for. A simple poboy served up at an improvised stand can knock you for a loop. The act of deep-frying is raised to high art, as drive-in onion rings and fried shrimp rightfully deserve "sublime" designation. Even the gas stations sport tiny short-order kitchens, where substantial plate lunches and links of hot boudin (spicy pork and rice sausage) eaten in the traditional manner (sitting on a pickup-truck tailgate or convenient car hood) can change your life.

The Roux

A persistent joke about Cajun food is that *every* recipe starts with the phrase "First you make a roux . . ."—even if you're making coleslaw.

And despite what you may have heard, roux preparation doesn't require magic, intricate rituals or incantations to Yoruba kitchen gods. Just a cast-iron pot, a single stovetop burner and a fair amount of patience.

This staple couldn't get any simpler—equal parts wheat flour and vegetable oil cooked gradually until the flour turns deep brown. A slow, low flame toasts the flour particles as the mixture develops a deep, nutty flavor.

The technique was adapted from classical French chefs, who use pale (blond) roux for thickening soups, gravies and sauces. For many Cajun gumbos, the process heads for the dark side of the spectrum—with tones described as peanut butter, medium brown, brick, chocolate and deep brown.

lafayette

Lafayette is a sprawling oilfield city, university town and de facto capital of Acadiana. It's also home to some of the legendary zydeco dance halls and celebrations of Louisiana's Cajun and Creole cultures.

Lafayette lacks the centralized infrastructure of urban New Orleans, but serves as a perfect jumping-off point for exploring the true treasures of Acadiana—the smaller towns located within 30 miles of the regional capital. With a hotel room in Lafayette, you can drive northward toward the Cajun prairie or eastward into the swampy basin in a matter of minutes.

Old Tyme Grocery
218 W. St. Mary, Lafayette, LA
337-235-8165

specialties: poboys and Cajun specialties
meals: lunch and dinner Mon–Sat (closed
  Sunday)

Popular corner store turned poboy shop just a few blocks off the University of Louisiana–Lafayette campus. During the hot months, they serve outstanding snowballs in a little stand in back of the store.

T-Coon's Restaurant
1900 W. Pinhook Rd., 337-233-0422
740 Jefferson St., 337-232-3803

specialties: home-style Cajun specialties
Jefferson Location: lunch Mon–Fri
Pinhook Location: breakfast and lunch
  Mon–Sat

Home-style Cajun food served cafeteria style. Outstanding crawfish étouffée, catfish courtboullion, fried chicken and gumbo (cold weather only). Smothered rabbit on Mondays. Always ask for an extra house-baked yeast roll.

Hot Boiled Crawfish

Take a few hundred pounds of live crawfish, plunge them into seasoned boiling water, spill the whole mess onto a newspaper-covered table. Pick up a steaming crawfish and rip it into two pieces—cephalothorax and tail. Strip shell from tail end, bite off exposed meat and inhale deeply through the head cavity. Take long quaff of fizzy beer, then throw shell onto towering mountain of empties. Repeat as needed.

Though it's anything but fancy, a crawfish boil is one of the cornerstones of Louisiana's culture. The preparation itself is amazingly simple—crawfish cooked with a few vegetables—but the scale required for a good meal complicates matters. For all their gustatory appeal, crawfish only provide a medium-sized morsel of tail meat, so the key to a well-fed crawfish crowd is high volume. Five pounds of boiled crawfish constitutes an average serving of the delectable beast.

During spring, locals hit Acadiana's backroads in search of "boiling points"— makeshift restaurants specializing in seasonal boiled seafood. As a rule, these low-brow joints aren't much for atmosphere (plastic chairs, Formica tables and shrimp nets decorating wood-paneled walls) but they're great for a simple sit-down meal or "Cajun fast food" (five pounds in an Styrofoam "go box"). Boiling points are the cure for midweek crawfish cravings, when peeling is about all you can handle.

By contrast, a backyard crawfish boil—a traditional Easter event throughout Louisiana—is an epic affair involving 40-pound sacks of wriggling crawfish and bubbling cauldrons big enough to be stirred with canoe paddles. Unlike a New England lobster boil, where ingredients fit into a single grocery sack, Louisiana crawfish boils require advance planning, a quasi-industrial outdoor kitchen, and at least one pick-up truck for hauling.

The proper "kitchen tools" for a crawfish boil are spiritual descendents of oilfield equipment. Many families in south Louisiana own oversized propane-powered gas burners—the perfect portable stovetop for crawfish boils (and summertime fish-frying extravaganzas). When fired up to full strength, these burners can bring a 10-gallon pot of water to a rolling boil in minutes. The cooks season the water with halved lemons, quartered onions, prepackaged seafood seasoning—a mix of bay leaves, mustard seed, allspice, clove and other aromatics—and copious amounts of cayenne pepper. When the mixture is brought up to temperature, properly spiced, it resembles a pot of boiling blood.

While the water boils, the crawfish are transferred from their sacks to a huge container (oversized ice chest or plastic wading pool) filled with heavily salted water. This purging process cleans the crawfish's digestive tract, literally taking the mud out of the mudbug.

Following a thorough post-purge rinsing, the cooking crew loads about 10 pounds of crawfish into a colander-style metal basket that fits snugly into the pot. Red potatoes and short cobs of sweet corn—traditional "cook-along" side dishes—are usually thrown in as the boiling crawfish change color from dull greenish-brown to bright, spicy red. After 10 to 12 minutes, the cooked crawfish are lifted from the water, drained and spilled onto a large picnic-style table covered with a protective coating of newspapers. The vibrant red mountain shimmers with fragrant steam and sunlight, and the basket heads back to the pot for another batch.

Prejean's Restaurant

3480 I-49 N. (on the access road)
337-896-3247

specialties: traditional and updated
  Cajun
meals: breakfast, lunch and dinner daily

Fantastic all-around restaurant serves up the classics (fried seafood and seafood-stuffed red snapper) and updated Cajun dishes (yellowfin tuna Rockefeller). Outstanding gumbo.

Deano's Pizza

305 Bertrand Ave.
337-233-5446

specialties: south Louisiana pizza
meals: lunch and dinner nightly

OK, you'll have to trust me on this, but the seafood including the savory étouffée-like CrawFest and the crabmeat-covered Marie Laveau will change the way you think about pizza.

Best Stop

511 Hwy. 9, Scott, LA
337-233-5805

specialties: specialty meats, sausage,
  boudin, stuffed meats
meals: snacks

Tiny off-highway grocery selling exceptional examples of all the meat market standards. Their green-onion spiked boudin and smoked sausage are worth the 10-minute interstate detour.

abbeville

In most of Acadiana, Abbeville is known for its active oyster culture. It's a local tradition in surrounding towns to make a pilgrimage to the little town for a night of shellfish slurping in one of the noted oyster bars. For years, family loyalties forced a choice between the two old-school shuckers—Black's or Dupuy's. Now a third oyster house, Shuck's, has further complicated life in this little Vermillion River town. But as the great philosopher once said, "These are good problems to have . . ."

Abbeville is also home to another Louisiana food classic—Steen's Cane Syrup. A few steps from the oyster bar axis, a huge storage at the Steen's plant is painted to look like an immense can of the sweet syrup.

Black's Seafood Restaurant and Oyster Bar

319 Pere Megret
337-893-4266

specialties: oysters
meals: Tues–Sat, closed Sun and Mon

This popular seafood destination started off in a tiny storefront few doors down, but moved over to a cavernous old mercantile store with an equally huge bar area. Fantastic fresh-shucked oyster cocktails, fried shrimp platters and Bloody Marys.

Dupuy's

108 South Main
337-893-2336

specialties: oysters
meals: lunch and dinner Mon and
  Wed–Fri, dinner only Sat, lunch only
  Sun, closed Tuesday

Old-school oyster house backing straight onto the bayou. The only Abbeville oyster house that sticks to an orthodox view of raw oysters during summer—no

Meat Market Menagerie

In the days before refrigeration, butchers developed methods of efficiently using ALL of a slaughtered animal and preserving meats without the benefit of an icebox—the sausage and the smokehouse.

Boudin—Cajun butchers proved to be particularly adept in their craft, and as a result, Acadiana sports a particularly active sausage culture. The two most famous examples of this are the omnipresent boudin (a heavily-spiced combination of pork and rice in a sausage, complimented by fragrant green onions) and andouille (a heavily smoked pork sausage used in a wide variety of dishes).

Tasso—From the charcuterie (butcher shop) comes another delicacy, the potent smoked meat known as tasso. Like the addictive Italian prosciutto, this amazing product is used sparingly, mostly as a flavoring agent in just about any slow-cooked stew (if you're lucky). A little goes a long way, but a good long way.

Graton (cracklins)—Known in other parts of the world as pork rinds, these tasty chunks of crispy pork skin rendered down in flavorful lard are about as healthy as you'd expect, and about five times as tasty. Grab a paper bag filled with these crunchy treats whenever you're in a meat market. Best when fresh.

Hogshead Cheese—Tender meat from a long-boiled pig's head (hence the name) is ground and cooled into a jellified loaf and served cold. Seriously, don't knock it 'till you've tried it.

Turducken—A novel variation on the standard stuffed chicken, the turducken is the crown jewel of hyper-complex meat market performance art. Imagine a poultry-based version of Russian nesting dolls—boneless turkey stuffed with a boneless chicken which has in turn been stuffed with boneless duck. And to further complicate matters, each bird is stuffed with a layer of moist rice or bread-based dressing. Long-baked and sliced like a savory jelly roll, it's one of those dishes that reads a lot better than it tastes. If you're going to try one, buy it from a meat market—life is too damned short to try this one at home.

Adventure Foods: Fried Turkey and Turducken

Despite alligator meat's reptilian reputation as the south Louisiana "adventure food," this local twist on the Thanksgiving classic ranks as the modern-day favorite of culinary thrill seekers.

Born in the Louisiana countryside in the 1950s, this admittedly extreme cooking technique became wildly popular across the US sometime in the mid-90s. And it's really no surprise, since it speaks to three things deeply valued by American males—deep-fried food, outdoor cooking and heavy machinery.

Bragging rights—the dramatic story after the meal—play a big part in the technique's popularity. Almost everybody has a buddy who will try anything once, especially if sounds like a bit from "Evel Knievel's Daredevil Thanksgiving Special." Large-scale cookery with a touch of danger—it's the perfect post-holiday story to tell around the office water cooler.

If you know about Cajun cooking traditions, then the whole Rube Goldberg setup makes perfect sense. Springtime in Louisiana is crawfish season, when thousands of families dust off propane-powered "cooking rigs" for large-scale crawfish boils. The rigs are masterpieces of oilfield ingenuity—free-standing metal burners fitted with wide-bore gas jets hooked up to tanks of compressed natural gas. Once lit, these rigs can boil 15-gallon batches of spicy seafood or fry a weekend's fishing catch in nothing flat.

So it makes sense that Cajuns would apply their outdoor cooking methods to the traditionally bland Thanksgiving dinner. The musical question "Why roast when you can fry?" transformed huge crawfish pots into improvised deep-fryers. The early innovators worked out many bugs in the system—such as getting super-sized poultry in and out of super-heated oil—and many developed products (narrow pots, metal "turkey lifters") to make the task easier. The legend grew and before long, the "Cajun fried turkey" became a long-lived national fad.

If the whole idea of frying a whole turkey sounds risky, that's because it is. Even experienced crawfish boilers quickly learn the world of difference between 212-degree water and 400-degree oil. Small oil spills can quickly turn into roaring grease fires. Excess water turns to sputtering steam and simple accidents often require emergency medical attention. City fire marshals issue annual warnings to keep fryers away from houses, trees and overhead power lines. One hot splash and you'll have new respect for the pimply kids working at burger-joint fry pits.

So if you're jonesing for a taste of this specialty, leave the cooking to the professionals. Many fried chicken joints and meat markets sell pre-fried turkeys around the holiday season.

halfshells in months without the R (see page 129).

Shucks!
701 W. Port St.
337-898-3311

specialties: oysters
meals: lunch and dinner Mon–Sat

Open since 1995, Shucks is the newest oyster palace in town, but the owners ran Dupuy's for the 21 years before moving across the bayou to this spacious, utilitarian space.

breaux bridge

The little town of Breaux Bridge calls itself the Crawfish Capital of the World, and backs it up with a no-holds-barred Crawfish Festival (held every first weekend in May). When the streets aren't packed with fans of the noble ecrevisse, the boutique-heavy little downtown district attracts antique hunters and other day-trippers.

Cafe des Amis
140 E. Bridge St.
337-332-5273

specialties: traditional and updated Cajun
meals: breakfast and lunch Tues–Sun, dinner Tues-Sat (closed Mon)

This airy storefront restaurant is a favorite for its updated takes on Cajun specialties, solid classic dishes and all-but-too-popular zydeco breakfast on Saturday mornings. Live music and specialties like boudin-stuffed *oreille de couchon* (crunchy, quick-fried pastries named for pig's ears) make for long lines, so arrive early on Saturday if you want a table near the dance floor.

Poche's
3015A Main Hwy.
1-800-376-2437, 337-332-2108

specialties: plate lunches, meat market specialties
meals: breakfast, lunch, and dinner daily

A few miles outside of Breaux Bridge proper, this meat market and restaurant complex does brisk business at both the grocery counter and the steam tables. The cafeteria-style setup doesn't look like much, but you're just not likely to find a better lunch than sausage-stuffed pork-chops and rice dressing ladled with deep brown gravy from pork backbone stew. Unless, of course, you get the crawfish étouffée, which elicited this near-heretical comment from a Lafayette native: "You know, I love my mama and all, but this is the best étouffée I've ever had." And in a mama-centric region like Acadiana, those are powerful words indeed.

Mulate's
325 Mills Ave.
1-800-422-2586, 337-332-4648

specialties: seafood and Cajun
meals: lunch and dinner daily

If you approach Breaux Bridge on Interstate 10, you'll recognize Mulate's sign from their billboards or their sister restaurant in New Orleans' Warehouse District. The Breaux Bridge location of this restaurant and dance hall is situated a mile or so off the main road, but it's pretty easy to find. The kitchen serves up the usual Cajun fare, while a tiny bandstand plays host to local Cajun bands nightly.

Cajun/Creole Seasoning Mixes

Call it enthusiasm over common sense, but novice cooks are often eager to add extra cayenne ("just a few BAMs' worth") to whatever's in their pot, only to learn a powerful lesson about third-degree afterburn. It's a tough way to learn an important Louisiana lesson—when it comes to spice, the key word is BALANCE.

For years, Cajun cooks have relied on pre-mixed spice blends for everyday cooking. A delicate mix of spices—salt for savor, black pepper for front flavor, cayenne for heat, paprika for color, etc.—simplifies the seasoning process and can come from an old family formula or a mass-market commercial product. In any beginner's kitchen, these seasoning blends take the guesswork out of spicing and reduce the odds of an accidental cayenne overload. The reddish-white dust is used to season meats and seafoods before cooking and often takes the place of salt and pepper for stoveside or tabletop flavoring.

eunice

North and west of Lafayette, the flat, mostly treeless Cajun prairie opens up as you enter the "higher and drier" section of south Louisiana. This is the land where cattle graze contentedly, flooded rice fields double as crawfish farms and locals celebrate Mardi Gras on horseback instead of waving from glitzy parade floats.

Most tourists know this small prairie town as the main turnoff to Mamou, an even smaller settlement that hosts a popular Saturday morning tradition—a French-language Cajun-music radio show broadcast from the tiny Fred's Bar. Locals and travelers head to Fred's jut after dawn to dance, drink a bit and go "dancin' on the radio."

But Eunice is also home to a well-preserved piece of the region's living heritage. The beautifully restored Liberty Theater hosts *Rendez-vous des Cajuns,* a Cajun French radio program that could be subtitled "A Cajun Prairie Companion." From 6 to 8 every Saturday night, host and folklorist Barry Jean Ancelet takes the stage for a two-hour broadcast of Cajun music, stories and culture that beams outward from the northern edge of Acadiana.

And of course, if you poke around a bit, there are always a few good meals to be found.

Ruby's Cafe
221 W. Walnut
337-550-7665

specialties: plate lunches, donuts
meals: breakfast and lunch daily

This tiny lunch counter isn't particularly frilly, but it is the next best thing to a Cajun grandmother's kitchen. This true country food—pork roast, peppery baked chicken and, if you're there on the right day, beef tongue—is usually accompanied by rice and gravy. Early risers can get fresh-fried donuts and appropriately strong coffee to wash it all down.

A. Johnson's Grocery
700 E. Maple Ave.
337-457-9314

specialties: boudin, specialty meats
meals: daytime meaty snacks

Johnson's is a few turns off the main road, but Cajun meat aficionados seek out the white clapboard grocery for its regionally-famous meat market. Johnson's boudin is high on both liver and spice, and is particularly tasty fried up into boudin balls. Grabbing a grease-spotted bag of these crunchy treats is a tradition on your way to (or back from) a beery morning at Fred's.

new iberia

Queen City of the Teche. Host of the Louisiana Sugarcane Festival and Fair.

Home of the Fighting Yellowjackets. I grew up in this mid-sized agricultural town and so for years overlooked a lot of the charms that strike many first time visitors to the city. New Iberia's defining waterway, teh Bayou Teche, is pretty damned picturesque, as are the oak-shaded historic mansions on Main Street. Over the last twenty years or so, bed and breakfast operations have sprung up in the historic sections of town, and downtown has also undergone a post-oil bust renaissance. Shadows-on-the-Teche, an antebellum plantaion house that's on National Historic Trust property, draws its share of tourist, as does Avery Island. Located seven miles southeast of New Iberia, the privately-owned salt dome of Avery Island contains the famed McIlhenny Tabasco Factory and stunning Jungle Gardens bird sanctuary.

CLASSIC

Boudin

The first bite of boudin can be a real challenge for all but the most adventurous food-folk. Plucked from an ever-present electric steamer, the plump links of rice-based specialty don't resemble the smoked products that Americans consider safe sausage. The most common "what's in it?" explanation (pork bits, organ meats and rice stuffed into pig intestines) usually doesn't do much to assuage the squeamish.

The slightly milky casing can be eaten, but usually isn't—which poses a problem of technique for the uninitiated. The whole "bite and pull" method is pretty easy to master, but usually requires a quick demonstration to truly understand.

But if you pass on the boudin, especially if you're driving through Acadiana, you're missing out on a universal snack food of south Louisiana and one of the highest forms of the butcher's art.

The two primary flavors in boudin are liver and spice. If you're still not sold, try it in the form of boudin balls. Restaurants make the specialty more approachable by removing the skin and forming the sausage into balls, which are deep fried to a crispy crust.

Cajun Spice: Not What You Think

The most unfortunate myth to emerge from the Acadians' turn on the world culinary stage is that "Cajun," loosely translated into English, means "dipped in red pepper." Though the popular view of Cajun cookery invariably involves ungodly amounts of palate-searing cayenne (or red) pepper, the traditional flavors tend toward more rounded flavors. Cajun cooks never shy away from the trademark heat of their highly visible exports (Louisiana pepper sauces, secret spice blends), but rarely partake in "heat for heat's sake" common to other culinary subcultures that prize products like 43-Alarm Chili or "Sign This Legal Release" Habenero Salsa. If it's gotta be hot (as is the case in fresh-boiled crawfish) it's gotta make sense to your palate.

The key to Cajun cooking is BALANCE—balancing the heat of red pepper with the bite of black pepper or the lush "green" fragrance of chopped parsley with the rich flavors of onion and garlic. (Buddha, it has been theorized, may have actually BEEN a very round, very worldly Cajun. He just shaved before heading east to pose for all those statues . . .)

Victor's Cafeteria
109 W. Main St.
337-369-9924

specialties: early breakfast, plate lunches
meals: breakfast and lunch daily (no Sat lunch)

Dave Robicheaux eats here. Cafeteria-style setting will be familiar to fans of James Lee Burke's mystery novels. Belly up to the steam table and ask the nice ladies what *they're* eating today.

Brenda's
409 W. Pershing St.
337-364-6820

specialties: plate lunch and soul food

Follow the railroad tracks to this homey, no-frills soul food emporium. The savory baked chicken with peppery gravy is a standout, if you get there early enough.

The Boiling Point
7413 Hwy. 90 W.
(about 4 miles east of New Iberia)
337-365-7596

specialties: boiled seafood
meals: lunch Mon–Fri, dinner daily

Another metal shack on Highway 90, This bare-bones serves impeccably boiled seafood. Specialties depend on the season: crawfish in spring, crabs and shrimp in warmer months.

Jim's Kountry Pies
3606 Romero Rd.
337-365-7465

specialties: pies, pralines, sweet dough tarts
meals: open most days, call ahead

Actually, it's outside of town in the rural settlement of Coteau, but well worth seeking out. Jim Romero practices some serious pastry-related art from his little bakery. Fruit pie fans should check out his impossible lattice work; coconut folk will marvel at his mile-high meringues. If you're lucky, he'll also have a few of his sweet dough tarts—a baked version of the fried pie filled with homemade vanilla or coconut custard.

celebrations

Festival International de Louisiane
Lafayette
Third week in April

Lafayette throws its share of amazing cultural festivals, but their most notable party is the spring celebration *Festival International de Louisiane*, when all French hybrid cultures converge and unite through music, food and art. Lafayette's *Festival* now provides an attractive alternative Jazzfest which runs its first weekend concurrently with *Festival*. With its manageable crowd sizes and spirited performances the *New York Times* called "the best unknown folk music festival in the United States."

Held annually during the third week of April in Lafayette, *Festival International* showcases the performing and visual arts of the French-speaking world. Known to Acadiana natives only as *Festival*, the annual celebration routinely draws energetic performers from five continents and the best musicians from all over Louisiana. Home-grown zydeco rhythms share the stage with driving Quebecois rock and the Central African drumbeats of Barundi. Traditional musicians from Martinique and Madagascar follow powerful New Orleans gospel choirs. Belgian stilt-walkers roam the streets along with hard-strutting bands of technicolor Mardi Gras Indians, the Crescent City's famous neighborhood dance-and-drum troupes.

Festival attracts audiences of around 100,000 instead of Jazzfest's 450,000, with most participants coming from Lafayette and smaller towns around Acadiana. During the evening and weekend performances, *Festival* transforms Lafayette's downtown district into a roped-off pedestrian mall, making it easy to walk among the four stages. Countless catering and concession trailers sell tempting local and unusual specialties without price gouging typical of other festival food courts. *Festival's* manageable size make it a distinctly relaxed, family-friendly event. And best of all, since *Festival International* is sustained both spiritually and economically by the community of Lafayette, five days of open-air performance, artistic expression, and cultural cross-pollination are provided free of charge for anyone willing to dance along.

Festival Acadiens
Lafayette
Third week of September

Similar to Festival International, but with a local focus. Plenty of Cajun and zydeco performances along with craft demonstrations of indigenous ethnic groups and more festival food than you can shake a shrimp at.

Mardi Gras
All over the state
Springtime—varies by year

Though Carnival isn't celebrated with the same month-long fervor as in New Orleans, Mardi Gras is usually commemorated with parades and street dances in nearly every town. (After all, it's a state holiday.)

In the rural areas of the Cajun prairie, residents still practice the *Courir de Mardi Gras* tradition, where costumed celebrants ride from farm to farm on horseback, singing for chickens and other ingredients for a communal feed back in town.

Small-Town Celebrations
All over Louisiana
All year

Thanks to a long growing season and well-honed celebration reflex, nearly every community celebrates some kind of natural harvest (be it animal, vegetable or mineral) during an annual free-for-all festival. Any time of year, you're never too far from a celebration, cultural fair, street dance or world championship cookoff of some local specialty—all you need to do is wait for the next weekend.

- Alligator Festival, Franklin
- Frog Festival, Rayne
- Garfish Festival, Baldwin
- Duck Festival, Gueydan
- Rice Festival, Crowley
- Shrimp Festival, Delcambre
- Swine Festival, Basile
- Yambilee (sweet potato celebration), Opelousas

No Chinese Crawfish, No Tiger Prawns

Just so you know: the bumper stickers emblazoned with the phrase "No Chinese Crawfish" aren't signs of a new crustacean immigration policy, but rather Louisiana's response to illegal "seafood dumping" in U.S. markets by importers based in the Middle Kingdom.

Over the past few decades, Chinese importers have flooded the U.S. market with peeled, frozen crawfish tails for well below their costs, resulting in lower prices for already strapped Louisiana crawfish producers. The practice is designed to bankrupt domestic producers and over the long haul remove local competition. Sound familiar? A similar practice is happening with farm-raised shrimp from various continents.

The imported product is usually less flavorful and soggy in texture than Louisiana crawfish, but at a third of the cost, some people can't resist the cheaper price point. Nevertheless, it's always a good practice to specifically ask your server about your crawfish's country of origin.

THE LOUISIANA pantry

Local Ingredients & Resources

NEW ORLEANS SPECIALTIES
Crystal Hot Sauce

In the now-crowded Louisiana hot sauce market, Crystal is considered the "city sauce" and is as common a sight on restaurant tables as saltshakers. Part of its popularity is based in tradition—local producer Baumer Foods dominated the New Orleans market before statewide distribution brought other sauces into the urban market.

Like most other hot sauces, Crystal uses only three simple ingredients—peppers, vinegar and salt—but the resulting liquid is more about flavor than heat; more about tickling the palate than overwhelming it. A few solid shakes of the bottle provide pleasing heat and a slightly bright flavor to seafood poboys or dark-roux gumbos. It's also a primary component of mix-your-own oyster sauces at local raw bars.

Baumer Foods, Inc.
4301 Tulane Ave.
P.O. Box 19166
New Orleans, LA 70179-0166
504- 482-5761
www.crystalhotsauce.com

Barq's Root Beer

Before this regional soda became a property of the Coca-Cola corporation, Barq's (pronounced BARKS) was a favorite in south Louisiana's iceboxes and convenience stores. Billed as an "Olde Tyme Root Beer," this spicy sweet concoction is a popular longneck fallback for teetotalers and underage kids alike. In local restaurants, you're also likely to find the other trademark flavor—a ruby-hued crème beverage that locals just call "red soda."

Barq's Olde Tyme Root Beer
www.barqs.com

Coffee

Just like tomato in jambalaya, the "chicory factor" used to be clear boundary between Creole city and Cajun country. New Orleanians grew up drinking their CDM (the grocery-store version Cafe Du Monde's chicory-enhanced coffee), while residents of Cajun country were much more likely to drink straight-ahead dark roast (usually Community or Mello Joy). Improved shipping and distribution networks have removed some of the regional differences, but chicory coffee (sometimes called "New Orleans Blend") remains a city phenomenon.

Cafe Du Monde
1039 Decatur St.
New Orleans, LA 70116
1-800-772-2927
www.cafedumonde.com

Community Coffee
P.O. Box 2311
Baton Rouge, LA 70821
1-800-525-5583
www.communitycoffee.com

Mello Joy Coffee Company
101 Row 3
Lafayette, LA 70508
1-866-355-6569
www.mellojoy.com

Hubig's Pies

Sweet, heavy and absolutely addictive, these fried turnovers are a standard snack food available only in New Orleans. They run for less than a dollar and provide a substantial and sugary bite in between meals.

The pies are a fresh product with a seven-day shelf life, which poses problems for cross-country shipment. A few web-based outlets sell the sweet specialty, but only in large lots (5 dozen or more).

Simon Hubig Co.
2417 Dauphine St.
New Orleans, LA 70117-7801
504-945-2181

Olive Salad

The trademark spread on New Orleans' muffuletta sandwich, this pre-jarred mix of olives, pickled vegetables, spices and olive oil makes a great pantry staple for quick stir-and-serve pasta dishes and quick marinara sauces. You can find several brands on local grocery shelves, but I prefer Central Grocery's chunky, garlicky version of the classic.

Of course, the tradition-bound grocery hasn't quite gotten around to figuring out Internet shipping, so if you want to get a jar, you'll need to contact them by phone or mail.

Central Grocery
923 Decatur St.
New Orleans, LA 70116
504- 523-1620

New Orleans Rum

With sugar plantations situated not far upriver and rum drinks flowing in the bar, you'd expect the city to have at least one active distillery to serve the local liquor trade. Local businessman James Michalopoulos recently revived the rum production industry, distilling a smooth aged rum from Louisiana sugar cane syrup.

His company, Celebration Distillation, recently expanded its line to four different barrel-aged rums, two for mixing (New Orleans Amber and New Orleans Crystal) and two for sipping (Cane and Cane Amber).

Celebration Distillation Corp.

2815 Frenchmen St.
New Orleans, LA 70122
504-945-9400
www.neworleansrum.com

Sicilian Cookies and Candies

The popular Midcity ice-cream destination also produces its own line of pre-bagged Italian sweets for sale through local markets and mail order. Durable biscotti (almond or anise flavored) are great for coffee dipping; sticky-sweet iced *cucidata* (fig cookies) and *pigniolata* candy make for a more immediate sugar rush.

Angelo Brocato Ice Cream and Confectionery

214 North Carrollton Ave.
New Orleans, LA 70119-5109
504-486-1465
www.angelobrocatoicecream.com

Zapp's Potato Chips

Available anywhere fine poboys are sold, these familiar metallic-striped bags contain crunchy kettle-fried chips produced in Gramercy, just upriver from New Orleans. Zapp's is famous for its locally-themed flavor names, including cayenne-dusted Cajun Crawtator, sour cream and Creole onion, and Cajun dill. Local markets often carry their limited-edition flavors and sweet potato chips as well.

Zapp's Potato Chip Company

Gramercy, LA 70052-1533
1-800-HOT-CHIP
www.zapps.com

Creole Mustard

In addition to making a damned fine poboy condiment, this tangy, coarse-grained mustard is a common ingredient in cream sauces and vinaigrettes. It's made from whole mustard seed, so it packs a little bit of heat as well. Zatarain's is the most common local brand.

Zatarain's
82 First St., P.O. Box 347
Gretna, LA 70053
1-888-264-5460

SOUTH LOUISIANA SPECIALTIES
Andouille

The Louisiana town of LaPlace, about thirty miles upriver from New Orleans, is the state-sanctioned "Andouille Capital of the World." And since 1928, LaPlace-based Jacob's has produced their andouille using the family's traditional recipes and old-world smoking techniques. The result is a firm, somewhat dry sausage with pronounced pecan wood flavor and the perfect amount of garlic and spice.

And though LaPlace is a stronghold of traditional andouille producers (most of whom use the word "Famous" in their business name), Jacob's is the only one that ships their product to out-of-state customers.

Jacob's World Famous Andouille
505 W. Airline Hwy.
LaPlace, LA 70068
985-652-9080, toll free: 1-877-215-7589
fax: 985-652-9022
www.cajunsausage.com

Creole Cream Cheese

Though it shares a name with the familiar Philadelphia variety, this Louisiana classic is actually closer in to French Neufchâtel or fresh farmer's cheese. This light cow's milk cheese has a lighter texture and tangier flavor than the popular bagel spread, and used to be a common item made in local grocery stores. The rise of the modern supermarkets put Creole Cream Cheese on the endangered species list before local dairy farmers and food producers recently revived the tradition. New Orleans chefs have been quick to integrate the local product to dishes such as cheesecakes and ice creams.

Mauthe's Dairy
Folsom, Louisiana
Available in neighborhood groceries and the Crescent City Farmer's Market.

Bittersweet Plantation Dairy
Gonzales, Louisiana
www.jfolse.com

Chef John Folse's artisan cheese operation offers online ordering and nationwide shipping. Also available in groceries across the state.

Filé Powder

Based in Rougon, just outside of New Roads, Lionel Keys still uses techniques that are well over a century old. He collects and dries his own sassafras, then works the leaves using his uncle's century-old wooden tools until the texture is just right. Other spice companies pack a mass-produced version, but the flavor just doesn't approach Key's hand-processed product.

At farmer's markets and craft festivals across Louisiana, Key scoops the intensely fresh filé straight from the stump's worn bowl into tiny jars for waiting customers. Back home, he runs a mail-order spice business, shipping his filé to dedicated fans across the country.

Uncle Bill's Creole Filé
P.O. Box 169
Baton Rouge, LA 70821
225-267-9220
www.unclebillspices.com

Roux

Even though roux is a snap to cook at home, it's a time-consuming process that doesn't quite fit in with the mostly microwavable modern kitchen. In recent years, it seems that just about every Louisiana food company responded to the quick-cook contingent by producing a pre-cooked roux in a jar.

Opelousas-based Savoie's bottles two versions of the oil/flour mixture (light or dark) along with a fat-free "dry roux" that's gained popularity in recent years. The dry version (called instant roux or gravy thickener) is flour that's been carefully baked in industrial ovens—browning the flour without the oil—and packaged for health-conscious cooks. Available in specialty grocery stores or on the web.

Savoie's Sausage and Food Products
337-942-7241
www.savoiesfoods.com
www.cajungrocer.com

Creole/Cajun Spice Mixes

Just about every Louisiana cook keeps some kind of pre-mixed spice blend close at hand. The varieties run in the hundreds, mixed by a local meat market or well-known regional spice company.

My personal preference is the spice mix that I grew up on—Tony Chachere's Creole Seasoning. The distinctive green and red shaker is a kitchen staple for good reason—the peppery mixture is well balanced on the tongue, with a whiff of fragrant garlic powder and just enough cayenne to get your tastebuds' attention. Over the years, the enterprising Tony has also developed low-salt, no-salt and more-spice versions of the mix for a wide variety of palates.

For the record, the last name is pronounced SHA-shu-ree, though just about everybody just calls the product "Tony's."

Tony's has made the jump from regional specialty to mainstream commodity. Look for it on supermarket shelves or visit their website (www.tonychachere.com) for an online "store finder."

Tony Chachere's Creole Foods
P.O. Box 1639
Opelousas, LA 70571
1-800-551-9066

Louisiana Seafood Box

If you're longing for real Gulf seafood but live well outside the "fresh zone," the Louisiana Seafood Marketing and Promotion board wants to ship you the state's freshest fish. And oyster. And shrimp. (Whatever's in season.)

The board's online shipping program allows computer-savvy shoppers to locate the freshest Louisiana seafood and hooks shoppers up with seafood vendors who can ship via the major overnight carriers.

Louisiana Seafood Promotion & Marketing Board
1600 Canal St.
New Orleans, LA 70112
1-800-222-4017
www.louisianaseafood.com

Steen's Cane Syrup

What did you expect in the middle of sugar country—Vermont maple? This thick, dark syrup is often mistaken for molasses, but Louisiana cane syrup contains all the sugary goodness of pure cane juice. (Molasses is a byproduct of the refining process—essentially cane syrup with the sugar crystals extracted.) Real cane syrup is served on top of just about any bready breakfast treat (biscuits, pancakes, or the local versions of French toast, *pain perdu).* Steen's of Abbeville has been making this Cajun staple for almost ninety years.

C. S. Steen's Syrup Mill
P.O. Box 339
119 N. Main St.
Abbeville, LA 70510

Tabasco Hot Sauce

Before the McIlhenney family got on the modern marketing train, their iconic red and green bottle was known worldwide for containing THE hot sauce—an aged mix of hot red peppers, salt and vinegar. The bright red classic sauce, a standard sight on diner tables and well-stocked bars, is heavy on the heat and best doled out by the drop. The current line of Tabasco sauces includes a green jalapeño, garlic enhanced, smoky chipotle and DAAAAAMMMMNTHATSHOT habeñero versions. The McIlhenneys have also branched out into everything from barbecue sauce to jellybeans and neckties.

McIlhenney Company
Avery Island, LA 70513
www.tabasco.com

andouille—A smoked sausage made using lean pork and spices, most often used as a flavoring meat. Not to be mistaken for French andouille, a tripe-stuffed sauce.

amberjack—A firm-fleshed fish native to the Gulf of Mexico.

beignet—New Orleans' answer to a "light breakfast," the beignet is a crispy, puffy square of deep-fried dough sprinkled liberally with powdered sugar.

black drum—A common Gulf fish and cousin to the red drum (redfish); often substituted for redfish in restaurant settings.

crawfish—The Louisiana name for crayfish, a small freshwater crustacean related to the lobster that thrives in the swamps and waterways of Louisiana.

Creole cream cheese—A tangy fresh cow's-milk cheese native to south Louisiana; similar to French Neufchâtel.

Creole tomato—A flavorful tomato native to south Louisiana.

escolar—A full-flavored Gulf fish that's closely related to the tuna. Also called oilfish.

filé—The pulverized leaf of the native sassafras tree, used as a flavorful thickener in Creole and Cajun cuisine.

grouper—A member of the sea bass family native to the Gulf of Mexico.

gumbo—Somewhere between flavorful stew and thick soup, hearty Louisiana gumbo can be made with anything from Gulf seafood (oysters, crabs, shrimp) to wild duck and Cajun sausage. Every Louisiana cook has his or her own version of this dish—thickened with okra, filé or a dark roux. In others even flavored with tomato (a New Orleans tradition).

Herbsaint—A locally produced anise liqueur, used in oysters Rockefeller and numerous New Orleans cocktails.

jambalaya—A savory composed rice dish that can include meats, poultry or seafood and rice cooked in a flavorful broth; the Louisiana cousin of Spanish *paella*.

mirliton—A light green squash common in Louisiana cooking; known as *chayote* and *vegetable pear* in other cultures.

poboy—Louisiana's entry in the "big sandwich" pantheon. These monstrous loaves of fresh local French bread are stuffed with any manner of fillings—from gravy-soaked roast beef to fresh-fried shrimp tails or tender soft-shell crabs.

pompano—A delicately flavored Gulf fish considered the most prized of Gulf fish.

redfish—Another name for the red drum, a mild-flavored fish native to the Gulf of Mexico.

roux—A thickener made of flour browned in fat (butter, oil or lard); used in gumbo and a wide variety of Louisiana dishes.

sheepshead—A reef-dwelling Gulf fish known for its flaky texture and delicate flavor.

tasso (TAH-so)—A spicy, long-smoked flavoring meat used in Louisiana cooking. Slices of lean pork are rubbed with peppery spice mixture and smoked until similar in texture to beef jerky. Tasso is a meat market specialty in Cajun Louisiana, but used sparingly throughout the state in red beans, jambalayas and contemporary cream sauces.

triggerfish—A Gulf fish with dry, firm flesh.

wahoo—A full-flavored Gulf fish and member of the mackerel family.

Parasol's Restaurant and Bar, 167
Slim Goodie's Diner, 191
Sophie's Ice Cream, 200
Uglesich's Retaurant and Bar, 67

Midcity

Angelo Brocato Ice Cream, 192
Café Reconcile, 171
Crescent City Steakhouse, 57
Fair Grinds, 186
Gabrielle, 76
Liuzza's by the Track, 164
Liuzza's, 163
Mandina's, 51
Pho Tau Bay, 180
Parkway Bakery & Tavern, 139
Ralph's on the Park, 99
Ruth's Chris Steak House, 89

Tremé

Dooky Chase, 40
Willi Mae's Restaurant, 177

Uptown

Barrow's Shady Inn, 170
Brigtsen's, 71
Camellia Grill, 55
Casamento's Restaurant, 128
Clancey's, 72
Cooter Brown's Tavern and Oyster Bar, 162

Creole Creamery, 195
Dante's Kitchen, 74
Dick and Jenny's, 75
Domilise's, 135
Dunbar's Creole Cooking, 173
Franky and Johnny's Restaurant and Lounge, 51
Gautreau's, 77
Guy's Poboys, 136
Hansen's Sno-Bliz, 196
Jacques-Imo's Café, 64
La Crepe Nanou, 122
La Petite Grocery, 107
Lilette Restaurant, 123
Martinique Bistro, 124
Martin's Wine Cellar, 207
Mat & Naddie's Café, 78
Pascal's Manale, 148
Tee-Eva's, 175
Upperline, 79
William's Plum Street Snowballs, 203
Ye Olde College Inn, 69
Zara's Lil' Giant, 209

Various (around town)

CC's Coffee House, 185
Crescent City Farmer's Market, 204
PJ's Coffee & Tea Café, 189
Popeye's Fried Chicken and Biscuits, 181
Rue de la Course, 189

general index

A

Abbeville, LA, 231
Abbeville, LA establishments
  Black's Seafood Restaurant and
    Oyster Bar, 232
  Dupuy's, 232
  Shucks!, 237
Abita Brewing, 169
Acadiana region, 226
Acme Oyster & Seafood House,
  126–128
A. Johnson's Grocery, 238
alcoholic beverages
  Bloody Mary, 95
  frozen daiquiris, 216
  mint julep, 219
  New Orleans Rum, 245
  Peychaud's Bitters, 221
  Pimm's Cup, 214
  Ramos Gin Fizz, 220
  Sazerac, 49
Alligator Festival, 242
American Bistro, 107–108
andouille sausage, 119, 246
Angelo Brocato Ice Cream and
  Confectionery, 192–194, 245
Antoine's, 37
Arcadiana region, 6
Arnaud's, 38
art galleries, 19
artichokes, 147
art museums, 19, 27
Atlas Brewing, 169
Aunt Sally's Praline Shop, 194
automobile impoundment, 29
Avondale, LA, 147–148

B

Bacco, 99
Balcony Bar, 218
Baldwin, LA, 242
Bananas Foster, 94
barbecue, 119–120
barbecue shrimp, 149
barbecue shrimp food, 148–151
barfood
  Coop's Place, 116–117
  Fiorella's Cafe, 60–61
  Liuzza's by the Track, 164–165
  Rocky and Carlo's, 151–152
  Verti Marte, 142
Barrow's Shady Inn, 170–173
bars and clubs
  Balcony Bar, 218
  Bull Dog, 218
  Circle Bar, 217
  Columns, 222
  DBA, 219–220
  Delachaise, 218
  Donna's Bar & Grill, 213
  F&M Patio Bar, 222
  Funky Butt, 213
  House of Blues, 213
  Howling Wolf, 217
  Kingpin, 222
  Lafitte's Blacksmith Shop, 215
  Le Bon Temps Roule, 222
  Loa Lounge, 218
  Loft 523, 218
  Maple Leaf Bar, 222
  Mid City Lanes Rock N Bowl,
    220–221
  Mimi's in the Marigny, 220
  Miss Mae's, 222
  Molly's in the Market, 215

F

S

T

Tabasco hot sauce, 248, 248–249
tarts, 238
tasso, 235
taxis, 15
T-Coon's Restaurant, 232
Tee Eva's, 174–175, 175–177
The Boiling Point, 238
The R Bar, 220
The Saint, 219
Tipitina's, 223
Tommy's Cuisine, 145–146
Tony Chachere's Creole Foods, 248
Tremé establishments
    Dooky Chase, 40–41
    Willie Mae's Restaurant, 177–178
trout amandine, 61
trout meunière, 61
Tujague's, 52–53
Tulane University, 22
turducken, 235, 236
turkey, 236
turtle soup, 50
24-hour establishments
    barrooms, 217
    Verti Marte, 142

U

Uglesich's Restaurant and Bar, 67–69
Uncle Bill's Creole Filé, 247
University, 22
Upperline, 79–81
Uptown (orientation), 12, 13
Uptown establishments, 14, 22, 23
    Barrow's Shady Inn, 170–173
    Brigtsen's, 71–72
    Camellia Grill, 55–57
    Casamento's, 128–130
    Clancy's, 72–74
    Columns, 222
    Cooter Brown's Tavern & Oyster Bar,
        162–163
    Creole Creamery, 195–196
    Crescent City Farmer's Market,
        204–206
    Dante's Kitchen, 74–75
    Dick and Jenny's, 75–76
    Domilise's, 135–136
    Dunbar's Creole Cooking, 173–174
    F&M Patio Bar, 222
    Franky and Johnny's Restaurant and
        Lounge, 61–62
    Gautreau's, 77–78
    Guy's Poboys, 136–137
    Hansen's Sno-Bliz, 196–199
    Jacques-Imo's Café, 64–65
    Kingpin, 222
    La Crepe Nanou, 122–123
    La Petite Grocery, 107–108
    Le Bon Temps Roule, 222
    Lilette Restaurant, 123–124
    Maple Leaf Bar, 222
    Martinique Bistro, 124–125
    Martin's Wine Cellar, 207–208
    Mat & Naddie's Cafe, 78–79
    Miss Mae's, 222
    Pascal's Manale, 148–151
    Snake & Jake's, 223
    St. Joe's, 223
    Tee Eva's, 175–177
    Tipitina's, 223
    Upperline, 79–81
    William's Plum Street Snowballs, 203
    Ye Olde College Inn, 69–70
    Zara's Lil' Giant, 209–210

V

Vaughn's, 217
vegetables, 110. *See also* produce
Verti Marte, 142
Victor's Cafeteria, 238
Vietnamese, 181
Vietnamese food
    Kim Son, 178–179
    Pho Tau Bay, 180–181
Vietnamese Market, 208–209
Vieux Carré (Old Quarter), 18

W

walking, 25

Warehouse District, 17–19

Warehouse District establishments. *See* Central Business District/Warehouse District establishments

West Bank, 28, 178–179

William's Plum Street Snowballs, 203

Willie Mae's Restaurant, 177–178

X, Y, Z

Yambilee (sweet potato celebration), 242

Ye Olde College Inn, 69–70

Zapp's Potato Chips, 245

Zara's Lil' Giant, 209–210

Zatarain's, 246

Zydeque Bayou Barbecue, 119–120